"Nolo's home
bookmarking."
...L

W9-AYN-949

LEGAL INFORMATION ONLINE ANYTIME

24 hours a day

www.nolo.com

AT THE NOLO.COM SELF-HELP LAW CENTER ON THE WEB, YOU'LL FIND

- **Nolo's comprehensive Legal Encyclopedia, with links to other online resources**
- **SharkTalk: Everybody's Legal Dictionary**
- **Auntie Nolo—if you've got questions, Auntie's got answers**
- **Update information on Nolo books and software**
- **The Law Store—over 250 self-help legal products including:**
  Downloadable Software, Books, Form Kits and E-Guides
- **Discounts and other good deals, plus our hilarious Shark Talk game**
- **Our ever-popular lawyer jokes**
- **NoloBriefs.com, our monthly email newsletter**

Quality LAW BOOKS & SOFTWARE FOR NON-LAWYERS

Nolo.com legal books and software are consistently first-rate because:

- A dozen in-house Nolo legal editors, working with highly skilled authors, ensure that our products are accurate, up-to-date and easy to use.

- We know our books get better when we listen to what our customers tell us. (Yes, we really do want to hear from you—please fill out and return the card at the back of this book.)

- We are maniacal about updating every book and software program to keep up with changes in the law.

- Our commitment to a more democratic legal system informs all of our work.

OUR "NO-HASSLE" GUARANTEE

Return anything you buy directly from Nolo for any reason and we'll cheerfully refund your purchase price. No ifs, ands or buts.

An Important Message to Our Readers

This product provides information and general advice about the law. But laws and procedures change frequently, and they can be interpreted differently by different people. For specific advice geared to your specific situation, consult an expert. No book, software or other published material is a substitute for personalized advice from a knowledgable lawyer licensed to practice law in your state.

1st Edition

BEAT YOUR TICKET

Go to Court & WIN!

by Attorney David Brown

nolo.com
LAW FOR ALL

Keeping Up to Date

To keep its books up to date, Nolo issues new printings and new editions periodically. New printings reflect minor legal changes and technical corrections. New editions contain major legal changes, major text additions or major reorganizations. To find out if a later printing or edition of any Nolo book is available, call Nolo at 510-549-1976 or check our website: www.nolo.com.

To stay current, follow the "Update" service at our website: www.nolo.com. In another effort to help you use Nolo's latest materials, we offer a 35% discount off the purchase of the new edition of your Nolo book when you turn in the cover of an earlier edition. (See the "Special Upgrade Offer" in the back of the book.)

This book was last revised in: **April 1999**.

First Edition	**APRIL 1999**
Editors	RALPH WARNER
	SPENCER SHERMAN
Cover Design	TONI IHARA
Book Design	TERRI HEARSH
Illustrations	LINDA ALLISON
Index	THÉRÈSE SHERE
Proofreading	ROBERT WELLS
Printing	BERTELSMANN INDUSTRY SERVICES, INC.

Brown, David Wayne, 1949-
        Beat your ticket : go to court and win! / by David Brown.
                p.   cm.
        Includes index.
        ISBN 0-87337-465-7
        1. Traffic violations--United States   2. Defense (Criminal
procedure)--United States.   I. Title.
KF2231.B76   1999
345.73'0247--dc21
                                                98-56031
                                                CIP

For information on bulk purchases or corporate premium sales, please contact the Special Sales Department. For academic sales or textbook adoptions, ask for Academic Sales. Call 800-955-4775 or write to Nolo.com, Inc., 950 Parker Street, Berkeley, CA 94710.

Dedication

To my wife Kwi Soon, my daughters Laura and Kate, my stepsons John and Jay, and my stepdaughter Sumi. And to my former wife and good mother of my children, Nancy Brown Selvy.

Acknowledgments

This book could not have been published without the assistance and efforts of many people:

- First and foremost Nolo's visionary publisher Ralph ("Jake") Warner, a kind but demanding editor who never tolerates quitting or skimping, without whom this book would not exist.
- Spencer Sherman, the Nolo editor who magically transformed crudely crafted words into a polished product.
- Susan ("Lulu") Cornell, a dedicated Nolo editor, whose excellent editorial suggestions were of great assistance in preparing the 50-state Appendix.
- Peter Hartley, of Monterey County, California, my secretary/assistant who tirelessly typed various drafts of many chapters from dictation and chicken-scratching.
- Jane Fajardo, of Palo Alto, California. Thanks, Mom, for your loving and supportive help.
- My loving wife, Kwi Soon, and all my children and stepchildren, for your love, support, and tolerance as I stayed up many times till 5:00 a.m.
- The National Motorist's Association of Waukaunkee, Wisconsin, (http://www.motorists.com), a freedom-loving organization that provides first-class assistance to the motoring public.

Table of Contents

Introduction

You Can Beat Your Ticket

1 First Things

2 What Are You Charged With?

3 Should You Fight Your Ticket?

Appendix

Traffic Court Rules for 50 States (And the District of Columbia)

Index

Introduction

You Can Beat Your Ticket

We don't advocate speeding. Or running stop signs. Or making illegal U-turns. Safe, drug- and alcohol-free driving is always best. But unsafe driving is not the only reason police hand out tickets. Traffic fines are a significant source of revenue for local governments and police feel pressure to contribute their part of the revenue stream. True, most court challenges to ticket quota systems have failed. But that's because most local governments are smart enough to encourage police to keep the money rolling in without admitting they have quotas. And sometimes a ticketing officer is just plain wrong. Lots of tickets are given out for reasons that have little relationship to enforcing sensible highway safety rules. Which helps explain why we believe you should study your ticket to see if you really deserved it. If not, fight it.

There are times when you should just go ahead and pay the ticket—and/or go to traffic school—and move on, because you are without-a-doubt guilty or the hassle-factor is just too high for the pay-off. If you just got your first ticket in ten years, and are determined that it will be ten more years before you get another, it may be best to cough up the money and forget it. But if, through bad luck or indiscretion, you are facing your second ticket in three to five years, you may decide to fight it to avoid higher insurance premiums or other problems described inside. But no matter whether this is your second or 22nd ticket, always remember this: Even if the police officer says you are guilty, the law may not back him up. It is always worth carefully checking out the legal realities you face before writing out a hefty check.

If you are reading this introduction, you probably have received a ticket you want to fight. While we can't guarantee you'll be successful, we can and do present much useful information that should make your task far easier. With a little research and preparation, there is a good chance that even many "unbeatable" tickets can be beaten.

Consider these facts:

- In my experience, the police officer fails to show up in court to testify in traffic cases about 20% of the time. If he doesn't show, you usually win.
- In many states, speed limits are not "absolute." If you show it was reasonable to drive over the posted limit, you win.
- If you go back to the scene of the "crime" you may find that what the officer said he saw was not possible from where he said he saw it.
- Many traffic laws have wiggle room in them, which often makes writing a ticket a "judgment call." As we'll explain, these types of tickets are often easy to beat.

One final note before we dive in. Procedures for fighting traffic tickets vary a lot from state to state. We can't write 50 separate books or have 50 separate chapters with every detail from every state. But we do have something unique: a 50-state Appendix that details the most important specifics of each state's traffic laws and traffic court procedures. You will want to take a look at the Appendix often to learn the specific procedures in your state. ■

Chapter

1

First Things

In Oklahoma, anyone who kills another person in an auto accident must immediately stop and give the deceased their name, address and vehicle registration.

—*Oklahoma Statutes (Section) 47-10-104*

A. A Typical Ticket

It's late. You're driving home from a party. You're thinking about what a good time you had. Then you realize you've missed a turn. You're in the middle of a quiet residential district with no cars moving in either direction. All you see is a car parked a few blocks away with its lights on. You make a U-turn.

Suddenly, in your rear view mirror, you see flashing lights racing towards you. You pull over to let the police car pass. Instead, it follows you to the curb. You realize you've just been pulled over. Even before your car is fully stopped, the officer has his high-intensity spotlight pointed at you. Then you hear a door slamming, the sound of pavement under boots and you are blinded by the beam of an industrial-strength flashlight.

Before you get a chance to ask, "What's the problem?" a voice from behind the flashlight says, "May I see your driver's license, please?" You fumble through your wallet, slowly and carefully, since the light from the flashlight is glinting off the handle of what looks like a very big gun. Finally, heart pounding, you hand your license over.

The officer returns to his car. His radio crackles in the night. A few minutes later he comes back, returns your license on a clipboard that also holds a traffic ticket. "You made an unlawful U-turn in a residential district," he says. "Please sign on the dotted line." When the officer goes on to explain that your signature is not an admission of guilt, but merely a promise to appear in court, you meekly do as he asks. A moment later as the officer pulls away, you eye your ticket, stunned at how quickly you've been made to feel like a criminal.

Chances are, as you drive the rest of the way home, you'll repeatedly wonder, "Why did I get a ticket for making a perfectly safe turn on an empty road?" Which will lead you to consider the following:

- Should I just pay the ticket and forget it?
- Is there a way to wipe this stupid ticket off my record?
- If I pay the ticket, will my insurance rates go up?
- Do I have legal grounds to fight the ticket?
- Can I lose my license?

If you decide to fight the ticket, several things will happen:

- You will spend at least several hours and probably many more preparing to fight the ticket.
- You'll worry about making a good court presentation.
- You'll spend half a day or more getting back and forth to court and arguing your case.

If you don't fight the ticket, you could end up doing some or all of the following:

- Spending money and many hours in traffic school to clear your record
- Paying a hefty fine and having the ticket appear on your driving record
- If you have had another recent ticket, paying higher insurance premiums for the next three to five years
- If you have had several recent tickets, losing your driving privileges.

B. Are Tickets Impossible to Beat?

The answer is: Absolutely not. Many are given in situations where even the cop knows that a motorist who puts up a spirited defense might win. But this doesn't necessarily mean the cop will cut back in handing out marginal tickets. That's because the officer also knows that only about 3% of ticketed drivers contest their citations.

And furthermore, many of those who do fight are so unprepared and nervous that they beat themselves, not their citation.

Getting a Ticket Doesn't Equal Guilt

Here is a great example of why you shouldn't just assume you are guilty because you are ticketed. In San Francisco, police use automatic cameras at some busy intersections to catch red-light runners. About 30% of all those pictures used to be thrown out by the police because the picture was fuzzy, blurred or otherwise deemed to be unusable. But in 1998 the police chief decided that everyone photographed would get a $271 ticket—no ifs, ands or buts. That means that 30% of these tickets are so marginal they used to be thrown away because the police themselves believed the evidence was not strong enough for a conviction.

Does it make sense for you to fight a particular ticket? Common sense would say "no" if there is a small chance of winning (say, you were going 50 mph in a school zone) and "yes" if the officer clearly screwed up. But as we'll see later, even a seemingly hopeless case can be won if the police officer fails to show up in court to testify. Still, for most tickets, guilt or innocence is not so clear cut, meaning that you'll normally want to consider a number of factors, including the consequences of paying your fine—which is the same thing as pleading guilty.

Before assuming the ticket can't be beaten and resigning yourself to writing out that big check, we encourage you to take a hard look at the facts to see if you have a reasonable chance of success. (We show you how to assess your ticket in Chapter 2.) There are a surprising number of good legal grounds on which many tickets can be beaten. For example, in about one third of the states—including California, Colorado, Texas and Massachusetts—many posted speed limits are not "absolute." This means if you were driving slightly above the posted speed limit, but can convince a judge you were driving safely, you may be found not guilty (see Chapter 5, Section C, on presumed speed limits). And to take another common example, where a ticket is given for an "unsafe lane change" it may be fairly easy to show that you changed lanes with reasonable safety. That's because it involves a quick judgment call on the part of the cop—a decision you may be able to successfully challenge if the lane change did not result in an accident (see Chapter 7 for defenses on a variety of moving violations).

To test the legality of the ticket you received, you must learn how to research the law and court procedure. Legal research is now much easier than in the past because of new innovations, particularly on the Internet (see Chapter 2, Section B). Once you locate the law you are accused of violating, you will want to closely examine its words and phrases. Many times, you will find the officer did not fully understand every technical aspect of the law or has taken great liberties in interpreting it. Some readers may be uneasy searching for legal technicalities to keep their record clear. But consider that lawyers and judges build their careers on doing just that. It is the way they think and the way they believe the law should be practiced. Or in the words of an anonymous rap song, "If the law's not precise, it's no vice!"

C. How This Book Is Organized

Chapters 2 and 3 provide the information you need to sensibly decide whether to fight your ticket, attend traffic school, or simply pay your fine. To help you make these decisions, Chapter 2 will also teach you how to locate the exact law you're charged with violating, so you can analyze it and decide for yourself whether you committed the offense listed on your ticket.

In Chapter 4, we discuss when you should hire a lawyer to represent you, particularly in serious cases like reckless driving and driving under the influence of alcohol or drugs. We also discuss how to evaluate lawyers and get help from an expert at an affordable price.

Chapters 5, 6 and 7 summarize what lawyers call the "substantive law" on the most common types of violations and provide many hints on how to fight them. Because speeding tickets are by far the most common, we use all of Chapter 6 to focus on how to defend yourself from police methods of nabbing alleged speeders, including pacing, VASCAR, radar and laser devices.

Chapter 8 is devoted to initial court procedures, including learning how to delay a trial for your advantage and obtaining the officer's notes to build your case. Chapter 9 helps you prepare for your day in court, including preparing your testimony and the testimony of your witnesses. Chapter 10 helps you prepare to cross-examine the police officer. Chapters 11 and 12 prepare you for jury and non-jury trials.

Because we want to keep this book brief, we do not cover:

- The most serious offenses, like drunk driving or hit-and-run; most people should not represent themselves against these and other charges that could land them in jail

- Contesting the loss or suspension of your driver's licenses by the state Department of Motor Vehicles
- The details of appealing to higher courts after a guilty verdict.

Icons Used in This Book

Look for these icons to alert you to certain kinds of information:

 A caution to slow down and consider potential problems

 Lets you know when you may skip reading some material that is not relevant to your situation

 Gives you practical suggestions for handling a legal or procedural issue that may arise

 This icon refers you to related information in another chapter of this book.

We also include useful information in sidebars, which you will find in shaded boxes throughout the book.

Chapter

2

What Are You Charged With?

If war is too important to be left to the generals, surely justice is too important to be left to the lawyers.

—Robert McKay

A. Determine What Your Ticket Says

The first thing you need to do is find out what you are charged with—not just what your ticket says, but the exact words of the law you are charged with breaking. In some states, traffic laws are set out in a law book called the "Vehicle Code," while in others they are gathered as part of a "Transportation Code," "Motor Vehicle Laws," or under some similar name. No two states have exactly the same traffic laws, but most are very similar. This is hardly surprising, since traffic signs, signals, and rules are basically the same all over the United States.

While the law of every state requires drivers to stop at red lights and stop signs, more minor details of each state's vehicle laws can be different. Perhaps surprisingly, this is especially true when it comes to speed laws. For example, California, Colorado, Massachusetts, Texas and at least ten other states allow drivers on some or all roads to go faster than the posted speed limit if it's safe to do so (See Chapter 5, Sections A and C, for more on what are called "presumed" speed limits). But a majority of states, including Florida, Georgia, Illinois, New York and Pennsylvania have "absolute" speed limits, which are illegal to exceed regardless of whether it is reasonable to do so (see Chapter 5, Sections B and D).

There is clearly not enough space here to include the fine print of every state's laws. Fortunately, they are easy to find. Here's how:

Closely examine your ticket. Look for a number that corresponds to the law (often called a "statute" or "vehicle code section") you are charged with violating. Sometimes it will have been hand-printed by the officer in a box or blank; other times it's preprinted on the ticket with the officer simply checking the appropriate box. In either case, near the statute number you will often find a very short description of the law (for example, "VC [Vehicle Code Section] 22350—exceeding posted speed"). For speeding violations, in most states you'll also find the speed the officer claims you were going, as well as the posted speed limit on the road where you were stopped.

B. Finding What the Law Says

Now you must look up and read the law the officer claims you violated.

1. Public and Law Libraries

Most libraries have copies of your state's vehicle laws. This could range anywhere from a single dog-eared volume containing just the fine-print text of traffic laws to a complete multi-volume set of all your state's laws. The bigger the library, the more likely it is to have a more comprehensive collection. Often it's a good idea to call the reference librarian to see what's available before making a trip. In most states you can also normally use a courthouse or public law school law library, which will almost surely have a complete set of laws. If you are simply looking up the law you are charged with violating, any up-to-date copy of the vehicle code will do. If you are planning to do more research to fight your ticket (as outlined below) you will need a more comprehensive collection of law books. But, call first to be sure the library is open to the public.

At the library, you must look in the proper code book to find the text of the law you are charged with violating. The easiest way is often to show your ticket to the research librarian and ask him to direct you to the proper book. If there is no librarian available, find where your state laws are kept (see our Appendix). Look first for the Vehicle Code or a similar sounding name (many states organize laws by subject, such as crimes, corporations and vehicles). If you find one, look for the number of the law you violated. If you do not find a book containing traffic laws, look for the index volume to the general laws of your state, as some states simply organize all laws by numbers. Look inside for the number listed on your ticket. (Be sure to read the rest of this chapter to learn other important research steps you should take.)

2. Legal Help on the Internet

You can also use the Internet to look up the text of most state laws. All you need is a computer equipped with a modem and a subscription to an Internet service provider. Also, most public libraries now have Internet access for free. The address (called a "URL") for the Website that sets out your state's laws is listed as part of your state's information in the Appendix. Or you can easily go to one of several legal Websites that will in turn provide you with direct access to your state's Website (see sidebar, "Useful Internet Resources").

Useful Internet Resources

- http://www.legalonline.com/statute2.htm (Maintained by Legal Online, a private company that provides links to state-law Web pages)
- http://www.findlaw.com/casecode/state.html (Maintained by Findlaw, another private company that also provides free links to state-law Web pages).

There are also several other good Websites where groups and individuals provide valuable ticket-fighting information and strategies. The ones we like best are:

- http://www.speedtrap.com
- http://www.mrtraffic.com
- http://www.motorists.com

Once you find a Web page for your state laws (see the Appendix), that page may assist you in looking for the law listed on your ticket. Typically, you may be able to use a search box to type in the particular vehicle code section number or you might need to type in a word that relates to your violation (e.g., "speed," "stop sign," "left turn") to find the exact law. And in some states, Web pages will not include search engines at all. Instead, you'll need to work with a table of contents listing your state's laws. Once you've found the correct law, you'll want to print it out. As we'll see below, it really is a big help to have your hands on the exact law you are accused of violating.

Check Local Court Sites to See Your Options

Researching state laws and court decisions isn't the only way to use a computer and the Internet to help you gain information about how to fight your ticket. More and more local courts are developing their own Web pages that often contain helpful information on your traffic-ticket options. The National Center for State Courts, a nonprofit organization in Williamsburg, Virginia, has a Website that provides links to numerous state-court Web pages, listed by state, city and county. Its Website address is: http://ncsc.dni.us/court/sites/courts.htm#state.

Be sure you are reading current law. Once you've found your state's motor vehicle laws, make sure you have your hands on the latest version (in the year 2002, this should normally include laws adopted in 2001). This is particularly important if you use hardbound code books. Republished fairly infrequently, these law books are updated with paperback supplements inside the back cover. Be sure you always check.

3. Reading the Law Carefully

Once you find the law you are charged with, study it carefully to determine which facts the prosecution will have to prove to convict you. Many laws are famously complex. In fact, they are often so convoluted that it's not uncommon to find, upon careful reading, that what you did was not, technically speaking, a violation of the exact words of the statute. Always ask yourself the question: "What are the elements (or parts) of the offense I am charged with committing?"

For example, in most states, the law making U-turns illegal reads like this:

"No person in a residence district shall make a U-turn when any other vehicle is approaching from either direction within 200 feet, except at an intersection when the approaching vehicle is controlled by an official traffic control device."

You should break this law down into its legal elements by drawing a line between each clause, like this:

"No person in a residence district / shall make a U-turn / when any other vehicle is approaching from either direction / within 200 feet / except at an intersection / when the approaching vehicle / is controlled / by an official traffic control device."

Focusing on each element of a law is often the key to unlocking an effective defense. That's because, to be found guilty of having made this illegal U-turn, the State must prove you violated each "element" or clause of the offense. In this case, the State would have to show specifically that:

1. You were driving in a "residence district"
2. You drove your vehicle in a 180-degree or "U-turn"
3. Another vehicle was approaching within 200 feet or less, in front of or behind you, and
4. An "official traffic control device" at an "intersection" was not controlling the vehicle approaching you.

If you can show that your conduct didn't violate even one element of a traffic law, you are home and dry. For example, if the area where you were ticketed was not a "residence district," *or* the vehicle the officer claims was approaching was over 200 feet away, *or* you were at an intersection controlled by an "official traffic control device," you should quickly be found not guilty.

But will a judge really follow such a technical reading of the law? You bet. This type of hyper-technical, word-by-word reading of statutes is the key skill all lawyers and judges learn in law school. In fact, they know of no other approach. This even makes sense when you realize that the American legal system is built on the concept that you are innocent unless the government can prove you violated a law that prohibits clearly defined conduct (for example, driving a motor vehicle faster than 65 mph on a public road). And doing this necessarily means proving you were guilty of violating every "element" of the law. But even if you conclude you really have violated every element of a law, your case is not hopeless. In Chapter 3 we discuss other ways you can challenge your ticket or offer legally recognized excuses for your actions.

C. The Importance of Doing Legal Research

Most of what lawyers know about law they didn't learn in law school. Instead, the key skill they learned is how to research and understand the laws that apply to the particular legal problem or case they are currently dealing with. Fortunately, legal research isn't difficult; you certainly don't need a law degree to do it. The techniques needed for even fairly sophisticated legal research on traffic tickets can be learned in several hours. An excellent tool for helping you do this is the book *Legal Research: How to Find and Understand the Law*, by Steve Elias and Susan Levinkind (Nolo Press). Below I'll briefly cover several key research techniques.

1. Using Case Decisions

As discussed, our first step is to dissect the wording of the violation you are charged with to see if you committed every element of the offense. If, after doing this, you are not certain you can challenge the law on this ground, there are further steps you can take to build a strong defense.

Once a law is written, judges use real-life situations to interpret it. Sometimes these decisions (called cases) will make a huge difference to your situation.

For example, in all states, speeding to show-off to people watching you is a crime called "exhibition of speed." But an appeals court in California expanded the law to include screeching a car's tires (or burning rubber) to impress *listeners* who can't necessarily see you. This unusual expansion of the words "exhibition of speed" is something you would never know by reading the law alone.

In another example, Ohio's speeding law says you must drive at a "reasonable and prudent" speed. But it does not say whether it is legal to drive over the posted speed limit. A state appeals court ruled, however, that the wording of the law allowed motorists to drive above the posted speed, if they are being "reasonable and prudent." Without reading the appeals court decision, the average person would not know that it was legal to drive above the posted speed limit in Ohio.

Don't waste time researching a law that is simple and clear. If you are charged with failure to make a complete stop at a stop sign, you probably do not need to research case law. Reading the law itself is probably enough. It's usually a pretty clear law and unlikely to have been changed through court decisions. On the other hand, if the law you're charged under is a bit more complex, case law research can help you to answer questions that the statutes or laws themselves don't address. For example, this could be true in a case involving a "presumed" speed law, where your right to see a copy of the officer's notes in advance of the trial has been denied. (See Chapter 5, Sections A and C, and Chapter 8, Section C, on using "discovery".)

The best way to find written court decisions that interpret a particular law is to look in a set of "annotated" codes or laws. This is simply a set of your state's laws that list summaries of court decisions interpreting what the law means. These summaries are found just below the text of each law. Annotated laws can be found in all law libraries in your state. Those at publicly funded law schools and at principal county courthouses are usually open to the public. Private law schools also often allow access to members of the public. Even some larger public libraries stock annotated codes, but because these multi-volume sets are expensive, smaller branch public libraries usually can't afford them. Annotated codes have comprehensive indexes by topic, and are kept up-to-date each year with paperback supplements (called "pocket parts") located in a replaceable pocket in the back cover of each volume. Don't forget to look through these pocket parts for any law changes or case decisions occurring since the hardcover volume was printed.

Once you find the law you are accused of violating in the annotated law books, skim the brief summaries of the court decisions that interpret the law. Look first for relatively recent cases that involve situations similar to yours where a judge ruled in favor of the defendant because of some circumstances that you, too, might be able

to prove. Assuming you find a summary that you think might apply to you, you'll need to read the court's full written opinion (often called a "case") to see if it really makes a point that helps you beat your ticket.

Step One is to write down the "citation" for the relevant case. This consists of a shorthand identification of the page, volume and set of law books where the decision or case can be found. (See sidebar, "How Citations Work".) In most states, there are two different sets of volumes of books containing the court decisions and you'll be given a citation to each, one after the other. It makes no difference which one you use.

> ### How Citations Work
>
> Decisions of a state's highest court look like this: 155 Cal 422. The first number refers to the 155th volume of California Supreme Court decisions (Cal = California) and the second number directs you to page 422. Similarly, 55 Pa. 345 refers to the 55th volume of the decisions of the Pennsylvania Supreme Court, page 345. In addition, many case citations also may list a 2d, 3d or 4th after the state abbreviation. Each refers to one of the chronological series of case volumes for that state. For example, the 2nd series might cover cases from 1960-1985 and the 3rd series 1986 to today.

If you find annotations to several cases that fit your facts, you will want to look first at the most recent one (newer cases often reinterpret or supersede older ones) which is decided by your state's highest court (called the Supreme Court in every state except New York and Maryland). Cases from your state's intermediate level appeals courts are valid unless overruled by that state's Supreme Court. Step Two is to find the actual case. Fortunately, help is available:

- In the law library—Show the law librarian your citation and he'll put your hands on the right book.
- Online (free)—Nolo's Website (www.nolo.com) contains detailed information on how to do legal research, including how to find and interpret cases.
- Online (pay)—See sidebar "Finding Cases on the Internet."

2. Check to See If Other Laws Can Help Your Case

Understanding the specific law you violated—and the cases that interpret that law—is just part of your job. Since each law is written to deal with a very specific action (for example, exceeding the speed limit), other laws may also have a bearing on your case. Or put another way, the legal interpretation of one traffic law can sometimes be affected by another.

Here are some examples:

- Section 123.45.678 of your state's motor vehicle law forbids exceeding 25 mph in a residential district. But section 123.45.605 says all your state's speed limits are "presumed" limits. This means even though you may have technically violated Section 123.45.678, you might be able to successfully claim that it was legal to do so because Section 123.45.605 allows you to exceed the speed limit when driving safely under the circumstances (see Chapter 5, Sections A and C, for more on "presumed" speed limits).
- You are ticketed for a violation of Section 123.45.654 of your state's vehicle code for making a U-turn in a "residential district." But Section 123.45.666 defines a residential district as an area with at least four houses per acre of land. Since you made your U-turn in an area with fewer houses-per-acre than are listed in statute 123.45.666, you can argue you are not guilty of *every element* of Section 123.45.654 and are, therefore, not guilty.
- You are charged with speeding based on the reading of a radar gun used by the police officer. Your ticket says you are charged with a violation of Section 123.45.765 of the vehicle code, speeding. But, Section 345.67.898 of the Vehicle Code says an officer must follow certain procedures in using radar and you can prove she did not follow the proper procedures (see Chapter 6, Section B.4, for more on radar defenses).

To find information about other laws related to your case, like these here, you will have to look in the index of the annotated codes under subjects that you believe relate to your ticket. Then you need to look up the laws related to those subjects and look for the "annotated" cases listed below the code. (Then you need to review those cases that look relevant to your case, just as you did in Section 1 above.)

Finding Cases on the Internet

To actually read court cases on the Internet, you need to work with a private company. The best and cheapest 50-state Internet case law provider is "Versuslaw," of Redmond, Washington. It's Web address is: http://www.versuslaw.com. You can use your credit card to sign up immediately, paying about $15 to $20 for 24 hours of access, or $7 to $10 a month for unlimited access until you cancel. You can find cases from your state for the past several decades.

Chapter

3

Should You Fight Your Ticket?

In the state of Washington, it is illegal for a driver to watch television.

—Revised Code of Washington (Section) 46.61.665

A. Understanding Traffic Offenses

By now you should have analyzed the law you are charged with violating and have a clear understanding of all the elements you are supposed to have transgressed. Perhaps you have already thought of at least one compelling defense. You may be so excited about fighting back that you are ready to jump into your trusty old car and drive (carefully, of course) to traffic court to demand your day of redemption. Full stop, please. Before you consume energy, time and money fighting your case, you'll first want to think about whether it makes sense to move in this direction.

Always prepare to contest serious violations. If you're charged with anything that could land you in jail—like reckless or drunk driving—it is almost always wise to at least take the first steps necessary to fight the charge. In most states, this consists of telling the court clerk you want to plead not guilty and then actually going to court to enter your plea. Doing this will give you time to research the charges you face, including searching for information that might help you fight to reduce the charges to a less serious offense through a plea bargain. It also gives you time to find and consult a lawyer, if you decide one is necessary (see Chapter 4).

A first step to doing this is to understand the category of offense you are charged with and the consequences you'll face if you fight and lose, or simply pay up. Traffic offenses are classified somewhat differently in different states. You'll learn how this classification system generally works below, and more about your state's system in the Appendix.

1. "Civil" or "Administrative" Traffic Offenses (Some States)

About ten states, including Florida, Massachusetts, Washington and Oregon (see the Appendix for others), have "decriminalized" ordinary traffic violations. They call them "civil infractions," or similar terms. Although this may sound good, in some instances it can make it harder to fight a ticket. Typically, where tickets are treated as civil offenses, states make it easier to be convicted. Here's how:

- The state does not have to prove guilt "beyond a reasonable doubt"—you can be convicted if a judge decides 50.01% of the evidence (see sidebar) tends to show you violated the traffic law.
- In Massachusetts, Washington and the District of Columbia, the ticketing officer is not required to show up at the hearing, greatly reducing your chances of casting doubt on his version of events. (Always insist that the officer appear, if you have that choice.)
- Your right to see the evidence against you in advance of the hearing (called "discovery") may be severely limited.

Even if you are charged with a civil traffic offense, you'll find much valuable information in Chapters 9 and 10 on preparing for trial.

What Does 50.01% Really Mean?

In a "civil" traffic ticket case, the burden of proof necessary for a conviction is not as strict as in a criminal case. The judge or jury must only find that over 50% of the evidence—called "a preponderance of the evidence"—goes against you. The total quantity of evidence is not critical as long as the most convincing and accurate evidence demonstrates that you are guilty. For example, the testimony of a single, credible eyewitness to a traffic accident will prevail over the accounts of a dozen people who arrived on the scene after the accident happened.

2. Traffic Offenses As Crimes (Most States)

In most states, traffic violations are still considered criminal offenses. Typically, there are three levels of these offenses: 1) infractions, "petty" and "summary" offenses, 2) misdemeanors and 3) felonies. The rights you have to fight a ticket, and the way they are handled in court, depend on which level of offense your state assigns to traffic violations. The consequences will also vary.

a. "Petty" or "Summary" Offenses or "Infractions"

In the majority of states, routine traffic violations are classified as petty or summary offenses or infractions. As these words connote, these are extremely minor criminal offenses. But fortunately, when it comes to mounting your defense, you still have the right to demand that the ticketing officer appear at trial, still may cross-examine the officer, and the prosecution must prove you guilty beyond a reasonable doubt. Unfortunately—for reasons explained in the sidebar "Your Rights to a Jury

Trial Denied"—in states that classify offenses this way, you do not have the right to trial by jury or the right to a court-appointed lawyer if you can't afford to hire one. But, hey, all is not lost. You have this book to help you mount a great defense.

Your Right to a Jury Trial Denied

The "petty" offense category was invented several decades ago, primarily, in my view, as a way to deny jury trials to accused traffic law violators who had enjoyed this right when the tickets were handled as misdemeanors. It was a bureaucratic expedient aimed at easing revenue collection by limiting the time and expense of trials.

Here's how it happened. In 1968, the U.S. Supreme Court ruled that for "petty offenses" punishable by six months imprisonment or less, the Sixth Amendment to the U.S. Constitution didn't require states to provide a jury trial, (*Duncan v. Louisiana,* 391 U.S. 145) And in 1972, the Supreme Court ruled that a state would only have to appoint an attorney for a criminal defendant if they were too poor to hire their own *and* they faced possible jail time, (*Argersinger v. Hamlin,* 407 U.S. 25) Realizing that the vast majority of convicted traffic offenders weren't sent to jail anyway, many state legislatures quickly redefined traffic offenses as "infractions" or "petty" or "summary" offenses punishable by fine and/or license suspension only.

b. Misdemeanors

In most states a "misdemeanor" is an offense punishable by up to a year in jail and a fine of no more than one or two thousand dollars. First offense charges of reckless and drunk driving fall into this category in most states. (We do not cover these more serious offenses in this book.)

Ordinary traffic tickets are also considered to be misdemeanors in close to half of the states. When you are charged with a misdemeanor, you have all the rights discussed under "infractions" or "petty" offenses discussed above, plus the right to a jury trial.

c. Felonies

This is the most serious type of offense, usually including repeat offense drunk-driving and hit-and-run accidents causing injury or death. In some states, a third or fourth drunk-driving conviction, even if it does not involve injury or death, is treated as a felony. In other states even the second DUI/DWI can be treated as a felony. Conviction of a felony can be punished by a sentence of more than a year in state prison and a substantial fine, although judges in many states have considerable discretion. We do not cover felonies in this book.

Charged with a felony, get help fast. People charged with a felony need more help than this book can give. Normally you'll want to at least talk to a lawyer with lots of experience in fighting serious traffic cases. (See Chapter 4, Lawyers and What They Can Do for You.) Once you are fully informed of your rights and your chances of prevailing in court, it will be time to decide whether to fight back or enter a guilty plea.

B. Negative Consequences of Getting a Ticket

In all states, only those convicted of the more serious traffic violations, such as drunk or reckless driving, face the possibility of going to jail. State laws do not allow a judge to impose a jail sentence for speeding or failure to stop at a signal. Even where laws do give a judge the discretionary power to jail a traffic offender (sometimes for repeat offenders), he will very rarely choose to exercise it. Even though ordinary violations won't result in jail time, the other consequences of not contesting a ticket, or fighting and being found guilty, can be serious. As you doubtless know, you can face a stiff fine, a day in traffic school, significantly higher insurance premiums and possibly even the suspension of your driver's license.

1. Fines

A routine ticket for speeding, failure to yield, or failure to stop at a stop sign will normally cost you between $75 and $300, depending on your state law and sometimes your driving record. If the fine isn't written right on the ticket, it's easy to learn the amount by calling the traffic court. States normally have standard fines for particular violations, based on the type of offense. In speeding cases, the fine can be based on how much you exceeded the posted speed limit. Some states can also set the fine based, at least in part, on whether you have other recent violations.

Because it's expensive for the state if you fight your ticket, courts place hurdles in the way of people who insist on a court hearing, while establishing "no muss, no fuss" options to pay your fine (often called "forfeiting bail"). But while paying up may be easy, it can have lasting negative consequences, since the violation will appear on your driving record, normally for about three years. The big exception to this rule is if you pay the fine in conjunction with going to traffic school. Completion of traffic school normally means the ticket will not appear on your record.

2. Insurance Rates

Depending on your state law and your insurance company policies, your auto insurance rates will normally not increase if you receive one ordinary moving violation over three to five years. But two or more moving violations—or a moving violation combined with an at-fault accident—during the same time period might result in an increase in your insurance bill. Unfortunately, because insurance companies follow different rules when it comes to raising the rates of policyholders who pay fines or are found guilty of a traffic violation, it's not always easy to know whether it makes sense to fight a ticket.

Before you can make an informed choice as to whether to pay, go to school or fight, it makes sense to find out whether having the ticket on your record will result in your insurance rates being upped. The most direct approach is to call your insurance company and ask. The problem with this approach is that it risks alerting your insurer that you have been ticketed (something you don't want to do if you hope to successfully fight it or go to traffic school). One approach is to call your insurer anonymously and suggest you are considering switching insurance companies and want to gather information on a range of key issues, such as their criteria for good driver discounts and premium increases when covered drivers get ticketed.

3. License Suspensions

You won't lose your license for one or usually even two tickets for a routine moving violation like speeding, running a stoplight or stop sign, or many other garden-variety traffic scrapes. That is unless you are under 18 years of age, where you could lose your driving privileges in some states.

If you are over 18 years of age and have had at least three previous convictions for moving violations in the past three to five years, you could lose your license (parking violations don't count). If you are charged with drunk, reckless or hit-and-run driving, and have several previous convictions for moving violations, you can be pretty sure your right to continue to hold your license is in jeopardy. In most states, suspensions

are handled on a point system, with a license at risk of being pulled if a driver gets three or more tickets in a short period (see sidebar). Check exact rules with your state's Department of Motor Vehicles. Obviously, if you face losing your license, your incentive to fight a ticket goes way up no matter what your chances of winning.

How Point Systems Work

A "point" system assigns a certain number of points for each moving violation. A driver who gets too many points in too short a time loses his license. In some states, points are also assessed for accidents, even if no court has found you to be at fault. While the details vary from state to state, most systems typically work like this:

State A: Each ordinary moving violation counts as a single point, except two points are assessed for speed violations where the speed is greatly in excess of the speed limit. A license is suspended when a driver receives four points in a year, six in two years, or eight in three years.

State B: Two points are assessed for what are classified as minor violations (an illegal turn or slightly exceeding the speed limit), with three, four or five points assigned for more serious violations, like illegally running a stop sign or speeding. A license is suspended if a driver gets 12 points over three years.

No matter what type of point system is used, you are typically entitled to a hearing in front of a Motor Vehicle Bureau hearing officer before your license can be revoked. At that hearing it is often a good idea to explain why at least some of the violations were the result of mistakes by the ticketing officer, but for some good reason you didn't fight the ticket. It also helps to explain the specific steps you've taken to drive more carefully and safely since the violations.

In states that assess points for accidents, this may be your first opportunity to show the accident wasn't your fault, was difficult to avoid or was not part of an ongoing pattern of bad driving. Be prepared to do just that. Also, tell the hearing officers if it is essential that you commute to work or actually drive for your job, particularly if you will lose your job if you lose your license. Finally, if you drive 15,000 miles a year or more, you should mention this as well. Argue that since you drive more than average, your chances of getting tickets or having an accident are also above average.

C. The Traffic School Option

Almost every state allows a person ticketed for some types of moving violations to attend a six-to-eight hour course in traffic safety in exchange for having the ticket officially wiped from their record. Often attending traffic school is your best choice, even if you think you have a watertight defense. After all, while a trial is always some-thing of a gamble, traffic school is 100% reliable in keeping the violation off your record. (As long as you remember to set your alarm clock, of course, and make it to the class.)

Policies on allowing you to eliminate a ticket from your record by going to traffic school vary from state to state. (They can also occasionally vary within a state, where local courts have some discretion to set their own policies.) For example, in some states you can attend traffic school once a year, while in others you must wait 18 to 24 months before you can eliminate a new ticket with a new trip to traffic school. And in some states, you aren't eligible for traffic school if you're ticketed for exceeding the speed limit by more than 15 or 20 miles per hour.

Procedures for getting into traffic school also vary from place to place. Most courts allow you to sign up through the court clerk, but a few

require that you appear before a judge to make your request. How a traffic school attendee's ticket is handled is also different in different areas. For example, in some states, courts dismiss your case when proof is received that you've completed traffic school. In other states, courts require you to pay your fine (forfeit bail) with the understanding that the conviction will not be placed on your record if you complete traffic school by a prearranged deadline. Under this system you must pay twice—once for the fine and again for the school.

In brief outline, for those who are eligible, the advantages of attending traffic school are as follows:

- As long as you show up, it's normally a 100% sure way to keep a violation off your record.
- It reduces the possibility of your license being lifted or your insurance rates going up if you get new tickets, and
- If you pay attention, your driving skills may improve. (Or you may be so bored that you will drive more safely to avoid another day in traffic school.)

The disadvantages of traffic school include:

- It typically lasts six to eight hours.
- In many areas it is expensive. This is especially true if you are in a state where you must pay for traffic school plus the fine for the ticket.
- Depending on your state's rules, it may use up your traffic school option for 12 to 18 months. If you can beat this ticket, you can save the school option if you get a tougher ticket later on.

Erase that ticket through online school. In some states, erasing a ticket through traffic school may even be accomplished while sitting at home. For example, California is just one of a number of states where traffic courts authorize Internet-based traffic schools (which use tests and other devices to be sure you are paying attention). This trend is almost sure to spread. But be sure to check with the court in your particular area to make sure that an Internet-based program is acceptable. Do not pay any money to the traffic school unless you are sure that the court accepts that particular school's program.

⚠️ **You often get only one chance to opt for traffic school.** By opting to fight your ticket (whether you lose or just change your mind in the middle), you often forfeit the option of having your case dismissed in exchange for attending traffic school.

D. Deciding Whether to Fight Your Ticket

If you nix the idea of traffic school—or you aren't eligible—you must decide whether it makes sense to fight or pay up. The decision should be based largely on your informed assessment of whether you have a good chance of beating the ticket.

1. Prove a Necessary Element of Your Ticket Is Missing

As discussed in Chapter 2, your first step should be to study the exact language of the law (code section or statute) you were charged with violating. The key fact to remember: If you can prove even one element of the infraction is missing from the facts, you should be found not guilty.

Remember! No Matter Your Defense— You Normally Win If The Officer Fails to Show Up

Suppose you decide you don't have much of a defense. For example, you ran a stop sign right in front of an officer or were caught doing 90 mph on the freeway with a 65-mph limit by an officer who paced you for two miles. Obviously, the attractiveness of traffic school goes up as your chances of beating the ticket in court go down. But what should you do if you aren't eligible for traffic school? Automatically pay the ticket? Maybe not. You always want to at least consider the possibility that the officer will not show up in court. In that case, in most states your ticket will probably be dismissed.

And don't underestimate the possibility of this happening. For all sorts of reasons, including the officer being on vacation, having a scheduling conflict, having been transferred, or not being notified of the court date, cops often miss court hearings.

Here are a few tips to help you decide if the arresting officer is likely to be a no-show.

- **The more serious the violation, the more likely the officer will be there.** If you and a dozen others are ticketed at "quota time" for going 5 mph over the speed limit, the officer is less likely to show up than if you were cited for going 60 mph in a school zone.
- **The farther the officer is located from the courthouse, the less likely he is to appear.** In large counties this can really work to your advantage.
- **An officer isn't as likely to appear during his vacation.** There are usually more no-shows in summer.

2. Challenge the Officer's Subjective Conclusion

Remember, in many states, with many tickets, it's perfectly possible—and sometimes even fairly easy—to challenge the police officer's view of what happened. This is particularly likely in situations where a cop must make a subjective judgment as to whether you violated an element of the offense in a situation where no accident ensued. For example, when an officer gives you a ticket for making an unsafe left, you may argue that your actions were "safe and responsible," considering the prevailing traffic conditions. Of course, it will help your case if you can point to facts that tend to show that the cop was not in a good location to accurately view what happened or was busy doing other tasks (driving 50 mph in heavy traffic, for example). In Chapter 7 we discuss defenses to a number of other types of tickets where an officer must make a "judgment call."

In about 20 states, deciding whether it is safe to exceed the speed limit is another circumstance where a subjective judgment must be made. That's because in these states the posted speed limit is not an absolute limit, but only creates a legal presumption as to the safe speed for that road. This in turn raises the possibility of challenging the officer's judgment by proving it was safe to slightly exceed the posted limit. We discuss this important defense in detail in Chapter 5.

3. Challenge the Officer's Observation of What Happened

Assume now your state law requires an objective observation by the officer, not a judgment call about whether your action was safe. This would be true if you were cited for failing to come to a stop at a red light or making a prohibited turn. Defending this type of ticket often boils down to an argument about whose version of the facts is correct. For example, if you say, "The light was still yellow when I entered the intersection," the officer is likely to reply, "It was Red, Red, Red, ten feet before she got to the crosswalk." In disputes like this, the guy in the badge usually wins unless you can cast real doubt on his ability to accurately perceive what happened. Fortunately, despite the fact that most judges tend to believe cops, there are a number of techniques that may work to raise at least a reasonable doubt as to your guilt. (See Chapters 6 and 7 for defenses to many types of tickets.)

Why Judges Believe Cops

Judges give a lot of weight to police officers' testimony for several reasons. For one, the judge may know and respect the arresting officer based on his testimony in previous cases. In addition, because officers are usually experienced at testifying in court, they often make a more convincing presentation than does a ticketed motorist. Add to this the fact that the judge knows you have more at stake—a fine and possibly an insurance-rate increase or license suspension—than the officer does, meaning he probably suspects you have more reason to bend the truth. Finally, realize that police and prosecutors often have significant influence over the selection and retention of judges. A judge who rules too often against the prosecution may find himself running for re-election without the crucial endorsement of the police and prosecutors' associations, and perhaps even being challenged by a former prosecutor as "soft on crime."

Here are the types of evidence most likely to help you convince the judge that you—not the officer—are in the right:

- Statements of witnesses, such as passengers or bystanders, who testify to your version of events

- A clear, easy to understand diagram showing where your vehicle and the officer's vehicle were in relation to other traffic and key locations and objects, such as an intersection, traffic signal or another vehicle. Diagrams are especially important for tickets given at intersections, such as right-of-way, stoplight or stop sign violations. (For more on preparing diagrams, see Chapter 9, Section C.)
- Photographs of intersections, stop signs, and road conditions. These can be used to show conditions like obscured stop signs or other physical evidence that backs up your case. (For more on preparing diagrams, see Chapter 9, Section C.)
- Any other evidence that would cast doubt on the officer's ability to accurately observe your alleged violation. A classic way to do this is to prove his view was obscured—or that his angle of observation made it impossible to accurately see what happened.

4. Prove Your Conduct Was Based on a Legitimate "Mistake of Fact"

Even if you technically violated a statute, consider whether you have a good defense based on the argument that your conduct was based on a legitimate mistake.

Judges are allowed some leeway in considering circumstances beyond your control. If you can show that you made an honest and reasonable error, a judge might find you made a "mistake of fact" that means your ticket should be dismissed.

Here are several examples:

- You failed to stop at a stop sign after a major storm because the sign was hidden by a broken branch. If possible, you should take pictures of the obscured sign and show them to the judge to support your argument.
- You failed to stop before coming to the pedestrian cross-walk markers because they

were old and faded and could not be clearly seen.

Often this argument comes down to your claim that you weren't given fair notice as to the conduct that was expected of you. For example, a judge might dismiss a ticket for running a stop sign if it was brand new or was obscured by a broken branch. However, the judge would probably not buy this defense if:

- The sign had been up for more than a few weeks.
- In the case of a new sign, you had never stopped at that intersection before (and therefore shouldn't have been fooled by its sudden presence).
- You were traveling 50 miles per hour in a 25-mph zone.
- In the case of a sign obscured by a branch, you drove that route every day (in which case you darn well should have known the stop sign was there).

5. Prove Your Conduct Was "Legally Justified"

You may also successfully argue that your actions were "legally justified" considering the circumstances of your alleged violation. For example, if you were charged with driving too slowly in the left lane, it is a legal defense in all states that you *had to* slow down to make a lawful left turn. In this situation you do not have to deny that you were driving significantly below the speed limit and causing vehicles behind you to slow down, but can offer the additional fact that legally justifies your otherwise unlawful action. Such defenses can be very successful because they raise an additional fact or legal point, rather than simply contradicting the officer's testimony.

Here are a couple of examples of situations in which this defense might work:

- You are forced to stop on a freeway because your car began to make a loud and dangerous-sounding noise and you feared you would put other drivers in danger if you continued to drive without checking it out.

- You swerved into the right lane without signaling a lane change to pull over because a hornet flew into your car through your open window.
- You had sudden and severe chest pain and safely exceeded the posted speed limit to get to the doctor, whose office was only one half mile away.

6. Prove Your Conduct Was Necessary to Avoid Serious Harm

Emergencies not of your own making are often another legal "necessity" defense recognized in all 50 states. To take an extreme example, you should be able to beat a charge of speeding if you can prove you sped up to avoid an out-of-control truck. The key here is to convincingly argue that you were forced to violate the exact wording of a traffic law in order to avoid a serious and immediate danger to yourself or others. Here are some examples:

- Driving in the right or slow lane, you are boxed in from the back and the left side by speeding cars. To avoid colliding with a car entering the highway from the right, you accelerate well beyond the posted limit.
- Because there is a car just to your right, you briefly speed up to avoid being rear-ended by a super-aggressive big rig that is tailgating you. Once you are in the clear, you move to the right and resume a legal speed.
- You swerve across a double yellow line to avoid hitting another vehicle, pedestrian, animal, or other unexpected obstacle. If you had failed to take an evasive action, you will be at high risk of being involved in an accident.

But it's important to realize that there is a big difference between presenting a true necessity defense based on road conditions and coming up with an excuse for breaking the law based on your own inattention or personal need. Sorry, the judge is not likely to dismiss your speeding ticket because you needed to go to the bathroom or even pick up your sick child at school. Other excuses that are born to lose include:

- My mind wandered and I didn't realize I was speeding.
- My dog swallowed a chicken bone and I had to get to the vet fast.
- I couldn't fasten my seatbelt because my recently pierced nipples were supersensitive.
- I was arguing with Rush Limbaugh on my cell phone and I didn't see the stop sign.

E. Putting It All Together—How to Decide Whether to Fight or Fold

Here are some questions I always ask to determine whether going to court makes sense.

- Was the officer's view of what occurred obstructed by other moving vehicles or stationary objects like trees, fences or buildings? If so, this allows you to argue the officer could not have clearly seen the alleged offense and gives you an opening to sell your version of events to the judge.
- Did the officer stop the right car? It is quite possible in heavy traffic for an officer to see a violation committed by one white minivan (a 1995 Plymouth Voyager, for example) and to stop another (an almost identical white 1994 Dodge Caravan) further down the road. Your ability to claim this happened (*"the officer got the wrong driver, your honor"*) obviously goes way up if you can show that because of a curve in the road, construction project or just heavy traffic, the officer lost sight of the offending vehicle between the violation and pulling you over.
- Were you charged with speeding when you were driving safely, even though you were driving over the speed limit? In about 20

states, the law says it's legal to drive slightly over the posted speed limit as long as you can prove conditions made it safe to do so. (Check the Appendix to see if your state is a "presumed" speed limit state.)

- Was there an actual, provable error in the officer's approach or methodology? In citing you for speeding, did the officer correctly pace your vehicle or properly use VASCAR, radar or laser to establish your speed? We discuss what the officer needs to prove for many types of tickets in Chapters 6 and 7.
- Do any other legal defenses exist to the law you're charged with violating? For example, if you were charged with driving too slowly in the left lane of a multi-lane highway, it is a legal defense (provided for in most state's laws) that you were planning to turn left.

F. Defenses That Almost Never Work

Face it, saying "I didn't do it," or "The officer's lying," without presenting any specifics to back up your contention is highly unlikely to result in your being found not guilty. Similarly, generalized statements about the possible inadequacies of radar or laser techniques almost never result in your beating a speeding ticket. Even your successfully pointing out minor inaccuracies on your ticket, such as the officer having mistaken the color, make or model of your car when writing the ticket, will rarely get you off. (Assuming, of course, the officer appears in court and convincingly explains why your conduct was dangerous and illegal.)

Below we present a laundry-list of poor defenses. If you can't come up with anything better, it's probably a waste of time to fight your ticket, unless you really have no other choice but to play a long shot. (For example, you have used up your trip to traffic school and face license suspension.) You never know, the cop may fail to show up.

- You claim you were honestly mistaken about the law (as opposed to a particular fact, as would be the case with a hidden stop sign). For example, if you tell the judge that you honestly thought it was okay to just slow down instead stopping at a blinking red light, his reply is almost sure to be, "Sorry, ignorance of a law really is no excuse."
- You argue your violation didn't harm anybody. Again, sorry, you are still legally required to stop at a red light even if it's 3:00 a.m. and no other vehicle is moving within two miles. The fact that your illegal conduct was not dangerous is not a winning defense, except when you are cited for speeding in states where it can be legal to exceed the posted speed. (See Chapter 5 for more on how it can be legal to exceed a speed limit in a state where the posted speed limit is only presumed to be safe.)
- "The officer was picking on me." This is called "selective enforcement" and is often raised by a motorist who claims the ticketing officer ignored others who were also violating the law. It is almost impossible to win this one, since the law makes it plain that it does you no good to simply show that other drivers also violated the law and that the officer singled you out. To win with a "selective enforcement" defense, you have to take a huge additional step and show that the officer had a specific and improper motive to pick on you. If you had just won a libel case against him, had complained against him for an earlier incident or slept with his wife, you might have a chance—otherwise forget it.
- Tell a sympathetic story. The fact that your child, your mother or your parakeet was ill will not get you off. At best, the judge may reduce your fine a little (especially if you throw in the fact that you have a very low income and nine hungry mouths to feed).

- Hope the officer will trip himself up. As discussed in Chapter 10, it makes sense to cross-examine a cop with a clear idea of what your defense is and what you hope to prove. But just asking the cop a bunch of questions hoping he will say something stupid, is yet another strategy born to lose. ∎

Lawyers and What They Can Do for You

If you laid all of our laws end to end, there would be no end.

—*Mark Twain*

If you have bought this book, you are probably considering representing yourself. And why not? If you are fighting a ticket that could cost between $100 to $300, it makes little sense to hire a lawyer who will charge you upwards of $150 per hour whether you win *or* lose. There are two big exceptions to this go-it-alone rule.

1. If losing your license is a serious possibility, particularly if you need a car to do or get to your work, and

2. If going to jail or paying a huge fine are possibilities. This could happen if you are charged with driving under the influence of drugs or alcohol, reckless driving or hit-and-run.

Get help with serious charges. Even if you've had experience in civil court—in a divorce, name change or a simple lawsuit—it often isn't wise to go it entirely alone when charged with a serious criminal offense, such as drunk driving. It is true that lawyers are not the only people on earth who can learn to handle a relatively straightforward trial. But it is also true that a lawyer with lots of experience in traffic court is almost sure to be a lot further up the learning curve than you are. Even if you decide it doesn't pay to retain a lawyer to represent you, paying for a couple of "lawyer coaching" sessions by someone who can help fine-tune your strategy can be an excellent idea.

A. What Lawyers Can Do

There are three basic ways a lawyer can help when you are charged with a traffic violation.

1. Consultation and Advice

The lawyer can listen to the details of your situation, analyze your legal position and give you the pros and cons of several alternate courses of action. Ideally, she won't just give you conclusions, but enough good information to allow you to make your own informed choices. This kind of coaching is the least expensive, since it only involves an office call—or sometimes even a phone call. A charge of more than $75 for a half-hour consultation or $150 for an hour might be excessive. Find out the fee before you go in.

2. Negotiation

For more serious charges you may be able to use the lawyer's skill and experience to help you negotiate with the prosecuting agency. In some situations her previous relationships with the prosecution and experience with plea-bargaining might be helpful in limiting the price you might have to pay in terms of jail and penalties.

3. Representing You in Court

If you face driving under the influence charges or even an ordinary ticket that could result in your license being suspended, a lawyer may be able to present a more effective defense in court than you could muster on your own. Similarly, an experienced lawyer may help you put on a more effective presentation at a motor vehicles bureau license-suspension hearing. Aside from the fact that the lawyer probably does know more than you do about effective trial tactics, it's important to understand that if the consequences of losing are truly serious, you will likely be under significant pressure and stress. This helps explain why inexperienced defendants often tend to make two big mistakes. First, they are disorganized, with the result that their version of the facts is rarely clearly presented. Second, they often focus the court's attention on reams of insignificant details, forgetting to concentrate on the one or two key points that can influence the decision. In contrast, a lawyer well schooled in traffic court knows what defenses work and which do not.

Don't pay a big up-front fee. People are most scared right after they receive a serious ticket. Knowing this, some lawyers immediately ask for as much as a $5,000 retainer to be paid in advance in a serious case like drunk driving. Months later, they often advise their client to plead guilty—a result the client could have obviously achieved on her own at no cost. To prevent this from happening to you, follow these rules:

- Never hire a lawyer in a hurry. Nothing serious will happen in your case for at least a week or two after you are cited (and by posting bail or pleading not guilty you can further slow things down), so take your time.
- Make sure you know what you are charged with and have followed the techniques set forth in this book to analyze your chances of winning in court. (See particularly Chapters 2 and 3.)
- Make sure you hire one of the relatively few lawyers that have lots of experience in traffic court (see Section B below).
- Don't pay or agree to pay a big fee. Instead, pay the lawyer a small amount to help you thoroughly evaluate your case. Then, much later, armed with all the facts, decide if you want to pay more to hire the lawyer to represent you in court or represent yourself.

B. Types of Lawyers

Now let's look at the various kinds of lawyers and lawyer services that are available.

1. Private Attorneys

Most lawyers in private practice are not adequately equipped to help you mount a traffic court defense. Like physicians, most lawyers specialize. Just as you wouldn't want a foot doctor operating on your eye, you don't want a divorce lawyer defending you in a traffic or criminal case. Unfortunately, relatively few lawyers specialize in traffic-ticket defense. But in every metropolitan area, a number of attorneys will routinely handle more serious vehicle code violations, such as drunk driving. These people are usually competent to advise you on how to defend yourself against garden-variety tickets. To find one of these traffic court experts, use the same sorts of common-sense techniques you use to find quality services in other fields. Ask around among lawyers, legal secretaries or business associates for a recommendation of a traffic court pro.

Local is best. It's usually best to hire a lawyer who routinely works in the court where your case will be handled. That's because a local lawyer will know the idiosyncrasies of the judges and prosecutors who will handle your case. Just being able to chat with these folks on a first name basis can be a huge help.

Beware of referral panels of local bar associations. In most parts of America, lawyers listed by referral panels are not screened. Often, attorneys who place their names on these panels are either new to the practice of law or don't have enough business. While you could get an excellent lawyer this way, you may well end up paying to educate a lawyer who doesn't know as much as you'll read in this book.

Once you have the name of a lawyer or, preferably, several lawyers who handle traffic or criminal cases, it often makes sense to hire one for an initial consultation for an agreed-in-advance fee. Some lawyers will briefly discuss your case for free, or charge you $50 or $75 for half an hour. For a more detailed, hour-long discussion of the facts of a serious case and presentation of the lawyer's suggestions, payment of $100 to $150 is fair. A consultation should allow you to learn important information about your case while you evaluate whether it makes sense to work with the particular lawyer. In some areas you can attempt to do the same thing by looking for a lawyer who will provide a free initial consultation, but too often you'll end up with a bottom-of-the-barrel lawyer who doesn't have enough paying clients.

From the beginning, you should make it clear if you want to participate in your defense. Some lawyers are pleased to explain all the legal aspects of your case and involve you in making good strategic decisions. Others prefer an "I'm the expert, you're the novice" approach, under which they expected you to listen and follow their advice. Especially if you are handling some or all of your own case, this second approach clearly won't work, meaning you'll need to find someone else.

2. Group Legal Practices and Prepaid Legal Services

A growing number of people join prepaid legal plans, which typically charge between $80 and $250 per year. Many groups, including unions, employers, alumni associations and consumer action groups, are offering plans to their members under which they can get legal assistance for rates that are substantially lower than most private practitioners. Some of these plans are good, some mediocre, and a few are worthless. When it comes to traffic court cases, your first step is to see whether your plan provides coverage for your type of violation or one or more free consultations for any legal problem. Then, if you are eligible for

help, you should be sure you are referred to an attorney with real expertise in handling traffic or criminal cases.

Beware of reduced fee legal plans. Some low-end prepaid legal plans purport to give members legal services at a reduced cost. There are two problems with this. First, you have to go to a lawyer on the plan's local panel who may know little about traffic court. Secondly, the fee discount is often an illusion. Often, with a couple of phone calls you could negotiate the same fee with a real expert. The worst "prepaid legal services" plans provide for a free half-hour consultation with a lawyer, but little more. After that one meeting, you pay the lawyer by the hour, either at a standard or "reduced" fee. Since the plan reimburses the lawyer almost nothing for your consultation, the lawyer is highly motivated to talk you into buying expensive services you may not need.

3. Public Defenders

If you cannot afford to hire an attorney, and you face the possibility of jail time, you have the right to request help from a court-appointed attorney. Since most vehicle code violations do not result in jail time, you are not likely to get a court-appointed attorney unless you face reckless driving, drunken driving or other very serious charges, which are not covered in this book.

The legal determination of whether or not you can afford a lawyer depends upon the requirements specified by the particular state or county. A judge may appoint a public defender or private lawyer to represent you under the following circumstances:

- You have a relatively low-paying job or are unemployed.
- Your family is living on a tight budget.
- You do not have a savings account large enough to pay a lawyer.

C. Getting the Most out of Your Lawyer

Once a lawyer agrees to represent you, he has a duty to represent you to the best of his ability, whether or not you are guilty. Unfortunately, some lawyers don't take their responsibility to provide competent representation seriously. And too many others fall down when it comes to observing good housekeeping details, such as returning phone calls and letters and generally staying in close contact with their client. Again, in addition to finding competent and conscientious lawyers in the first place, your best approach is to pay the lawyer based on work produced, not an up-front retainer. A pay-as-you-go approach will give your lawyer an incentive to keep hustling and make it easier for you to politely but firmly fire the lawyer if you decide to end your relationship—something you have the right to do at any time.

D. Firing Your Lawyer

If you decide you have chosen the wrong lawyer, you may have to fire her. You have the right to do this at any time—whether or not your bill is fully paid. It is best to do this in writing. If you fax or e-mail your letter, follow up with an original copy and keep one copy for yourself. No need to say more than, "I no longer wish you to represent me." (If things get really bad between you and your lawyer, you might want to look at *Mad At Your Lawyer*, by Tanya Starnes, Nolo Press.) ∎

Speed Violations: Understanding the Laws of Your State

Judge: *Where were you when the officer pulled you over?*

Witness: *On the interstate highway.*

Judge: *What state were you in?*

Witness: *I was feeling no pain, your honor.*

Judge: *I mean were you in California or Nevada?*

➡ If you are not charged with speeding, you may skip this chapter.

Speeding tickets are, by far, the most common moving violation. For starters, there are two things you need to know about your speeding ticket. First, were you charged under an "absolute," "presumed" or "basic" speed law? (Don't worry, we'll explain this jargon below.) Secondly, you need to know how the cop determined your speed—through pacing, aircraft, radar, laser, VASCAR or other means. We discuss types of speed limits in this chapter and methods of speed detection in Chapter 6.

A. Three Types of Speed Limits

The 50 states basically use three types of speed limits. We call these "absolute," "presumed" (or "prima facie" in legalese) and "basic" speed limits. Because each type of speed limit violation often requires a unique defense, it is key to understand which you are charged with violating. (See the Appendix under "Speed Laws" for the rules of your state.)

Most states have an "absolute" speed law. There is no trick to how this works: if the sign says 40 mph and you drive 41 mph or more, you have violated the law.

"Presumed" speed limit violations are a little more complicated, but give you far more flexibility in building your defense (see Section C below). In states that use this system for all or some of their roads—California and Texas, for example— it's legal to drive over the posted limit as long as you are driving safely. For example, if you are driving 50 mph in a 40-mph zone you are "presumed" to be speeding. But if it is 6 a.m. on a clear, dry morning with no other cars on a wide, straight road, *and* you can convince the judge that you were driving safely given those conditions, you should be acquitted. That's because you present facts that "rebut the presumption" that by going over the limit you were driving at an unsafe speed. (We'll give you more information about this below.)

The concept of the basic speed law is even trickier. It works like this: In all states you can be charged with speeding by violating the "basic" speed law, even if you were driving *below* the posted speed limit. The ticketing officer must simply decide that you were going faster than you should have, taking into account the driving conditions at the time. Or put another way, if you are driving 40 mph in a 45-mph zone on an icy road in heavy fog, a cop could sensibly conclude that by driving too fast for road conditions you are in violation of the "basic" speed law. This type of ticket is mostly handed out after an accident. We discuss this violation in Section D, below.

To find out which system your state or locality follows, start by looking up your state's law under "speed laws" in the Appendix, and then study the law itself.

Here are a few samples:

- Pennsylvania: All speed limits are "absolute."
- Texas: Almost all speed laws are "presumed."
- California: Speed limits are "absolute" on freeways, but "presumed" almost everywhere else.
- Colorado: Some speed limits on city streets and county roads are "presumed." But most limits are "absolute."

⚠ **Read the law, not just our Appendix.** Before preparing to defend your speeding ticket, be sure to read the exact law you're charged with violating. To find the exact speed law you are charged under, refer to Chapter 2, where you will learn the tools necessary to find and analyze the law. Unfortunately, it is sometimes hard to tell from simply reading your state speeding law whether it follows the "absolute" or "presumed" method. Here are a few things to keep in mind:

If your state's laws refer to a "maximum" speed limit, it is most likely "absolute," so that it is illegal to exceed by even 1 mph, period.

If your state's laws refer to a speed limit above which it is "unlawful to exceed," or your state's law says something like "no person shall drive in excess" of that posted or set speed limit, that speed limit is "absolute."

If the law sets speed limits, but then just says it's "lawful"—in the absence of a hazard—to drive below the speed limit, without flatly saying it's illegal to exceed that limit, the speed limit is probably "presumed."

If the law says it's merely "prima facie unlawful" to exceed the posted speed limit, without reference to "maximum" limits, and it doesn't flatly forbid driving at a speed over the limit, the speed limit is likely "presumed."

B. "Absolute" Speed Limits

➡ You may skip this section if you were ticketed on a road covered by a "presumed" speed limit. But you should read Sections A & C of this chapter.

When you're charged with exceeding a posted speed limit in an area where the limit is "absolute," the law is simple. You are guilty if you drive over the speed limit.

Your only defenses are:
- Attacking the officer's determination of your speed. To do this you must discover what method the officer used to cite you and then learn about the ways to attack that particular method. (See Chapter 3, Section D, and Chapter 6 for ideas on how to do this.)
- Claiming an emergency forced you to exceed the speed limit to avoid serious damage or injury to yourself or others. If you had to speed up to avoid a jet making an emergency landing on a freeway, you would have a good case. (See Chapter 3, Section D, for help with this defense.)
- Claiming that the officer mistook your car for another car. With so many similar looking late-model cars, it is very possible that a cop could see a speeding car, lose sight of it around a corner, and then wrongly pick out your car further down the road.

In Chapter 6 we will help you build your defense by showing you how to challenge all common methods used to determine whether you were speeding. These methods will work whether you were ticketed in an "absolute" or "presumed" speeding area.

C. "Presumed" Speed Limits

➡ After reading Section A and your state's speeding laws, you may go back to Section B if you are sure you have been charged with violating an "absolute" speed limit.

In areas with "presumed" speed limits, the law usually reads something like this:

"No person shall drive a vehicle upon a highway at a speed greater than is reasonable or prudent having due regard for weather, visibility, the traffic on, and the surface and width of, the highway, and in no event at a speed that endangers the safety of persons or property. Unless conditions require a lower speed, the speed of any vehicle upon a highway below the limits established as authorized herein is prima facie lawful. The speed of any vehicle on a highway, in excess of the speed limits herein, is prima facie unlawful, unless the defendant establishes by competent evidence that the speed in excess of said limits did not constitute a violation at the time, place and under the road, weather, and traffic conditions then existing."

State statutes vary. The wording of each state's law will vary slightly, so be sure to read yours carefully.

If you're accused of violating a "presumed" speed limit, you have two possible defenses:

1. Claim you weren't exceeding the posted speed limit, just as you would if you were charged with violating an "absolute" speed law, or

2. Claim that, even if you were exceeding the posted limit, you were driving safely given the specific road, weather and traffic conditions at the time.

Occasionally an officer will incorrectly measure your speed. (We discuss how this happens and possible defenses in Chapter 6.) But even if he does, it can be hard to convince a judge to accept your version of what happened. In short, if you were ticketed in a "presumed" speed area, it is most sensible to rely on the argument that you may have been driving slightly over the posted speed limit, but it was safe to do so considering all the highway conditions at the time. For example, if you know you were driving 33-35 mph in a 25-mph zone, and the officer can probably prove it, you should concentrate your defense on showing that you were driving at a reasonable speed, considering the conditions at the time you were stopped.

Tailor your defense to what the officer says.
Before you testify, you'll have a chance to listen to what the officer says and to cross-examine him (see Chapter 10). If you are a quick study, you'll have the opportunity to tailor your testimony to his answers. For example, if the officer testifies he paced your car for a very short distance (see Chapter 6, Section B.1) or simply eyeballed you and concluded you were speeding, you could attempt to cast doubt on the accuracy of the officer's determination of your speed. But if his testimony as to how he established your speed seems foolproof (he carefully paced you at a constant distance for a quarter mile), you could concentrate on arguing that you were driving safely under prevailing conditions at the time you were ticketed.

As mentioned, being charged with violating a "presumed" speed limit means you are accused of driving at an unsafe speed, considering the conditions at the time you were ticketed. But most cops don't look at it this way. They reason that if you are over the posted limit, you are a law-breaker. That's why you really do have a good chance of prevailing if you can show you were just slightly over the limit and road, weather and traffic conditions were good.

But be aware that the "presumed" speed-limit law works both ways. On a pleasant summer morning on a wide, uncrowded highway, it may be safe to drive above the posted speed limit. However, on a wet day when visibility is limited by fog, it may not even be safe to drive at the posted speed limit. In short, an officer can still ticket you for driving *at or below* the posted limit, if it is unsafe to do so. This is true in all states (see Section D, below).

Now let's focus on how you might successfully mount a defense to a "presumed" speed limit ticket. Start by understanding it is not like a typical criminal defense, where the prosecution must prove you committed an illegal act beyond a reasonable doubt. (See Chapter 12, Section E, for an explanation.) In a "presumed" speed law defense, you (the defendant) have the burden of proving your speed was safe and prudent. In other words, the speed law presumes the posted speed limit is the fastest safe speed. It is up to you to prove that going faster at the time you were ticketed is also safe.

EXAMPLE: Bill was clocked by radar driving 43 mph on a street where 35-mph signs were properly posted. The law of his state contains a presumption that the posted speed limit is reasonable or prudent. To fight this ticket based on a claim that it was prudent to drive 43 mph, Bill will have to overcome the presumption that 35 mph was the only safe speed at the time he was ticketed. He might do this by showing there was no traffic at the time he was stopped and that weather was clear and dry.

No question, proving that your speed was safe becomes more difficult the more your speed exceeds the posted limit. Convincing a judge it was reasonable and prudent to go 38 mph in a 35-mph zone may not be too hard. (Which helps explain why police officers rarely write tickets for speeding less than 5 mph over the speed limit.) But proving that it was safe to go 65 mph in a 35-mph zone will be close to impossible.

But remember that there are many wide, straight roads designed for safe driving at 35 to 50 mph that have lower posted speed limits because of political pressure on public officials to crack down on speeding. Your testimony, backed by photographs, could show that your speed was safe on these broad, straight roads, even though you were driving faster than the posted limit. If you have weather, visibility and traffic factors in your favor, a judge might find you not guilty, even if you technically violated a "presumed" speed limit.

EXAMPLE: You are somewhat grumpily taking your kids to a soccer tournament at 7:00 Saturday morning. Realizing that you are running a few minutes late (and not wanting Mandy and Maude to be chewed out by their coach) you are doing 35 mph in a 25-mph zone on a wide two-lane arterial street when a cop nails you for speeding. Deciding that a red-blooded soccer mom can only take so much crap, you go to court and argue:
1. Few other cars were on the road, and
2. Traffic lights controlled traffic at all major cross streets, and
3. Visibility was great and the sun was shining.

Regardless of whether you were driving five or 25 miles per hour over the speed limit, the strategy for attacking a speeding ticket in a "presumed" speed state is usually the same. You should attempt to prove that good weather and visibility, road configuration and lack of traffic combined to make a higher speed perfectly safe. But it's rarely enough to simply tell the judge that the road looked safe to you. Instead, you'll want to introduce convincing proof to back up your position.

Here are important ways to build your case:
- Go back to the scene and take photos at the same time and day of the week you were cited. Also, take a photo from the driver's viewpoint. It's obviously to your benefit if you can establish the road was straight, with good visibility. It helps if you can show you were not in a residential area where children might run out into the street or cars could back out of driveways. It could also help if you were pulled over at a time when few cars or people would normally be present (see Chapter 9, Section C.2).
- Diagram the road, showing the location of your vehicle, the officer's vehicle, and any other traffic. (See Chapter 9, Section C.1, on preparing your testimony for trial.) It helps

if you were not ticketed in a busy commercial district where cars enter and exit parking lots and businesses. And it will almost surely help if you can show you were ticketed on a wide, straight business street with a low posted speed limit early on Thanksgiving morning when there was no vehicle or pedestrian traffic to justify the restricted speed. If you were going over the speed limit, it helps if there were few intersections along your route. If there were many intersections, be prepared to show that they were clearly controlled by lights and stop signs. (Sorry, uncontrolled intersections and speed don't go well together.)

- Although proving traffic was light is best, all is not lost if the road was busy. Indeed, the presence of heavy traffic can sometimes be a plus if you present your case skillfully. With lots of other cars on the road your argument could be that "everyone was exceeding the speed limit by about 10 mph and I would have endangered myself and others by driving slower than the flow of traffic." You might even want to argue that, had you driven more slowly, you would have violated your state's law on illegally impeding traffic. (Make sure you look up the exact law in your state's vehicle code and quote it to the judge. See Chapter 2.)

- Get a copy of the officer's notes (see Chapter 8, Section C) so you'll know what he's likely to say at trial. If he didn't make any specific notes about other traffic or pedestrians, curves, hills or obstacles, he probably won't mention them at trial. This gives a good opening to cross examine him on those issues to show that in fact the road was relatively wide, straight and free of obstacles (see Chapter 10).

Radar speed results are suspect when traffic is heavy. If radar was used to document your speed in a heavy traffic situation, you may be able to successfully argue that the officer's

radar unit may have focused on another vehicle instead of yours. (See Chapter 6, Section B.4, for more on how to do this.)

D. The "Basic" Speed Law

"Absolute" speed states set an upper limit, above which your speed is considered illegal. Drive one mile over the limit and you are a law breaker. But these states also have a way to ticket you when you are driving under the speed limit if the cop concludes your speed was unsafe. Called the "Basic" Speed Law, it prohibits driving at an unsafe speed, even if that speed is below the posted limit.

"Presumed" speed limit states also have the same law, although it is usually written into the "presumed" law. Or put another way, since the posted speed limit is only presumed to be safe when road or traffic conditions are good, the presumption can be rebutted by the police officer and the safe speed can be much lower.

But technicalities aside, in all states, tickets for driving under the speed limit, but too fast to be safe, are often referred to as "driving too fast for conditions."

For example, driving exactly at the 65-mph posted limit on the freeway would be really dumb amidst slower and heavy traffic, in a dense fog, or in a driving rainstorm or blizzard. In common-sense terms, such unsafe driving is unlawful, regardless of higher speed limits. Police most often rely on the "Basic" Speed Law after an accident. They reason that you were driving too fast, no matter how slow you were driving, because you were in an accident.

The difference between fighting one of these tickets and a speeding ticket for going over the speed limit is that here the prosecution has the burden of proving you were driving unsafely. (Again, that's because the posted speed limit is presumed to be safe.) This means the officer must testify that given the unusual road, weather or traffic conditions, your below-the-limit speed was unsafe. This can be tough to do unless you were involved in an accident, since the cop may be hard put to come up with enough hard evidence to rebut the presumption established by the posted limit. If you were in an accident, the officer will probably try to show that it was evidence you were driving at an unsafe speed, and if your speed had been lower, you would have avoided the accident.

However, you do not have to despair even if you were in an accident and are charged with violating the "basic" law for driving at an unsafe below-the-limit speed. The fact that you've had an accident is not absolute proof that you were driving unsafely. Accidents, after all, are not always caused by your violating the law. Often they are caused when another driver screwed up.

If the police officer argues that the accident itself is *evidence* that you were driving at an un-safe speed, even though you were not technically speeding, you must be prepared to challenge him. Your best bets are normally to claim, and hopefully prove, that the accident could have occurred for a number of reasons. For example, it could have been:

- Entirely or partly another driver's fault, or
- The result of a freak act of nature, in the form of a sudden wind gust, a tree falling or other natural occurrence, or
- A defect in the highway, signs or signals, which would happen if kids stole a stop sign or a stoplight fails.

Never plead guilty to a ticket issued to you following an accident. Seek the advice of an attorney. Even if you don't want to fight the ticket, you should enter a "nolo contendere" plea, which is a way of not fighting the charges (see Chapter 8, Section B.2). A guilty plea can be used against you if anyone involved in the accident sues you for damages. By contrast, if you fight a citation and lose, a guilty verdict might be used against you in a civil lawsuit arising from the accident. If you have been involved in an accident, you may want to contact a lawyer for advice and/or representation. ■

Speed Detection: Pacing, Aircraft, VASCAR, Radar and Laser—How They Work, How to Fight Them

Judge: *How did you leave the scene of the accident.*

Witness: *Scared.*

A. Getting Caught

There may be only one way to speed, but there are half a dozen ways to get caught. Generally, police use the following methods to catch you:

- **A visual estimate.** The officer sees your car and estimates how fast you are going.
- **Pacing.** The police officer follows your vehicle at the same speed you are traveling and checks her speedometer to see how fast you are going.
- **Timing.** The officer times your vehicle along a pre-measured stretch of road and is able to calculate how fast you were going.
- **VASCAR.** The officer uses a computer program to mark your time between two points and calculate your speed.
- **Radar.** The officer points a radar gun at your car and it calculates your speed.
- **Laser.** The officer points a laser gun at your car and it calculates your speed.

Not all methods are allowed in all places. California, for example, forbids the use of timing devices over fixed distances, outlaws VASCAR, and forbids radar on some roads. In Pennsylvania, only the state police—not local law enforcement —can use radar, and VASCAR can only be used if the measured speed exceeds the posted speed limit by 10 mph or more. (See Appendix for details on your state.)

Research your own state law. If you are going to challenge the method used by the police officer to nab you for speeding, you will have to track down the state laws that authorize and control the method used against you. We explain how to do the needed research in Chapter 2.

Be aware of hearsay. In challenging your ticket you will want to be aware of a key legal rule called "hearsay" that could help your case. The "hearsay" rule prohibits any testimony that quotes information from somebody other than the witness. This is sometimes called the "he said" rule because it forbids a witness from testifying to what somebody else said he saw. There is a huge catch to this hearsay prohibition—just like Perry Mason, you must affirmatively object or the judge will allow the testimony. Here are the most common situations in which a prosecutor is most likely to use hearsay evidence to prove a speed violation:

- An officer testifies about what another driver told her about your behavior.
- The officer who wrote your ticket testifies about what another officer told her. This is particularly likely to happen where an aircraft monitored your speed and relayed the information to a patrol car that stopped you.
- Where two officers were in a patrol car, and one of them observed your driving. The officer who did not see your driving may not testify to what the other officer told him about your driving.

B. How Was Your Speed Measured?

The key to challenging a speeding ticket is to know what method the officer used to determine your speed. It may not be obvious to you which method was used. First, remember to politely ask the officer when you are stopped. Second, you'll want to obtain a copy of the officer's notes before your trial (see Chapter 8, Section C, on "discovery") to learn what method was used.

Here we discuss the five most common methods of speed detection. If you know for certain what method was used to nab you, go directly to that section.

1. Pacing

Many speeding tickets result from the police officer following or "pacing" a suspected speeder and using her own speedometer to clock the suspect's speed.

a. How Pacing Works

With this technique, the officer must maintain a constant distance between her vehicle and the suspect's car long enough to make a reasonably accurate estimate of its speed. Some states have rules that the officer must verify speed by pacing over a certain distance. (For example, at least one-eighth or one-fourth of a mile.) In practice—even in states that don't require pacing over a minimum distance—most traffic officers will usually try to follow you for a reasonable distance to increase the effectiveness of their testimony, should you contest the ticket.

Road configuration may help prove inadequate pacing. Hills, curves, traffic lights and stop signs can all help you prove that an officer did not pace you long enough. For example, an officer following your vehicle a few hundred feet behind will often lose sight of it at a curve, not allowing enough distance to properly pace the vehicle. Similarly, if you were ticketed within 500 feet of starting up from a stop sign or light, the officer will not be able to prove that she paced your car for a reasonable distance.

b. How Pacing Fails

Now let's discuss the most common ways pacing can be shown to be inaccurate.

i. The Farther Back the Officer, the Less Accurate the Pace

For an accurate "pace," the officer must keep an equal distance between her car and your car for the entire time you are being paced. The officer's speedometer reading, after all, means nothing if she is driving faster than you are in an attempt to catch up with you. That's why an officer is trained to "bumper pace" your car by keeping a constant distance between her front bumper and your rear bumper. Doing this correctly requires both training and good depth perception, and becomes more difficult the farther behind the officer is from your car. (The most accurate pace occurs where the officer is right behind you.) But patrol officers like to remain some distance behind a suspect, to avoid alerting a driver who periodically glances at his rearview and sideview mirrors. So if you know an officer was close behind you for only a short distance, your best tactic in court is to try to show that the officer's supposed "pacing" speed was really just a "catch-up" speed. You will want to ask the officer the distance over which she tailed you. (See Chapter 10, on cross-examination techniques.) If she admits it was, say, only one-eighth mile (between one and two city blocks), it will help to testify (if true) that you noticed in your rear view mirror that the officer was closing the gap between your car and hers very quickly. This would have the effect of giving her a high speedometer reading. Represented graphically, it looks like this:

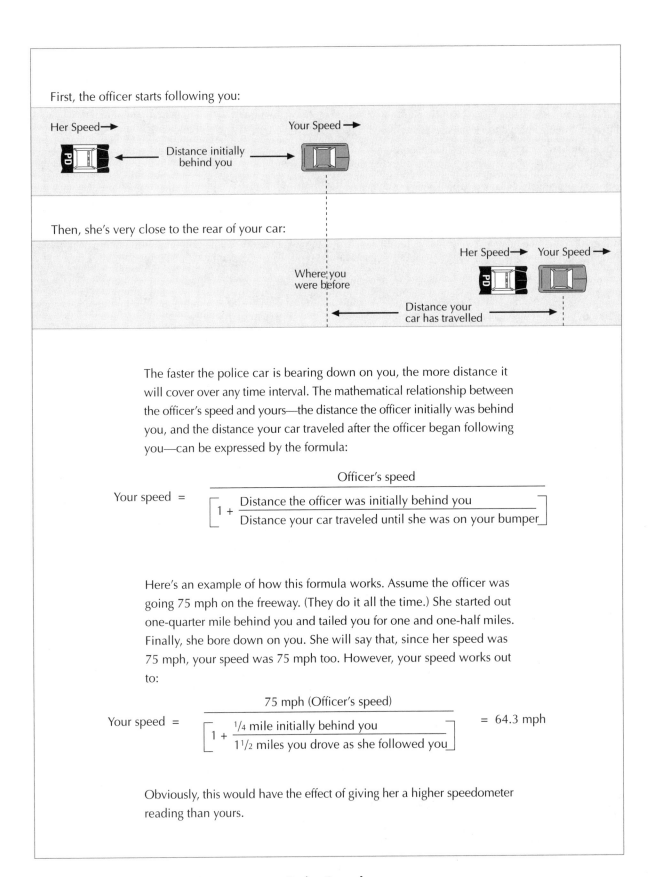

First, the officer starts following you:

Her Speed ➡   Your Speed ➡

← Distance initially behind you →

Then, she's very close to the rear of your car:

Her Speed ➡ Your Speed ➡

Where you were before

← Distance your car has travelled →

The faster the police car is bearing down on you, the more distance it will cover over any time interval. The mathematical relationship between the officer's speed and yours—the distance the officer initially was behind you, and the distance your car traveled after the officer began following you—can be expressed by the formula:

$$\text{Your speed} = \frac{\text{Officer's speed}}{\left[1 + \dfrac{\text{Distance the officer was initially behind you}}{\text{Distance your car traveled until she was on your bumper}}\right]}$$

Here's an example of how this formula works. Assume the officer was going 75 mph on the freeway. (They do it all the time.) She started out one-quarter mile behind you and tailed you for one and one-half miles. Finally, she bore down on you. She will say that, since her speed was 75 mph, your speed was 75 mph too. However, your speed works out to:

$$\text{Your speed} = \frac{75 \text{ mph (Officer's speed)}}{\left[1 + \dfrac{\text{1/4 mile initially behind you}}{\text{1}\text{1/2 miles you drove as she followed you}}\right]} = 64.3 \text{ mph}$$

Obviously, this would have the effect of giving her a higher speedometer reading than yours.

Pacing Formula

The Math of Pacing

Vyou = your speed

Vcop = the officer's speed as she closes

Dyou = the distance you travel during the "pace"

Dcop = the distance the officer travels during the "pace"

Dcop0 = the distance the officer was behind you, when she started the "pace"

t = the time the officer took to start from **Dcop0** behind you, to catch up to you and wind up on your tail.

This formula can prove the officer improperly paced you. But there is one problem. The judge may not allow it as evidence. Normally, in court, legal rules of evidence require a mathematician or expert to use this kind of testimony. But you may be able to present it in your closing argument, where the rules of evidence don't come into play.

Here's how it's derived:

Speed equals Distance divided by Time and Time is equal to Distance divided by Speed. In mathematical symbols, since $v=d/t$, then $t=d/v$. The time, **t,** over which the pacing occurred will be the same for you and the officer. Therefore, This time "**t**" will equal both (**Dyou/Vyou**) and (**Dcop/Vcop**), which are equal to each other, both being equal to time " **t**." Therefore, (**Dcop/Vcop**) = (**Dyou/Vyou**). It's also true that if the officer drove faster to gain on you, then **Dcop = Dyou** + the distance the officer was originally behind you (**Dcop0**). Also from rearranging (**Dcop/Vcop**) = (**Dyou/Vcop**), we get **Dcop = (Dyou** x **Vcop)/Vyou**. These last two "**Dcop**" equations are equal to each other, so, **Dyou + Dcop** behind = (**Dyou** and **Vcop)/Vyou**. Rearranging this last equation gives: **Vyou = (Dyou** x **Vcop)/(Dyou + Dcop** behind). Dividing both numerator and denominator by **Dyou**, we get: **Vyou = Vcop/** [1 + (**Dcop** behind/**Dyou**)].)

Your goal is to use the speeds that the officer testified to for her car while she was "pacing" you to argue that she used her speed while closing in on you as you were driving under the speed limit. Here is how to do this:

1. Read the material on how to cross-examine the officer in Chapter 10.

2. Pin down the officer during cross-examination on the distance she was behind you during the pace and the distance she paced you. (See above for how to do this.) At that point, you can use a calculator to figure— based on the officer's answers, pacing and tailing distances— whether these speeds and distances, inserted into the formula, will result in a speed that is below the speed limit.

3. Later, when your turn comes to testify, emphasize (if true) how you initially saw the patrol car some distance back in your rearview mirror, then saw it bear down on you quickly.

4. Be sure to also testify (if true) that you periodically glanced at your speedometer, which indicated a steady speed, and that you didn't slow down when you saw the patrol car.

5. During your final argument, you should emphasize the point that your testimony and the officer's both show that she was actually closing in on you when she claimed to be measuring your speed, not truly pacing you at a constant speed. Then, if the above formula will result in your speed being below the limit, explain that there is a "simple mathematical formula" to show your true speed. Show how it is derived (see above), and how, when the numbers are "plugged in" it shows your speed was below the speed limit. (See Chapter 11, Section B.11, for closing arguments before a judge and Chapter 12, Section D.6, for closing arguments before a jury.)

Practice, practice, practice. If you are pretty sure your defense will turn on whether the officer really paced you properly, practice explaining the speed formula ahead of time. Bring a large piece of thick white paper to court so after the officer testifies to his speed you can plug this number in.

ii. Pacing at Dusk or Night

Pacing is much more difficult in the failing light of dusk or in complete darkness, unless the officer is right on your tail. In darkness, the officer's visual cues are reduced to a pair of taillights. Also, if an officer paces a speeder's taillights from far back in traffic, she'll have trouble keeping the same pair of taillights in view. In Chapter 10, Section B, we include a few cross-examination questions to bring this out during the trial.

iii. Road Conditions Can Affect Pacing

Pacing is easiest and most accurate on a straight road, with no hills, dips or other obstacles and where the officer can see your vehicle continuously as she follows you. This allows her to keep her car at a constant distance behind you while she paces your speed. Hills, freeway interchanges, dips, curves, busy intersections and heavy traffic make for a poor pacing environment. All of these obstacles can be used to challenge the accurate pacing of your vehicle.

2. Aircraft Speed Detection

Many drivers are ticketed for speeding when a ground patrol unit is alerted to their speeds by a radio report from an airplane. Obviously, this is especially common in states with lots of wide-open highway. If your ticket was based on information from one of these aircraft patrols, there are several possible ways you may be able to challenge it.

a. How Aircraft Speed Detection Works

There are two ways an aircraft officer determines your speed. The first is to calculate your speed by timing how long it takes for your vehicle to pass between two highway markings at a pre-measured distance apart. The second involves a kind of "pacing" (see Section 1 above on pacing) of the target vehicle, but from the aircraft. The pilot uses a stopwatch to time its own passage over highway markings that are a known distance apart. Then the aircraft is used to pace your vehicle's speed. As we'll see, this second method is less accurate and therefore easier to attack.

Under either system, if a car is found to be speeding, a waiting ground patrol car is radioed. If that ground patrol car does not independently verify your speed, your chances of successfully fighting your ticket go up. For starters, that's because both the aircraft and ground officer will have to be present in court. The aircraft officer must testify as to how he measured your speed and the ground officer must say that you were, in fact, the driver. If the pilot appears in court, but the ground officer does not, the prosecution cannot prove its case in the majority of states that treat traffic cases as minor criminal violations. In part, this is because you are not required to testify, since the Fifth Amendment to the Constitution gives you the right to remain silent. However, in states that treat traffic violations as "civil offenses," you may not have this right to remain silent (see Chapter 3, Section A).

Ask for a dismissal if either officer fails to appear. If both officers are not in court, ask the judge to dismiss the case. If the prosecution tries to introduce an absent officer's police report or other written record into court in place of live testimony, simply object on the basis that it is hearsay. Without an officer present, the written report is inadmissible hearsay testimony. For more on how to object and insist that the case be dismissed, see Chapter 10, Section A.

Even if both officers show up, you still may have a decent opportunity of winning a case where an airplane is involved. To maximize your chances, ask the judge to exclude one officer from the courtroom while the other is testifying. (See Chapter 11, Section B.2, for more on why and how to do this.) Don't worry, you are not being impolite but only exercising your right to prevent the two cops from taking cues from each other's remarks.

b. How Aircraft Speed Detection Fails

Fortunately for you, there are several good ways to challenge tickets based on an aircraft's measuring your speed.

i.   Stopwatch Error / Reaction Time

If the timing is not performed properly from the aircraft, the speed of your vehicle will be wrong. Since this speed is calculated by dividing distance by time, the shorter the distance your speed was measured over, the more likely it is that a timing error on the part of the sky cop will result in a too-high speed reading. If the officer hesitated even slightly before pushing the timer as you passed the first ground marker, the measured time would be shorter than the true time your vehicle took to traverse the distance to the second marker.

EXAMPLE: Officer Aircop sees Dawn Driver pass between two markings an eighth of a mile apart. At a speed of 65-mph—the speed limit—Dawn's car should cross the two marks in 6.9 seconds. But if Officer Aircop starts the stopwatch a second too late or stops it a second too early and gets 5.9 seconds, she incorrectly figures Dawn's speed to be (0.125 mile/5.9 sec.) x 3,600 = 76 mph.

The longer the distance between the ground markings, the more accurate the officer's reading

is likely to be. A one-second error in starting the stopwatch will only result in about a 1-mph error, where the distance between markers is a mile. (See Chapter 10, Section B, for cross-examination questions that highlight this error.)

ii. Difficulty in Keeping Your Car in View

If two markers are a mile apart, it takes a car doing 75 mph some 48 seconds to travel between the two markers. It's hard to stare continuously at anything for that long, especially from a plane. If many other cars are on the road, it would be easy for the sky officer to lose sight of your car while she is looking at her flight instruments.

You should raise this possibility on cross-examination by asking the airplane officer about procedures during her flight. Your goal is to get the officer to admit that she did not continuously watch your car during the pacing. Hopefully, you will learn that the officer must keep a log for every vehicle she paces, recording the vehicle's basic description, the time between the two points, and the calculated speed. In short, the officer is usually also keeping track of other cars. If you establish this during cross-examination, you can argue in your final argument that the officer might have started to pace your car, but mistakenly focused on another car that looked like yours after looking up from taking notes. (See Chapter 10, Section B, on cross-examination.)

iii. Using the Aircraft to Pace You

The second method by which an officer in an aircraft can determine your speed involves two steps: (1) timing the aircraft's passage over two separate highway markings a known distance apart, to get the aircraft's speed and then (2) using the aircraft to "pace" your vehicle. For example, if the aircraft passes over two markings a mile apart in 60 seconds, the aircraft's speed is 1 mile/60 seconds, or 0.0167 mile per second. Since there are 3,600 seconds in an hour, this 0.0167 mile per second is multiplied by 3,600 to get miles per hour, or 60 mph. If the car below stays ahead of the aircraft, it's going 60 mph; if it's pulling away, it's going faster. The officer in the plane then radios this information to the officer on the ground. This method is less accurate than timing a car's passage between two points for the following reasons:

- **Inconsistent distance while pacing.** It's much more difficult for an aircraft pilot, than for the driver of a police car, to maintain the same distance behind the paced vehicle.
- **Inaccuracy in ascertaining reference points from the air.** For the officer in the air to determine his speed, he has to time the passage of his plane over two markers several thousand feet below. This is done by starting a stopwatch as the plane passes the first marker on the roadway and by stopping the watch as the second marker is crossed. The speed is then determined by dividing the distance between the markers by the elapsed time. This sounds reliable enough, but it often isn't. For starters, it is difficult for a pilot to know exactly when she passed a spot on the ground. An inconsistency in the aircop's body position within the aircraft, by even a few feet, as she times the passage, can add several miles per hour to your estimated speed.
- **Wind conditions can also affect the ground speed of the aircraft.** If a headwind comes

up after the aircraft has timed its passage over two markers its airspeed would be decreased. That would make it appear to the aircop as if you were going faster than you actually were.

iv. Problems Identifying the Vehicle

After testifying about how the speed was computed, the aircraft officer will next testify about radioing the information to the ground officer who stopped you. Here you'll again want to raise the possibility that the ground cop stopped the wrong car. Given that license plate numbers are too small for the airborne officer to see, and many modern cars look very much alike, this is a real possibility.

Ask the pilot how many cars she fingered for speeding. Often aircraft officers relay information on several speeding cars at the same time. This, of course, increases the possibility that the ground officer might confuse several. If the ground-unit officer is excluded from the courtroom, she will take the copy of the ticket with her, since she issued it. This means the aircraft officer won't be able to use the ticket to "refresh her memory" while testifying. In Chapter 10 we discuss cross-examination techniques, including suggested questions for this situation.

rush hour

More About Aircraft Tickets

When the aircraft officer identifies a car going too fast (either by pacing it, or measuring its speed between two marks), he normally records the time, speed, vehicle color and type, along with brief notes on the car, in what's usually called an "observation log." As noted in Chapter 8, Section C, you have the right to request a copy of this log before trial. It really does pay to examine this log. Here are some things to look for:

- References to multiple vehicles, thus raising identity problems
- Hard-to-believe identical speeds for multiple vehicles
- Short distances between markers, and hence higher reaction-time errors
- Long distances between markers, and hence possible vehicle identity problems.

You may also see that the timing occurred over less than a minute, or even that your car was described as being a different make or color than it really is. Obviously, tidbits like these are extremely useful to prepare questions that cast doubt on the reliability of the pacer's observations.

If the patrol officer on the ground testifies that he independently checked your speed, by pacing, try to establish that he overly relied on the radio report and didn't really pace you for an extended period. See Section 1, above, for how to challenge the accuracy of pacing.

recorded by the stopwatch) by the time it took to travel that distance. For example, a car passing between two points 200 feet apart, over two seconds, is traveling an average speed of 200/2 or 100 feet per second, which converts to 68 miles per hour.

Converting Miles Per Hour to Feet Per Second

Some judges will insist that you explain your math when you talk about translating miles per hour into feet per second. Here is how to do it: There are 5,280 feet in a mile, so one mile per hour is 5,280 feet per hour. Since there are 60 seconds in a minute and 60 minutes in an hour—or 60 x 60 seconds in an hour (3,600 seconds)—one mile an hour, or 5,280 feet per hour, is really 5,280 feet per 3,600 seconds, or 1.47 feet per second. If one mile per hour is 1.47 feet per second, you multiply the speed, in miles per hour, by 1.47, to get the speed in feet per second."

MPH	FT/SEC
20	29.4
30	44.1
40	58.8
50	73.5
60	88.2
70	102.9

3. VASCAR

Most states allow police officers to catch speeders using technology called "VASCAR" (Visual Average Speed Computer And Recorder). Despite the fancy name, VASCAR amounts to a stopwatch coupled electronically with a calculator. The calculator divides the distance the target vehicle travels (as

a. How VASCAR Works

VASCAR is not like a radar or laser gun, which gives a read-out of a vehicle's speed by simply pointing and pulling the trigger. A VASCAR unit requires far more human input than radar or laser guns. As we will see, this also greatly increases the possibility of mistakes.

VASCAR works like this: The officer measures the distance between the two points by using a measuring tape or uses her vehicle's odometer, which is connected to the VASCAR unit. When the officer sees the target vehicle pass one of two points, she pushes a button to start the electronic stopwatch, then pushes it again to stop it when the vehicle passes the second point.

EXAMPLE 1: On a busy street, the officer uses a tape to measure the distance between two road signs, which comes to 234 feet. She then goes back to her car and dials this number on her VASCAR unit. When a car passes the first sign, the officer presses the "time" switch, then presses it again when the car passes the second sign. If the elapsed time is 2.75 seconds, the VASCAR unit calculates the average speed as 234 feet divided by 2.75 seconds, or 85.1 feet per second (57.9 mph).

EXAMPLE 2: Another officer picks one point at a marked crosswalk and another at a manhole cover in the street. The officer drives the distance between the two points, making sure to press the distance button on the VASCAR unit when she drives over the crosswalk and again when she reaches the manhole cover. The odometer connected to her VASCAR unit measures a distance of 0.12 mile or 633 feet and records this in its memory. The officer then picks a hidden spot where she has a clear view of both points, and waits. A motorcycle passes the crosswalk line and the officer clicks the "time" button, then clicks it again when the vehicle crosses over the manhole cover 6.78 seconds later. The VASCAR unit calculates the speed as 633 feet in 6.78 seconds, or 93.4 feet per second (63.5 mph).

A VASCAR unit is normally connected to an officer's odometer to allow her to measure a distance between two pre-selected points while driving past them. This also allows her to use the unit while moving. VASCAR units are engineered to take into account the police unit's speed and the suspected vehicle's speed by pressing the

"time" switch twice as your car passes the two pre-selected points, and by pressing the "distance" button twice as her car traverses those same two points.

The officer can use a VASCAR unit in five ways:

- While stationary. The officer manually measures a certain distance with a tape or other measuring device, dials that measurement into the VASCAR unit, then clicks the "time" switch when the car passes the first and second distance marks.
- While stationary, after having driven a set distance in her vehicle and using the odometer to enter that distance into the VASCAR unit. Again, the cop clicks the "time" switch when the car passes the first and second distance marks.
- While following you and allowing the VASCAR unit to take into account that her patrol car is also moving.

EXAMPLE: While 200 feet behind you on a downgrade where the officer has a good field of vision, he watches you pass a no-parking sign and clicks the "time" switch. He pushes the "distance" switch as he passes the same sign, then pushes the "time" switch again after you pass a shadow made across the road by a telephone pole. Finally, he pushes the "distance" switch a second time as he passes that same phone-pole shadow. The VASCAR calculator divides the distance by the time to calculate the speed.

- While ahead of you, by pressing the "distance" switch twice as she passes between the two points, then the "time" switch twice as she watches you—in her rearview or side view mirror—pass over the same two points.
- While driving in the opposite direction, by clicking the "time" switch as you pass a point well ahead of her and by simulta-

neously pressing the "time" and the "distance" buttons as your cars go past each other—setting the second point. Then the officer presses the "distance" switch as she reaches the first point where she started to time you. (She then makes a quick U-turn to pull you over.)

VASCAR is obviously a much more flexible tool than pacing, since the officer does not have to be going the same speed as you are or follow you over any particular distance. As long as she manipulates the "time" and "distance" switches correctly and consistently, while accurately observing when your vehicle and hers pass over the same two points, she can accurately track your speed.

But fortunately, from your point of view, correctly using VASCAR isn't one bit easy. For example, it is no easy thing to accurately push the "time" and "distance" buttons while observing the target pass between two points, at least one of which is almost sure to be far away from the officer. And, of course, doing this accurately is even harder when the patrol car is moving.

b. How VASCAR Fails

Since speed is defined as distance traveled per unit of time, nothing could be seemingly more accurate than timing an object's passage between two measured points. But, because VASCAR measurement depends entirely on human input—accurately pushing the button for "time" and "distance"—it is easy for errors to creep in. The most common three mistakes that can cause error in a VASCAR measurement are:

- The inability of the officer to accurately see when a distant car passes a distant point
- The officer's reaction time. (How long it takes her to push the button when a car passes a marker.)
- The accuracy of the odometer on the officer's car.

Different Types of VASCAR Errors

Short Distances. At short distances, generally less than 500 feet, reaction-time error is most likely to produce an incorrect VASCAR result. If the officer is late to the trigger when you cross the first measuring point, but accurate as you cross the second point, you will be clocked as going faster than you actually were. For this reason, a federally commissioned study of VASCAR (J. Gavin Howe, Transportation Research Center, East Liberty, Ohio, DOT HS 807 748, NTS No. PB92-125178, republished in the Winter 1994 edition of *Auto and Traffic Safety*) recommends that to obtain accurate VASCAR readings, officers measure speeds over elapsed times of at least 4 seconds for stationary police units and 5 seconds for moving units.

Long Distances. When VASCAR is used at distances over 1,500 feet, reaction-time errors are less of an issue. (Half a second one way or the other won't make much difference.) Here, significant errors usually result because the officer simply doesn't see when you pass the marker point farthest from her car because it is too far away.

In its "Legal Defense Kit" for defending traffic tickets, the National Motorists Association of Waunaukee, Wisconsin, (http://www.motorists.com) includes a scientific study entitled "An Error Analysis of VASCAR-Plus" by Kenneth A. Moore of JAG Engineering, Manassas, Virginia. Through numerous calculations, charts, and graphs, Moore demonstrates that VASCAR is most prone to error where the distance between the two clocking points is 1,500 feet or more. (He also agrees that it is prone to error below 500 feet.)

The possibility of VASCAR error is so well known that Pennsylvania lawmakers have taken action. Pennsylvania law (Title 75, Section 3368), forbids a VASCAR speeding conviction—where the speed limit is less than 55 mph—if the VASCAR speed readout isn't more than 10 mph over the limit. That's another way of saying, "We don't trust the accuracy of a VASCAR unit that says '44 mph' when the speed limit is 35."

If you're charged with speeding and the officer used VASCAR, you should try to bring up these possibilities for inaccuracy at trial. The best way to do this is to cross-examine the officer, knowing what questions to ask (see Chapter 10, Section B).

i. Officer's Observation of Distant Point

When an officer times the passage of a car between two points, she must accurately record when the car passes each. This becomes more difficult, the farther the officer is from either point. This is especially true at dusk, at night, and during bad weather, particularly fog or rain. For example, while VASCAR can be used at night, the officer will need to be able to tell when vehicle headlights pass objects that may be illuminated poorly or not at all. Obviously, this is far more difficult than watching a car pass two nearby points at noon in good weather.

> EXAMPLE: At dusk, the officer is parked near the first point—a crosswalk. The second point—a phone pole—is 500 feet away. The officer can see and accurately react to your car passing the crosswalk near him. But due to poor visibility and a poor visual angle, he slightly misjudges when you passed the distant shadow of the telephone pole. It took you six seconds to drive that distance (your speed was 500/6=83.3 feet per second or 56 mph.) However, because the officer misjudges when your car passed the second point, he clicks the VASCAR "time" switch after only five seconds and your speed is calculated erroneously at 500/5=100 feet per seconds or 68 mph. In short, his one-second error results in your speed being recorded as 12 mph too fast.

It follows that in court, whenever a VASCAR ticket turns on an officer's ability to record when your car passes a distant spot, you'll want to challenge her testimony that she could see your vehicle clearly. (See Chapter 10, Section B, on cross-examination.)

ii. Officer's Reaction Time

"Reaction time" is the time between observing something and responding to it. Especially where the distance between the two points is only a few hundred feet, an officer's reaction time will greatly affect the speed calculated by the VASCAR unit. Here's why: The less distance between the two points, the lower the elapsed time a speeding car will take to pass through those two points. For example, if the distance is only 100 feet the car will pass the second point in only a second or two, meaning a reaction time error of only a few tenths of a second will affect the accuracy by 20 or 30 percent. On the other hand, if the distance between the two points is 1,000 feet—which takes 15 seconds for a car going 40 mph to pass—a reaction time error of a few tenths of a second will affect the accuracy by only one to two percent.

> EXAMPLE: The speed limit is 45 mph. The distance between the two points is 100 feet and your car covers that distance in 1.54 seconds. Your speed is 100/1.54=64.9 feet per second or 44.2 mph—legal. But if the officer pushes the "time" switch 0.124 seconds after you pass the first point (the average reaction time of race-car drivers) and your passage past the second point is done correctly (more likely because she can anticipate, rather than react), the VASCAR elapsed time will be 1.42 seconds. Your speed will be incorrectly read as 100/1.42=70.4 feet per second or 48 mph—illegal.

In promotional materials, VASCAR manufacturers claim reaction time isn't a factor, because they assume that the officer will anticipate, rather than react to your car passing each point. They also argue that any delayed reaction will be the same for each click of the VASCAR unit, thereby canceling out the error. This is faulty reasoning. There's no guarantee that the officer will delay the same interval when pushing the button as you pass the first and then the second points. In fact, she may do a much better job at the second point since her eyes have now been fixed on your car for quite some time, making her better prepared to press the button. The result can easily be that she's erroneously shortened the time and, thereby, increased your recorded speed.

Reaction time error is likely to be worst in the situation where the officer's vehicle is approaching yours from the opposite direction. For example, if you're doing 65 mph northbound, and an officer is doing the same speed southbound, your closing speed is 130 mph or 191 feet per second. If you're 500 feet away, the officer has little more than two seconds to look ahead, watch your vehicle pass one point, hit the "time switch," then hit the "time" switch again simultaneously with the "distance" switch as your cars pass each other. The officer then has a few more seconds to hit the "distance" switch a second time, hopefully just as she passes the same point you passed when she hit the "time" switch the first time. Operating VASCAR in the "opposite direction" is so difficult to do well that some police agencies discourage officers from using it this way.

Your main goal is to attack the officer's reaction time through cross-examination (see Chapter 10, Section B), particularly relating to the difficulty in timing a car's passage past a distant point. When it is your turn to testify, tell the judge in detail (if true) that your speed was at or under the limit— or safely above it in a "presumed"-speed-limit state. Finally, be prepared to argue during your closing argument (see Chapter 11, Section B.11, and Chapter 12, Section D.6), how your testimony as well as the officer's responses to your cross-examination questions raise a reasonable doubt over whether you were violating the speeding law.

iii. Odometer Error

The VASCAR unit's accuracy depends on the accuracy of the police vehicle's odometer, except where the distance between the two points is independently measured with a tape and dialed into the VASCAR unit. That is because the VASCAR gets its distance information via the patrol vehicle's speedometer/odometer, to which it is connected.

As the patrol vehicle moves forward, the cable linking the VASCAR unit to the speedometer/odometer turns, calculating how far the vehicle has moved from Point A to Point B. It is supposed to be re-calibrated at least once a year. Tire wear and pressure can affect the accuracy of a speedometer. These factors will also affect odometer accuracy, since the odometer and speedometer both run off the same cable.

For example, low tire pressure and tire wear on the police vehicle can result in a tire with a slightly smaller circumference than a new and properly inflated tire. The smaller wheel must make more revolutions to cover the same distance as a new tire. This results in erroneously high speedometer readings and in an exaggerated odometer distance reading. Since speed is distance divided by time, an erroneously high odometer distance fed into the VASCAR unit will result in an erroneously high speed reading.

This type of error, however, is usually fairly small. For example, a 24-inch diameter tire that has lost 1/4-inch of tread will be 23.75 inches in diameter, a mere 2% less, so that the recorded distance and speed will only be 2% high. Still, this type of error, when added to other types of errors —like the ones listed above—may well result in an erroneous VASCAR reading. So, during cross-examination, ask when the VASCAR unit was last tested. If it was not tested recently, or the officer does not know when it was tested last, you should attack the accuracy of the test in your closing argument. (See Chapter 11, Section B.11, and Chapter 12, Section D.6.)

4. Radar

Since so many speeding tickets involve the use of radar measurement systems, let's briefly examine how radar works. Of course, the point of doing this is so you'll be well positioned to cast doubt on the accuracy of your radar ticket. It can sometimes be an uphill battle trying to convince a judge that a sophisticated electronic radar device is fallible. But it is definitely possible to do this. After you've read what follows, you'll know more about radar than most judges and some police officers, and may be able to use your knowledge to beat your ticket.

Don't confuse radar with laser. You need to determine how you were caught. You can ask the ticketing officer what method she used, and testify to that in court. Or you can demand to see the officer's notes, which will indicate what method was used to clock your speed. (See Chapter 8, Section C, on "discovery.") While radar and laser detection systems work in a similar way, the way to fight them in court has significant differences. Be sure you know which one was used against you.

a. How Radar Works

The word "radar" is an acronym for "Radio Detection And Ranging." In simple terms, radar uses radio waves reflected off a moving object to determine its speed. With police radar, that moving object is your car. Radar units generate the waves with a "transmitter." When they bounce back off your car, they are picked up and amplified by a receiver so they can be analyzed. The analysis is then reflected in a speed readout device.

Radar systems use radio waves similar to those involved in AM and FM radio transmissions, but with a higher frequency—up to 24 billion waves per second as compared to one million per second for AM radio. Why so high? Because the higher the frequency, the straighter the beam, the truer the reflection and the more accurate the speed reading. It's important to know this because, as we discuss below, the primary defense to a radar speeding ticket is to attack its accuracy.

To better understand how radar works, remember what it was like to blow peas out of a straw as a kid. If you blew the peas at the trunk of a stationary car, they would (at least theoretically) take the same amount of time to bounce back and hit you in the forehead. If the car had been moving away from you, the peas would each take a longer time to hit and bounce back. The radar beam sends out billions of electronic pulses (like peas) per second and sends back reflected waves whose pulses are slightly farther apart.

The greater the difference between the transmitted and reflected waves, the greater the relative speed or difference of speed between the target vehicle and the police car.

Although radar signals can be bounced off stationary or moving objects, they cannot be bent over hills or around curves. To clock your speed with radar, this means you must be in an officer's "line-of-sight." However, don't expect to see the radar unit. Officers can hide it behind roadside shrubbery or stick it out unobtrusively from behind a parked car.

Unfortunately for errant motorists, modern radar units are fairly easy to operate. Officers using them do not have to be certified or licensed. But it's also true that to operate radar units with a high rate of accuracy under all sorts of road and weather conditions takes practice and skill. The best way to learn is with the help of an experienced instructor. It follows that it will usually look bad in court if an arresting officer admits she's never had any formal instruction in the use of radar equipment. Realizing this, most officers will say (either when making their presentation or in answer to your cross-examination questions) that they have taken a course in how to use radar. It's important for you to know that this course can range anywhere from a short pep talk by a company sales representative to a few hours or even a day of instruction at a police academy.

Either way, most officers don't receive comprehensive instruction on the important fine points of using radar.

This gives you the opportunity to use cross-examination questions to try to pin the officer down (see Chapter 10, Section B) on just how few hours she actually spent on good instruction. Assuming you succeed in doing this, you'll then want to make the point, during your closing argument, that the officer could well have misused the unit. For example, the officer may not have realized that at a distance of a few hundred feet, a radar beam is wide enough to cover four lanes of traffic, and thus might have clocked a nearby vehicle instead of yours. And as we discuss in the rest of this chapter, there are a number of other ways officers commonly produce false radar readings.

b. How Radar Is Used/Types of Equipment

Although many brands of radar units are in use, they all fall into two types: car-mounted units that can be operated while the officer's vehicle is stationary or moving, and hand-held radar "guns" often used by motorcycle officers in a stationary position. Let's briefly look at the distinguishing characteristics of each with the idea of using our knowledge to mount an effective defense.

i. Car-Mounted Units

Most radar antennas used in patrol vehicles are shaped something like a side-mounted spotlight without the glass on the front. They are usually mounted on the rear left window of the police car facing towards the rear. If you're sharp-eyed and know what to look for, you can sometimes see one sticking out from a line of parked cars.

But no matter where the antenna is mounted, the officer reads your speed on a small console mounted on or under the dash. The unit has a digital readout that displays the highest speed read during the second or two your vehicle passes through the beam. This means that once you go through the radar beam, slowing down does no good. These units also have a "speed set" switch that can be set to the speed at which the officer has decided a ticket is appropriate. This allows the officer to direct his attention elsewhere while your car travels through the beam. If the speed reading exceeds the "speed set" value, a sound alarm goes off. The officer looks at the readout, then at your car, and takes off after you.

Most modern police radar units can also operate in a "moving mode," allowing the officer to determine a vehicle's speed even though her own patrol vehicle is moving. In moving mode, the radar receiver measures the frequency of two reflected signals: the one reflected from the target vehicle—as in the stationery mode—and another signal bounced or reflected off the road as the patrol vehicle moves forward. The frequencies of these two signals indicate the relative speed between the officer's vehicle and the target, and the officer's speed relative to the road. The target vehicle's speed is then calculated by adding or subtracting these two speeds, depending on whether the two vehicles are moving in the same, or opposite, directions. This calculation is done automatically, by the electronics in the radar unit.

EXAMPLE 1: Moving radar from opposite direction: A police car is going north on a two-lane road at 50 mph. Your vehicle is heading south at 45 mph. This means the vehicles are closing in on each other at a combined or relative speed of 95 mph. The radar unit in the 50-mph patrol car with its beam pointed at your car will receive a reflected radar signal indicating a 95 mph combined speed, as well as a signal indicating the officer's 50 mph speed relative to the road. After the police vehicle's 50-mph speed is subtracted from the 95-mph relative speed, your actual speed of 45 mph is obtained.

EXAMPLE 2: Moving radar from same direction: A radar-equipped patrol car is traveling 50 mph. A truck is traveling 70 mph in the same direction as the officer. The officer would like to know how fast that truck is going. Since both vehicles are going in the same direction, with the truck pulling away from the patrol car, the relative speed between the two vehicles is 20 mph. The radar beam reflecting back from the road shows the officer's 50-mph speed. The unit adds the 20-mph difference between the truck and the officer, to this 50-mph speed. The result is a reading showing that the truck is going 70 mph.

ii. Hand-Held Radar Units

Hand-held "radar guns" are used most often by motorcycle officers. A "radar gun" is simply a gun-shaped plastic mold containing the transmitter, receiver and antenna. The antenna is normally mounted at the front of the gun, and a digital speed readout is mounted on the back. A trigger is included, allowing the officer to activate the radar beam only when she sees a car that appears to be traveling fast enough to spark her interest.

Radar guns are hard to detect. Radar detectors have a difficult time detecting hand-held radar devices. That's because car-mounted police radar units often transmit a steady signal that can be detected hundreds of feet or even yards down the road. Radar guns, on the other hand, usually do not transmit steady signals. (The convenient trigger on the hand-held unit allows the officer to activate it only when the targeted vehicle is close enough for the officer to clearly see and aim the gun.) So, when the officer finally pulls the trigger and your radar detector beeps a warning, it's usually too late to slow down.

c. How Radar Fails

Contrary to police department propaganda, new technology has not completely ironed out problems known to cause radar malfunctions. Most screw-ups result from the radar's operation in "real world" conditions, which are often far less than ideal. And, of course, the fact that less-than-perfect humans must use radar devices creates plenty of additional room for error.

One good way to point out all the pitfalls of radar readings is to subpoena the radar unit's instruction manual. (See Chapter 8, Section C, for how to do this.) The manufacturer will usually include a page or two on inaccurate readings and how to avoid them. If you study the manual, you may find a way to attack its reliability in court using the manufacturer's own words.

The following are descriptions of common malfunctions and sources of inaccurate readings.

i. More Than One Target

Radar beams are similar to flashlight beams—the farther the beam travels the more it spreads out. And this simple fact often results in bogus speed readings, since it's common for a spread-out beam to hit two vehicles in adjacent lanes. Most radar units have beam angle or spread of 12 to 16 degrees, or about 1/25th of a full circle. This means the beam will have a width of one foot for every four feet of distance from the radar an-tenna. Or put another way, the beam width will be two lanes wide (about 40 feet), only 160 feet distant from the radar gun. Thus, if you're in one lane and a faster vehicle is in another, the other vehicle will produce a higher reading on the officer's radar unit, which the officer may mistak-enly attribute to you.

The mistaken reading of another vehicle's speed is especially likely to occur if the other ve-hicle is larger than yours. In fact, the vehicle con-tributing to the officer's high radar reading needn't even be in another lane; if a larger ve-hicle, such as a truck, is rapidly coming up be-hind you in your lane, the officer may see your car, while her radar is reading the truck's speed. Inability of the equipment to distinguish between two separate objects is called lack of "resolution."

Ask the officer, at trial, if his radar unit was on automatic. The chances of registering the speed of the wrong car go way up when an officer, who is stationary, points his unit at a highway and puts it on the automatic setting. This is true because the officer isn't pointing at a specific vehicle, and the beam angle width means the unit could be picking up one of several cars going the same, or even opposite, directions. In this case, you ask the officer whether there was other traffic in either direction. If the answer is "yes," ask him which direction. If there was traffic in the direction opposite you, follow up and ask him whether the unit responds to traffic in both directions. (See Chapter 10, Section B, for sample cross-examination questions of this type.) Either way, if there was other traffic, be sure to raise the possibility in your closing argument that the radar unit clocked the wrong vehicle. (See Chapter 11, Section B, and Chapter 12, Section F.)

ii. Wind, Rain and Storms

Although metal reflects radar beams better than most surfaces, pretty much any material will reflect radar waves to some extent. In fact, on windy days, windblown dust or even tree leaves are often "read." And sometimes these spurious readings can be attributed to your vehicle. You may have read newspaper stories about radar trials in which a hand-held radar gun was pointed at a wind-blown tree resulting in the tree being "clocked" at 70 mph!

Windblown rain can also reflect enough energy to give false signals, particularly if the wind is strong enough to blow the rain close to horizontal. The more rain or wind, the more likely an errone-ous radar reading will result. Pre-thunderstorm atmospheric electrical charges can also interfere with a radar unit. That's because electrically-charged storm clouds can reflect a bogus signal back to the radar unit even though they are high in the sky. If such a storm cloud is being blown by the wind at sufficient speed, a false radar read-ing may result.

Typically, you would attack the radar use by referring to the manual during cross-examination and getting the officer to admit that the manual says errors can occur due to adverse weather con-ditions. Then in your final argument, you might say something like this: "Your Honor, the officer testified that the radar unit's accuracy can be affected by windblown rain and storm clouds, and she also admitted that at the time, there were clouds and rain."

Make sure the manual is complete. Police departments have been known to tear out pages that discuss common radar screw-ups from the radar manual before responding to a sub-poena. So be sure to look to see if any pages are missing and, of course, point out any gaps you discover.

iii. Calibration Problems

Every scientific instrument used for measuring needs to be regularly "calibrated" to check its accuracy. Radar equipment is no exception. It must be checked for accuracy against an object traveling at a known (not radar-determined) speed. If the speed on the radar equipment matches the known speed, the unit is properly calibrated. In practice, the best way to do this is to use a tuning fork as the moving object. While this may seem a far cry from a moving car, the use of a tuning fork is scientifically sound; tuning forks, when struck against a hard object, vibrate at a certain frequency which we, incidentally, hear as an audible tone.

More About Tuning Forks

Tuning forks are supplied by the manufacturer of the radar equipment and "certified" to correspond to the speed marked on the fork. According to most operation manuals, a radar unit should be calibrated with the tuning forks before and after every shift. Ideally, several tuning forks vibrating at different speeds should be used to check the radar unit's accuracy. Since tuning forks can easily become inaccurate, it's important that they be protected from damage. (A good scratch or drop of a few feet can render one inaccurate.) Keeping the forks in a sturdy box usually protects them.

It is time-consuming to use a tuning fork as a calibration device. So a second, but far less accurate, method has been developed to check the accuracy of radar units. This consist of flicking on the "calibrate" or "test" switch built into the radar unit itself and seeing if it calibrates properly. The unit reads a signal generated by an internal frequency-generating device, called a "crystal." The resulting number is supposed to correlate with a certain predetermined speed. Unfortunately, there is a big problem with this sort of "calibration" testing. The test does not measure the two types of circuits in the unit, frequency circuits and counting circuits. Only the counting circuit is tested. In short, if the frequency circuit is not calibrated, the radar unit may well be inaccu-

rate. The Connecticut case of *State v. Tomanelli,* 216 A.2d 625 (1965), indicates that the use of a certified tuning fork is the only scientifically acceptable method of calibrating a radar unit.

The fact that an internal "calibrate" test isn't a substitute for a tuning fork explains why it's so important in any traffic trial involving the use of radar to cross-examine the officer and see whether she really did use a tuning fork before you were ticketed. Typically, they are required to use the tuning fork at the beginning and end of their shifts. If she says "yes," move on to another question. But if she says she didn't, then it's time to ask more specific questions. (See Chapter 10, Section B, for suggestions on cross-examination questions on this point.) Of course, if you discover that a tuning fork wasn't used, you'll want to emphasize this as part of your final argument.

iv. False "Ground Speed" Reading in Moving Radar

A radar unit used while a patrol car is moving must take into account:

- The speed of an oncoming vehicle relative to the patrol car, and
- The speed of the patrol car relative to the ground.

In subsections i, ii and iii above, we discussed common ways that a moving radar unit can incorrectly attribute high speed to your vehicle. Here we deal with the notion that radar units can also misjudge the patrol car's speed. This can most easily occur if the radar unit mistakes a signal reflected back from a nearby car or truck for the signal reflected back from the ground.

EXAMPLE: A patrol car is doing 70 mph southbound and passing a truck going at 50 mph. You are going 65 mph northbound, in the opposite direction. Your car approaches the officer's car at a combined speed of 70 + 65 or 135 mph. The officer's unit detects this 135-mph speed, and should subtract his 70-mph ground speed, to get your true speed of 65 mph. Instead, the officer's ground-speed beam fixes on the truck ahead and measures a false 50-mph ground speed. It subtracts only 50 mph from the 135-mph to get 85 mph for your speed, even though you're only doing 65 mph.

v. Pulling You Over As Part of a Group of Cars

In situations where several cars proceed over the speed limit, some especially zealous officers will take a radar reading on the "lead" vehicle and then pull it over, along with one or two followers. In court, the officer will try to use the reading for the first vehicle as the speed for everyone else. She may even be up-front about this, saying that she saw the vehicles behind following at the same speed ("There was no change in bumper-to-bumper distances"). Or she may even claim that she also used her radar unit to measure the speed of second and/or third cars. ("When they passed through the beam, there was no change in the reading.")

Either way, this is shaky evidence. To be really accurate, the officer would have had to simultaneously note the lead car's reading while also very carefully looking at the other cars. (This is something that is especially hard to do if the officer's car was also in motion.) If the driver of the second car can truthfully testify as to how the lead car was going faster and increasing the distance, it should be a big help to establish reasonable doubt in court. And the use of radar to measure the cars is also problematic, since by doing so the officer admits several cars were close together and that she was trying to measure all their speeds almost simultaneously. Here are some possible defenses:

- If you were the driver of the lead car, you may be able to claim that the officer inadvertently locked onto a higher reading of the second or third vehicles that were gaining on you. If the second or third vehicles were larger than yours, the chances of a false reading on your car go up, since the larger vehicle will reflect a stronger signal. In this situation it may help the driver of the lead car if he or she can truthfully testify to seeing (in the rear or side mirror) the second vehicle quickly gaining from behind and suggest that the radar reading was really for that vehicle.

- If you were the driver of one of the vehicles behind the lead car, the vehicles in front of you may have been traveling faster (as lead vehicles often do). If that vehicle was larger than yours, or closer to the officer's vehicle, this would result in that vehicle's reflected radar signal being stronger. You could argue here that the radar unit read the speed of the car ahead of you, not your slower speed.

d. About Radar Detectors

No discussion of radar would be complete without a few words on the technological ways of beating it, primarily with a radar detector. Usually this is a little black box you clip to your sun visor or put on your dashboard and plug into your cigarette lighter outlet. It consists of a sensitive radio receiver adjusted to pick up signals in the radar frequency range. But instead of powering a loudspeaker, this type of radio circuit activates a beeper or light to warn that your speed is being monitored. Many of the commercially available detectors have a sensitivity control that can be adjusted to give the best compromise between trying to detect even faint, far-away police radar signals and attempting to screen out off-frequency signals that come from sources other than police radar.

Radar detectors are illegal in Virginia and the District of Columbia, but legal in all other states for most drivers. However, federal regulations, which apply in all states, prohibit commercial big-rig drivers from using them. Where radar detectors are illegal, you can usually be ticketed for having one and have it confiscated. Often this occurs when officers use what, for lack of a better term, are called radar-detector detectors. These are, in essence, radio receivers that pick up the very-low-power signal emitted by most radar detectors.

Even when radar detectors are perfectly legal, some people believe that officers are more likely to issue a ticket—as opposed to a warning—when they see a radar detector in your car. It follows that the best types of radar detectors are inconspicuously wired into the vehicle, with tiny radar antennas worked seamlessly into the hood or grill. Fortunately, some of these hard-to-see units are also more sensitive, thus giving you more warning than dash- or visor-mounted units. Unfortunately, they also tend to be more expensive.

5. Laser

"Laser detectors" are the most recent addition to the traffic officer's arsenal of speed-measuring devices. Built to look and act like a hand-held radar gun, a laser detector uses a low-powered beam of laser light that bounces off the targeted vehicle and returns to a receiver in the unit. There, it electronically calculates the speed of the targeted vehicle. Laser detectors are supposedly more accurate than radar units.

One advantage for police officers of the laser gun is that the light beam is narrower than a radar beam, meaning that it can be more precisely aimed. This is true even though laser detectors use three separate beams, because the combined width of the three beams is still much narrower than a radar beam at the same distance. This technology reduces, but does not eliminate, the chance that the speed of a nearby car will be measured, instead of the speed of the car at which the operator aims the gun. Still, there is room for error.

Here's why:

Laser detectors measure distance (between the gun and the target car) using the speed of light and the time it takes the light, reflected off the target vehicle, to return to the laser gun. The detector makes about 40 of these distance measurements over a third of a second, then divides the

light's round-trip distance by the time, to get the speed. This means to be accurate the officer must hold the combined beams on the same part of the car during the test. While this is easier to do with radar because of its wide beam, it is tricky to do this with a narrow laser beam and it's impossible to be sure that it's been accomplished, since the officer can't see the beam. The result is its measurement is highly subject to error.

EXAMPLE: Officer Krupke fixes her laser gun on Jane's car, which is traveling 60 mph, about 90 feet per second. It travels about 30 feet in the one-third-second measurement the laser device uses. If the laser beam starts at the windshield and travels to the bumper, it adds about four feet to the 30-foot distance that the machine otherwise would have measured if it had stayed pointed at the windshield. It would incorrectly calculate that Jane went 34 feet, or 102 feet per second, or 68 mph in the one-third of a second it took to measure the speed of her car. The result is that the laser unit registers Jane's speed 8 mph faster than it was actually going. (See Chapter 10, Section B, for specific questions to ask when cross-examining the officer.)

It's also possible (especially in heavy traffic) for one beam to hit the target car, and another beam to hit a nearby car. The chances of this happening increase with traffic density and the distance between the laser unit and the measured vehicle. If the two cars are traveling at different speeds, the laser detector will read incorrectly.

Laser Reliability Still a Question

The scientific accuracy of laser speed detection devices has been given an unqualified legal seal of approval in only a few states, including New York, Maryland and New Jersey. In other states, it is up to the prosecutor to prove that a laser reading is accurate. For example, in 1999 an appeals court in Georgia ruled that scientific evidence of accuracy must be presented in every speeding case where a laser gun was used. (*Izer v. State*, No. A98A2475. Ct. App. Ga., Feb. 5, 1999.)

According to the Georgia appeals court, legislatures and courts in 47 states have not unequivocally decided whether laser guns are reliable, even though laser speed detection units are currently used in 39 of those states.

There are several ways you may be able to use this information if you are ticketed for speeding based on the use of a laser gun. Probably the best approach is to object at trial (in any state but New Jersey, New York or Maryland) if an officer testifies about the use of a laser gun without presenting scientific evidence that the particular gun was able to produce an accurate reading in your situation. And then in your closing argument, ask for the case to be dismissed because no scientific evidence was presented on laser gun reliability.

Other Moving Violations

Judge: *Was the intersection at Maple and Main a controlled intersection?*

Defendant: *I didn't have control at the intersection. That's why I crashed.*

In most states moving violations other than speeding tickets are treated as petty offenses or infractions not punishable with jail time. (See Chapter 3, Section A.) Your chances of successfully beating one of these tickets often depends on your ability to show:

- You did not violate every element of the law as written. (See Chapter 2 on researching the law you are charged with violating.)
- The officer was unable to clearly observe the alleged offense from where he was located.
- The officer lost sight of your vehicle between the time the offense was committed and the time you were stopped, opening up the defense that he mistook your car for the offending car.
- You made a reasonable mistake based on genuinely obscured signs or signals.
- You technically violated the law, but did so in an emergency situation.

Tickets involving judgment calls are often beaten. Statutes that prohibit "unreasonable" actions, like unsafe lane changes or turns, are based on subjective judgments. This gives you the chance to argue that what you did was safe and reasonable under the circumstances. The officer, of course, will probably claim just the opposite. But if you can present even a little evidence supporting your claim that you acted reasonably (and show that the officer didn't have as good a view of the traffic situation as you did), many judges will give you the benefit of the doubt.

Tickets Issued After Accidents

Police officers are rarely present when an accident occurs. Therefore, most tickets written after an accident are handed out without first-hand knowledge of what happened. To figure out what happened, the officer must rely on the positions of the collided vehicles, other people's statements and possibly your own admissions. Beware! Your own damaging statements can be used against you later in court. Therefore, it is unwise to admit any fault or to discuss what happened with the officer, the other driver, or anyone else.

Instead, it's perfectly legal (and can't be held against you later) to simply tell the officer that you're highly upset and simply don't wish to discuss what happened until later. Holding your tongue at the scene of the accident also allows you to quietly reflect on the circumstances to more carefully divvy up blame for the accident. Unlike your statements, which are admissible in court, things said by witnesses at the scene of an accident cannot properly be repeated in court unless the witness is called to testify.

A. Not Stopping at Stop Signs

Oh, those rolling stops! At quota time police love to hand out piles of tickets for not quite making a full stop. And it's easy to do, since every area has plenty of stop signs with infrequent cross traffic and good cover for a police cruiser.

Most stop sign laws say something like:

"The driver of any vehicle approaching a stop sign at the entrance to, or within, an intersection, shall stop at a limit line, if marked, otherwise before entering the crosswalk on the near side of the intersection. If there is no limit line or crosswalk, the driver shall stop at the entrance to the intersecting roadway or railroad grade crossing."

To be found guilty of this offense, in most states all the following conditions (legal elements) must be satisfied:

1. You must drive a vehicle and approach a stop sign.
2. The stop sign must be at the entrance to or within an intersection or railroad grade crossing.
3. You must fail to come to a complete stop at:
   a. A limit line (a white stripe painted at or near the beginning of the intersection), if it exists
   b. A crosswalk, if any
   c. The entrance to the intersection or railroad crossing, if there was no marked limit line or crosswalk.

Here are the most successful defenses:

1. You Stopped Farther Back

Most statutes say you must stop at the limit line, crosswalk or entrance to the intersection. Practically, this means you must stop slightly before you reach this line. Some conscientious drivers, however, stop further back from the white marker line or crosswalk. In these cases, an officer hiding behind a bush 50 feet down a side street might not be able to see whether the driver stopped or not.

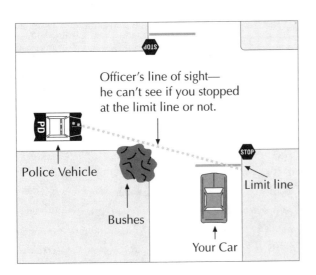

To mount this defense, first request a copy of the officer's notes (see Chapter 8, Section C). Then go back to the scene of the ticket and take pictures from exactly where the officer was sitting. Especially if you can document a visual obstruction—and convincingly testify you did stop—this defense is often a winner. Of course, it's a big help if you can produce a passenger or other witnesses who will sign on to your version of the facts.

2. The Stop Sign Was Obscured

Here you concede that while you may have run the stop sign, it wasn't your fault. This can occur if the stop sign is hidden by storm-blown branches, twisted the wrong way by kids or obscured for any of a variety of reasons. Called a "mistake-of-fact" defense by lawyers, what this amounts to is your claim that, given the information you had, you made a reasonable mistake and are therefore not guilty. But realize you have to prove your mistake was truly reasonable—it's never enough to say it was "a little hard to see the sign, Your Honor." (See Chapter 3, Section D.4, on mistake-of-fact defenses.)

Pictures are worth a thousand words. Pictures taken from different angles or distances are more convincing than your testimony. For example, if a stop sign is hidden from view by overhanging branches until a few feet before the intersection, take pictures from inside your vehicle (with someone else driving) as the car approaches the sign. Snap one from a distance of 75 feet, and others from 50, 25 and ten feet away from the sign. (Write on the back of each the exact distance from the sign.) In court, you may show your pictures to the judge and explain that they reveal the sign was obscured until it was too late to stop at the intersection. (See Chapter 11, Section B, on how to admit evidence.)

To video or not to video. Lots of judges are hostile to videos. Most traffic-court courtrooms are usually not equipped with video players and monitors and even if they are, some judges will resent the time it takes to set up and watch a video. And few judges will be willing to peer through the viewer of a portable video camera. But times change even in the courtroom, and some judges are a bit more modern. So while it's probably safer to stick with photographs, if you really feel you need to make your point with a very short video, contact the clerk well in advance to find out whether the judge will let you show it in court.

Ignorance is no excuse, even in a "mistake-of-fact" defense. It is not a "mistake of fact" defense to say you did not know it was illegal to do something illegal (roll through a stop sign, for example). You were taught the rules before you got your license and you are expected to know them. A "mistake-of-fact" defense only works if you reasonably lacked a piece of factual and important information when you broke the traffic law. This would be the case if a traffic sign was missing or seriously obscured, but not if it was front-and-center and you just failed to see or abide by it.

3. Newly Installed Stop Signs

Another possible "mistake-of-fact" defense can be tried if you are ticketed for blowing through a newly installed stop sign. No question, it is easy to miss a new sign on a familiar road. But this only has a hope of working if you can prove the sign really was recently installed and that you used the road frequently before the sign was installed. It will also help if you can introduce pictures into evidence showing the sign was also hard to see from a distance (just around a curve, for example).

The more the merrier when it comes to beating tickets. If you didn't see the newly installed sign, you are probably not the only one. Go back to the location a few days later, at about the same time you were cited, and watch. If you see others failing to stop, you can jot down how many drivers missed the stop sign and present the numbers during your testimony. You can say, *"Your honor, three days after I was cited, on another weekday, June 20th at about 8:30 a.m., I went back to the scene and kept records for a half hour, during which 65 vehicles passed through the same intersection. Of those 65, ten went through the intersection without stopping, and another fifteen came to a dangerous screeching halt, apparently after noticing the sign very late. My point is, until that sign has been present long enough for people to know it's there, giving tickets for failing to stop at it offends basic fairness."*

4. The Limit Line Was Faded

Crosswalks and limit lines fade. If you are ticketed at a stop sign for stopping a little too far into an intersection, you may win if you show that the limit line or crosswalk was too faded to see clearly. Here again, a picture is truly better than a thousand words. (See Chapter 9, Section C, on introducing photographs into evidence.)

B. Not Stopping at a Stoplight

Most state laws on stoplights read something like this:

"A driver facing a steady circular red signal shall stop (1) at a marked limit line, or (2) if none, before entering the crosswalk on the near side of the intersection or, (3) if none, then before entering the intersection."

The legal elements of this offense are basically the same as for driving through a stop sign (see

Section A above), with one big exception. That's based on the fact that while stop signs stay red all the time, traffic lights change colors. Of course, it's always legal to drive safely through an intersection when the light is green or yellow. In fact, in most states, as long as the front of your vehicle entered the intersection (passed the crosswalk or limit line) before the light turned red, you haven't broken the stoplight law.

Here are the most successful defenses:

1. Your View Was Better Than the Officer's

The only time an officer has a really good view of when your car entered an intersection is when he is sitting directly to the side of, and close to, the intersection (usually either standing on the corner or in a car on the cross street near the corner). But chances are the cop was someplace else—sitting across the street in the Burger King parking lot, perhaps.

To understand why it's so hard for a cop at another location to see whether you entered an intersection after the yellow light turned red, think about watching football on TV. How many times have you seen a football play where it looked like the wide receiver was off-sides, but no penalty was called? You thought you saw an off-sides, but you were wrong because your visual angle was not at field level looking down the line of scrimmage. Similarly, a police officer is rarely looking directly down the traffic "line of scrimmage" when you cross into an intersection.

Cross-examine the officer as to exactly where he was when he says he saw you run the red light. Try to get the officer to admit that other cars were in a position to obscure his view of the intersection, or that he was also doing something else, such as driving his car or eating a Whopper. (See Chapter 10, Section B, on cross-examination.) Then, when it's your turn, provide detailed testimony, making it clear where you were when you saw the light turn yellow, and how far you

were across the intersection when it turned red. (See Chapter 9, Section D.3, on preparing your testimony.) Make a simple diagram like this (adapted for your particular situation, of course) and show it to the judge. (See Chapter 9, Section C, for how to do this.) And especially if the cop really did see you from a bad angle, work in the wide receiver analogy—it's a real winner with jock judges.

Bring a witness to court. When a judgment call is involved (such as the location of your front bumper when a light turned red), two observers are always far better than one. If someone riding in your front seat can testify that the light was still yellow when you entered the intersection, you should present him as a witness. (See Chapter 9, Section E, on having a witness testify at trial.)

2. The Officer Didn't See Your Red Light

When a light turns green, we assume the light for cross-traffic has simultaneously turned red. For example, if an officer approaches an intersection with a green light and sees you drive across the intersection, he will assume you ran a red light and won't later check to be sure that the light changes were synchronized. Sometimes they aren't. If you can go back to the scene and document that the light was mistimed, you should be entitled to acquittal. And don't dismiss this possibility—neither machines nor the people who time them are infallible.

! Never claim a yellow light was too short. Traffic engineering practices require the duration of yellow lights to be at least the time it takes to stop if driving at the speed limit. This might tempt you to tell the police officer who stops you or the judge at trial that the yellow light was too short ("less than three seconds, Your Honor"). The problem with this defense is you come very close to admitting that you were driving too fast to stop in time, or entered the intersection when the light was red. No joy there.

C. Improper Turning

There are many ways to be ticketed for making improper turns. One of the most common is making an improper U-turn. Here we provide information on defending against a wide array of these violations.

1. Failing to Stay to the Edge of the Road to Turn

Most state laws read like this:

"The driver of a vehicle intending to turn upon a highway shall do so as follows:
(a) Right Turns. Both the approach for a right-hand turn and a right-hand turn shall be made as close as practicable to the right-hand curb or edge of the roadway.
(b) Left Turns. The approach for a left turn shall be made as close as practicable to the left-hand

Roadsigns

hair pin tern

edge of the extreme left-hand lane or portion of the roadway lawfully available to traffic moving in the direction of travel of such vehicle, and, when turning at an intersection, the left turn shall not be made before entering the intersection. After entering the intersection, the left turn shall be made so as to leave the intersection in a lane lawfully available to traffic moving in such direction upon the roadway being entered."

The term "as close as practicable" is your best friend in defending against this violation. You will want to present evidence that shows why what you did was the most "practicable" thing to do under the circumstances.

These include:

- Avoiding cars parked at the curb
- Steering clear of traffic pulling out of parking spaces
- Avoiding roadside construction
- Avoiding pedestrians.

EXAMPLE: As you approach an intersection, you see an old lady with a cane getting into her parked car. You swung wide before making your turn to prepare for any unexpected movements from the woman, who appeared unsteady. You're cited for making too wide a right turn. The officer says you went almost through the middle of the intersection, rather than staying close to the right curb as you turned. Your defense is that you drove "as close as practicable" to the right, leaving a wide berth on your right for the lady getting into the car.

2. Turns Prohibited by Signs or Marked Lanes

Here are edited versions of the three most common laws that make it illegal to make certain types of turns.

"When turning movements are required at an intersection, notice of such requirement shall be given by erection of a sign, unless an additional clearly-marked traffic lane is provided for the approach to the turning movement, in which event, notice as applicable to such additional traffic lane shall be given by any official traffic control device."

"When right- or left-hand turns are prohibited at an intersection, notice of such prohibition shall be given by erection of a sign."

"When official traffic control devices are placed as required by law, it shall be unlawful for any driver of a vehicle to disobey the directions of such official traffic control devices."

Basically, all these laws forbid right, left or other specified turns when "notice" of special turning requirements is given by a sign, signal, or white arrow painted on the road surface. For example, a sign at an intersection may prohibit all U-turns and left turns during certain hours.

Here is one possible defense:

You claim you weren't given proper notice of the prohibited turn. This is a version of the "mistake-of-fact" defense we discussed in Section A.1, above. For instance, assume you receive a ticket at an intersection where the sign or signal prohibiting a turn was difficult to see because it was turned the wrong way, obscured by a pole or not visible for some other reason. You argue and prove "reasonable notice" was not given and the judge dismisses your case.

EXAMPLE: You're driving home from your new job westbound on a road you have never been on before. It's 4:45 p.m. on a Wednesday in November and the sun is setting. You enter an intersection and turn left. The setting sun happens to be right next to the sign that says, "No Left Turn 4:00 PM-6:00 PM MON-FRI." Because of the strong glare, you don't see this sign until you have almost completed the turn. In court, you show the judge a photo you took the next day showing the sunset obscuring the sign. You argue that given the circumstances, the sign was poorly engineered. On cross-examination, the officer honestly admits the sign was right where the sun was and if he was in your shoes, he might have missed it. You win.

3. Prohibited U-Turns

In most states, U-turns are almost always illegal in business districts. In residence districts and other areas, they are likely to be legal except where traffic conditions make them unsafe. Because possible defenses to U-turn tickets greatly depend on where a turn was made, let's look at the most common situations.

U-turn laws vary considerably from state to state. Be sure to read the law you're charged with violating to see exactly what its elements are. Then try to figure how you can convincingly claim you didn't violate at least one of them. (See Chapter 3 for instruction on how to do this.)

a. U-Turn in Business District

Most state U-turn statutes say something like:

"No person in a business district shall make a U-turn, except at an intersection or on a divided highway where an opening has been provided."

In most states it is usually legal to make a U-turn unless you are in a business or residential district (see subsection b, below) or a sign prohibits it. A "business district" is typically defined as a place where over 50% of the property fronting the street is "in use for business" along a specified length often defined as several hundred feet and often longer. Even in a business district, it usually is legal to make a U-turn at a stoplight as long as you begin your turn in the far-left lane.

Your best defense to a charge that you made a U-turn in a business district is usually that you weren't, in fact, in such a district. Typically, this involves two steps: First, looking up your state's definition of the term business district (see Chapter 2 on how to find the right law) and then going back to the scene of your turn to see if the location meets your state's technical definition.

The officer must prove you were in a business district. Since making a U-turn in a business district is a key element of the offense you are charged with, it should be up to the officer to prove it. It follows if the officer provides no proof, you should win your case. Often it's best not to bring up this point until after the prosecution has finished presenting evidence, because you do not want to tip off the other side to your strategy. Instead, this point should be made in your direct testimony (see Chapter 9, Section D, for tips on preparing this) and closing argument. (See Chapter 11, Section B.11, and Chapter 12, Section D.6, on preparing your closing argument.) For example, you might say, *"Your Honor, the only reason my U-turn is said to be illegal was that it supposedly occurred in a business district. But Officer Kwota didn't say a word about what kind of area it was."* And then, if true of course, you could continue, *"In fact, while there are some businesses in the area where I made my turn, I do not think the state proved that it falls within the definition of a 'business district' under the law of this state."*

b. U-Turn in Residence District

Most state laws read something like this:

"No person in a residence district shall make a U-turn when any other vehicle is approaching from either direction within 200 feet, except at an intersection when the approaching vehicle is controlled by an official traffic control device."

To be convicted of this, the prosecution must prove that you did all of the following things (violated all of these legal elements):

1. You were driving in a "residence district," which is usually defined elsewhere in your state laws or code. You'll want to use the Appendix to find where the "rules of the road" or similar laws are located in your state's vehicle code, then look it up and read carefully.
2. You made a full 180-degree or U-turn
3. Another vehicle was approaching (not merely stopped) within the distance specified by the law, and
4. You were at an intersection not controlled by an "official traffic control device" (sign or signal).

The Poor Person's U-Turn Is Okay

Dividing your U-turn into several parts makes it legal. It is legal if you turn into a driveway or parking lot, make a full stop, then back out into traffic to complete the U-turn. Think of it this way: The left turn into a driveway is legal. Backing out of the driveway is legal, as long as you stay to the shoulder of the road, stop, activate your left turn signal, and enter traffic when safe to do so. And best of all, it's a way to make what amounts to a U-turn while keeping all those green portraits of Andrew Jackson safely in your pocket.

The best ways to beat this violation are to raise doubt as to whether another vehicle was approaching within the distance specified in your state law or whether the area was a "residence district." To demonstrate that other vehicles were not within the specified number of feet at the time you made your turn, it often helps to use maps or drawings containing a distance scale. (See Chapter 9, Section C, on introducing diagrams and maps into evidence.) One way to do this is to enlarge a city map to help show the judge where your car and the other vehicle was, noting that no vehicle was within 200 feet of you. Or you can draw your own map, carefully indicating the distances.

Or, you can use pictures of the street when no other traffic is present on it. That way you can mark, on the photograph, with felt-tipped or ballpoint pen, the spots where the other vehicles were. You can testify that you went back to the scene and measured the distances from where your car was to those points when you started the U-turn.

If your state law sets a more relaxed U-turn standard in rural or other non-residential areas (see Subsection C, below), you may want to try to show there weren't enough residences within the area for it to be a residence district. But be careful not to open up the possibility that you turned in a business district, which will almost always have even tighter U-turn rules.

c. U-Turns on the Highway (Not in Residence, Business or Other Restricted Districts)

The law usually reads like this:

"No person shall make a U-turn upon any highway where the driver of such vehicle does not have an unobstructed view for 200 feet in both directions along the highway."

This law applies to areas of any highway that are not labeled a "residence," "business" or other specified district. Here you are free to make a legal U-turn, provided you have an unobstructed view for the number of feet specified in your state law. It doesn't matter whether other vehicles are approaching within that distance, so long as you can see them clearly and it's safe to make the turn. You can often use maps, diagrams or pictures to demonstrate that you could see more than the distance specified by law. (For defenses to a charge that your turn was unsafe, see Section 4, below.)

d. U-Turns Across a Traffic Island

A "divided highway" is often a road with a traffic island or other physical barrier in the middle, separating the two directions of traffic. It's obviously against the law to make a U-turn over a physical barrier. Because it is very dangerous and potentially damaging to the vehicle, few sober drivers attempt it. However, a divided highway can also be designated by a "painted traffic island" consisting of two sets of double yellow lines at least two feet apart. And it's far more common for drivers to cross this type of artificial barrier.

A typical state law reads as follows:

"Whenever a highway has been divided into two or more roadways by means of intermittent barriers or by means of a dividing section of not less than two feet in width, either unpaved or delineated by curbs, double-parallel lines, or other markings on the roadway, it is unlawful to drive any vehicle over, upon, or across the dividing section, or to make any left or U-turn except through a plainly marked opening in the dividing section."

In other words, you can't legally cross two pairs of double white or yellow lines two or more feet apart or a highway divider strip, except at an opening or a place where the double-double lines drop to one set of double lines (or, in some states, become intermittent).

Your Best Defenses:

- The two sets of parallel lines were less than two feet apart. At your trial you can challenge the officer to say whether he measured the distance between the lines or just estimated them. Although technically this is a decent defense, most judges probably won't go for it (they will assume the two sets of lines were the correct distance apart) unless you measure them and prove they were not. Since people who paint highways aren't perfect, it can pay to wait until traffic is light and get out the old measuring tape.
- There appeared to be a break in the double-double lines to accommodate a driveway. Pictures help a lot with this one, although sometimes you can challenge an officer on cross-examination and get him to admit he can't remember. If so, when it comes to your turn to testify, you'll want to claim that the officer's inability to remember raises a reasonable doubt as to your guilt.

- You were forced to divert over a set of double lines to avoid a dangerous traffic situation. The burden of proving any "emergency defense" is squarely on you. Be sure your emergency really relates to road conditions (you had to avoid an out-of-control truck) and not just your personal situation (you needed to stop to adjust your seatbelt).

4. Unsafe Turns and Lane Changes

In addition to the specific turn laws outlined above, most states also have a catchall category called "unsafe turns or lane changes." Here is a typical statute.

"No person shall turn a vehicle from a direct course or move right or left upon a roadway until such movement can be made with reasonable safety and then only after the giving of an appropriate signal in the event any other vehicle may be affected by the movement."

Here is another violation where that fuzzy concept of "reasonable safety" applies. In theory, at least, it is up to the prosecution to prove facts that, taken together, demonstrate that you were not driving safely. But in a real courtroom, the ticketing officer will probably just testify that your actions were dangerous. Although this is a conclusion—not really proof—it is usually enough to shift the burden of proof to you. (The judge will now expect you to show your actions were safe.) It is, therefore, important for you to be prepared to produce evidence that this was the case. Following are some suggestions on how to do this.

a. Turning Left Against Oncoming Traffic

It is legal to make a left turn in front of oncoming traffic if you can do so with reasonable safety. If ticketed, you can start by testifying that, since there was no accident and the other driver did not have to swerve or brake sharply, your turn was safe. In addition, you may wish to point out that there was enough distance between your car and an oncoming car to make the turn safe. One good approach is to use a little mathematics to show the judge how much time you had to make your turn. Start by understanding that six car-lengths equals about 100 feet. Assuming the car approaching yours was traveling at 25 mph (or 37 feet per second), you would have about three seconds for you to make your turn. Twelve car lengths (or 200 feet) would allow about six seconds, and so on. This should be explained with the help of a diagram as part of your direct testimony and reiterated in your closing argument (see sidebar "Converting Miles Per Hour to Feet Per Second" in Chapter 6, Section B.3).

It helps to testify that the other driver signaled you to proceed. Motorists commonly make hand or head signals to tell another driver to go first. And sometimes signaling is done more subtly by simply slowing down or speeding up. If true, it will be a big help if you can testify that the other driver nodded or otherwise told you to go ahead with the turn. The officer may say otherwise, but chances are he wasn't in as good a position to see the other driver (a point you'll often want to develop in cross-examination. See Chapter 10).

b. Pulling in Front of a Vehicle Going the Same Direction

The law in most states also prohibits pulling out in front of another vehicle in an unsafe manner. This can happen when you turn right or left at an intersection in front of another car that is too close to your vehicle. And, of course, it can also occur when you change lanes abruptly, especially when you don't signal. Officers who cite for this offense will usually testify that your actions

caused another car to slow abruptly, indicated by brake lights and quickly reduced speeds.

Your best defenses are typically to show:

- You allowed enough space—diagrams and photos can help. (See diagrams in this chapter and Chapter 9, Section C.)
- The other driver did not come to a screeching halt (if true) and no accident occurred.
- The other driver overreacted by braking or swerving unnecessarily.
- The other driver was exceeding the speed limit.
- The officer had a poor view of the incident.

This last point can be the most important. Unless the officer was right behind your vehicle, in the case of a lane change, or sitting at the intersection in the case of a too-fast merge, he might not have been in a good position to be able to judge the relative speeds and positions of both vehicles. For example, suppose you turn right onto a road in front of a vehicle being followed by a police car. Even if the car slows quickly, which in turn causes the cop to brake, it would be difficult for the officer to see how close the car came to hitting you. In short, you would argue the officer could not see if you performed an unsafe maneuver as part of presenting your testimony—backed up by a diagram—that your turn was safe.

c. Pulling Onto a Road and Backing Up Unsafely

Typically, your state's law will say something like this:

"No person shall start a vehicle stopped, standing, or parked on a highway, nor shall any person back a vehicle on a highway, until such movement can be made with reasonable safety."

This ticket is almost always worth fighting unless you caused an accident. To win you must simply present testimony that you took reasonable precautions before you pulled onto the road and started backing up.

Start by explaining in your testimony what you did and why it was sensible and safe under the circumstances. Assuming your conduct might reasonably have looked dangerous to the officer, be ready to explain that the problem was really caused by the unpredictable or antisocial actions of the other driver. (Remember, this person won't be in court to contradict you.) This would be true if another vehicle suddenly did something truly dangerous like exceeding the speed limit or making a high-speed turn. If possible, present convincing eyewitness testimony to back up your story. Plan to use a diagram or map to help show why your conduct was safe. (See Chapter 9, Section C, on preparing and using diagrams.)

d. Failing to Signal a Turn

Your state law will say something like this:

"Any signal of intention to turn right or left shall be given continuously during the last 100 feet traveled by the vehicle before turning."

Officers write many turn signal tickets claiming the offenders didn't signal for 100 feet before making a turn. (Incidentally, it's fine to use hand signals—they're just as legal as electric signals.) To challenge the officer's memory, you should try to recall and testify to how many times you heard your signal click. The point of doing this is to determine how far you traveled by counting the number of clicks. Here's how. Count the number of clicks your signal indicator makes in five seconds. (Ten clicks in five seconds obviously means one click every half a second.) Next, convert the time you've arrived at into distance. (See sidebar in Chapter 6, Section B.3, "Converting Miles Per Hour to Feet Per Second.") For example, if you were traveling 35 mph (52 feet per second) and concluded you heard four clicks over two seconds (again assuming two clicks per second), you could testify that you had covered at least 104 feet.

⚠ Your dashboard turn signal indicator may blink and click even if a signal lamp is burned out. The fact that your dashboard turn signals are clicking does not mean your turn signal lights are blinking. If you check and see that the cop was right (you weren't signaling), you can claim that you made a reasonable "mistake-of-fact" (you shifted your signal lever, but didn't know your signal lamp had burned out). We discuss this defense in Chapter 3, Section D. However, to do this you need to testify that you learned of the broken bulb only after you were ticketed. If you had your car serviced recently and it got a clean bill of health, make sure you work this into your testimony, since it shows you to be a conscientious motorist.

D. Right-of-Way Violations

Tickets in this category are usually issued when, in the estimation of an officer, a driver rudely fails to yield to other motorists or pedestrians when required. Unfortunately, if the officer shows up in court, he is likely to remember this type of incident and make a forceful presentation. For example, he may explain in great detail why your failure to let an elderly person cross the street in a crosswalk was a dastardly act.

Here is a rundown of the most common violations for failing to yield to other vehicles, along with suggestions on to how to fight them.

1. Right-of-Way at Intersections

State laws typically read:

"The driver of a vehicle approaching an intersection shall yield the right of way to any vehicle that has entered the intersection from a different highway."

These statutes do not mean you have to wait until the intersection is completely clear before entering. Instead, they simply prohibit deliberate crowding or interfering with other vehicles already in the intersection. Fortunately, whether you really did improperly fail to yield the right-of-way to another driver is commonly a judgment call, meaning you usually have a pretty decent shot at beating this type of ticket.

EXAMPLE: You cautiously enter an intersection, even though there is another vehicle ahead of you. You wait a few seconds before you see that its driver is not sure whether to go straight or turn. To exit the intersection for safety reasons, you cut to the left of the vehicle and make your left turn. In court, you would testify that you first slowed to allow the other driver to leave the intersection. But when he didn't, you realized you were in danger of blocking other traffic and creating a dangerous situation, so you proceeded as cautiously as you could to leave the intersection. In short, with the help of a diagram, you could demonstrate that the other car, not your vehicle, caused the confusion in the intersection.

a. Failure to Yield at Uncontrolled or Four-Way Stop

There are laws controlling actions at intersections that have four-way stop signs or no lights or signs, called "uncontrolled" intersections. They typically say:

"When two vehicles enter an intersection from different highways at the same time, the driver of the vehicle on the left shall yield the right-of-way to the vehicle on his or her immediate right."

This ticket involves a violation at an intersection that has:

1. No traffic signal, stop sign or yield-right-of-way sign.
2. Four stop signs, one facing in each direction, or
3. Stoplights that, for an unknown reason, are inoperative.

Start by understanding that the first car stopped at a four-way intersection has the right-of-way. And that if two cars arrive at the intersection at the same moment from different directions, the vehicle to the right has the right-of-way.

The legal elements of this violation normally include all of the following:

1. The vehicle was "approaching a four-way intersection."
2. The intersection had four stop signs, one for each street in each direction. Or the intersection had no yield sign, stop sign or operative traffic light on any street approach.
3. Another vehicle entered the intersection from "a different highway." (That is, not directly across from you, but to your right or left.)
4. The other vehicle entered the intersection first or, if you both entered at the same instant, the other vehicle entered from the street or road to your right.
5. You failed to yield to the other vehicle.

This kind of ticket is often written after an accident. It follows that if you tell the officer that the other car entered the intersection first or that it arrived at the intersection to your right at the same time you arrived, you have all but admitted your guilt. Instead, to prevail, it's normally important to be able to claim you entered the intersection first, or would have if the other driver hadn't rolled through a stop sign. Obviously, it is a huge help to have a witness if you made a real stop while the other driver faked it.

A picture or diagram can help you out.. A diagram or picture of the intersection, showing where your car collided with the other car, may be helpful in showing the other driver rolled through the stop sign. For example, if you can show the collision occurred farther from the point where you entered an uncontrolled intersection than from where the other vehicle entered it, that supports the idea that you were in the intersection longer—or first. That would mean you had the right of way.

Roadsigns

traffic jam.

b. Failing to Yield at a "T" or Three-way Intersection

At three-way (or "T") uncontrolled intersections (or where the two roads are controlled by stop signs), the rules are a little different. The driver on the road that dead-ends must always yield to the other driver (the one crossing the "T"), no matter who got to the intersection first.

Here the law typically says:

"Where two vehicles enter an intersection formed by a continuing highway and a terminating highway, at the same time and from the different highways, the driver of the vehicle on the terminating highway shall yield the right-of-way to the driver of the vehicle on the continuing highway."

The elements of this violation are as follows:

1. A "T" or three-way intersection is formed by one road that terminates and another that goes through.
2. The intersection is not controlled by stop signs, or it has stop signs in all three directions, or an inoperative stoplight.
3. You were driving on the road that ends at the intersection.
4. Your vehicle and the other entered the intersection at the same time.
5. You failed to yield to the other vehicle.

Again, as is true for a four-way intersection, your main defense to this charge is that your vehicle entered the intersection first, or the other driver rolled through the stop sign, making it appear that he got to the intersection before you, even though this wasn't really true.

c. Failure to Properly Yield When Making Left Turn

Most state laws read like this:

"The driver of a vehicle intending to turn left on a highway, or to turn left into public or private property, or an alley, shall yield the right-of-way to all vehicles approaching from the opposite direction that are close enough to constitute a hazard at any time during the turning movement and shall continue to yield the right-of-way to the approaching vehicles until the left turn can be made with reasonable safety."

To be convicted, the prosecution must establish all of these elements:

1. One or more vehicles were approaching from the opposite direction.
2. Approaching traffic was "so close as to constitute a hazard" at any time during the turning movement.
3. You made the left turn anyway without "reasonable safety."

As with many other types of illegal turn tickets, this one involves a judgment call from the ticketing officer that your turn was "unsafe." It follows that in mounting your defense, it is often wise to focus your defense on the words "reasonable safety." For example, you might argue to the judge that if no other car had to suddenly brake or swerve to avoid hitting your turning car, there is at least a "reasonable doubt" as to whether your driving was unsafe. (See Chapter 12, Section E, for a discussion of why establishing "reasonable doubt" should lead to your acquittal.)

💡 **The officer probably had a poor look at the other driver.** If you can truthfully testify that the other driver waved or nodded for you to proceed (possibly while slowing slightly), chances are the cop won't be able to contradict you. One good technique here is to ask the cop on cross-examination to identify the type of car—or description of the driver—you allegedly turned in front of. If he fails to do that—and he probably will—you can later argue that he obviously didn't get a very good look at the driver.

d. Failing to Yield at Stop and Yield Signs

Even though you may have stopped as required at a stop sign, you may still be ticketed if you fail to properly yield to another driver who has the right of way. In most states, the elements of this violation are:

1. After encountering a stop sign or a yield sign, you entered an intersection.
2. One or more other vehicles approached on an intersecting street or road.
3. Approaching traffic constituted a hazard, and
4. You continued through the intersection anyway.

EXAMPLE: After signaling your intention to turn right, you stop at a stop sign. You turn even though a car is approaching from the left on the cross street. The other car must brake to avoid rear-ending you. You get a ticket. Your defenses:

- The other vehicle appeared to be turning left, right or stopping so that it shouldn't have presented a hazard.
- The other vehicle sped up suddenly just as you entered the intersection, creating a hazard where none should have reasonably existed (people really do this!).
- You were lawfully in the intersection (after having stopped) before the other driver got close to it.

- Obstructions on either side, such as hills or bends in the road, meant you couldn't see traffic from that direction, and that, given those obstructions, the other driver was driving too fast, thus creating the hazard.

As you can see, your defense should normally be based on raising the likelihood that another vehicle—not you—caused the dangerous situation. Or put in reverse, you want to convince the judge or jury that you acted with "reasonable safety." One way to do this is by clearly demonstrating that you had a better view of the developing situation than the officer did. For example, you might be able to testify that several other cars were between the officer and the intersection and, therefore, you were closer to what was occurring. Supplement this with pictures and diagrams showing where you were in relation to the other vehicle. (See Chapter 9, Section C.)

e. Yielding to Pedestrians

Let's now discuss the most common tickets issued for failing to yield to pedestrians:

This law typically states:

"The driver of a vehicle shall yield the right-of-way to a pedestrian crossing, or trying to cross, the roadway within any marked crosswalk."

In most states the elements of this violation are:
1. You drove a vehicle.
2. You approached a marked crosswalk.
3. There was a pedestrian actually crossing or trying to cross, and
4. You failed to yield to the pedestrian by either refusing to stop (even though there's no stop sign or traffic light) or coming very close to running the pedestrian down.

In thinking about how to successfully defend against this type of ticket, there is often plenty of opportunity to raise a reasonable doubt as to whether you improperly failed to yield to a pedestrian. For example, you could argue that the pedestrian appeared to be simply standing at the crosswalk, not preparing to walk through it. Or, assuming it is true, of course, you could argue that the pedestrian motioned you to go first.

The law in some states contains an additional requirement that you must yield to a pedestrian within any "unmarked crosswalk" at an intersection. In short, the law assumes that a crosswalk exists at any corner where two roads meet. If you get a ticket for failing to yield to a pedestrian who is not in a marked crosswalk, it is very important to check the exact wording of your state's law on this point. For example, you'll learn that if there is a crosswalk on one side of a major intersection and no crosswalk on the other, pedestrians are required to use the marked crosswalk side. In this case, it is not a violation to cross in front of a pedestrian on the non-cross-walked side. (See Chapter 2 on how to find the exact law you are charged with violating.)

To consider other ways to defend against this type ticket, it will help to look at a real life situation. Assume, as you approach a corner, a pedestrian begins to cross the street, walking slowly from your right to your left in a crosswalk. You see you have plenty of room to safely drive by after the pedestrian passes by. So you drive through the intersection while the pedestrian is still in the cross-walk. You are stopped and ticketed.

To contest the ticket, start by focusing on the exact words (legal elements) in your state's law. For example, in some states the law makes it clear that it is legal to cross through an intersection after a pedestrian has passed the path of your vehicle even if they are still in the crosswalk. But in other states, the pedestrian must be entirely off the street before you can proceed. If you are in a state that allows cars to proceed while pedestrians are still in the crosswalk, your defense should focus on proving that you gave the pedestrian plenty of room to pass by and then proceeded safely across the intersection. In states that absolutely prohibit you from moving across the intersection until the pedestrian has cleared the crosswalk, you must try to prove that you did wait for the pedestrian to leave the street and the

officer just didn't see clearly. In some courts, you may be able to succeed with an argument that the only reason the pedestrian was still in the crosswalk was that he unexpectedly stopped or reversed direction. But don't count on winning this one, as some judges may simply treat your argument as an admission of guilt.

E. Driving Too Slowly

There are several circumstances in which drivers may be ticketed for illegally blocking or impeding traffic by driving too slowly or failing to yield to a long line of vehicles behind them. Let's look briefly at the most common.

1. Driving Too Slowly in Left Lane

Your state's law will say something like:

"Any vehicle proceeding upon a highway at a speed less than the normal speed of traffic moving in the same direction at such time shall be driven in the right-hand lane for traffic or as close as practicable to the right-hand edge or curb, except when overtaking and passing another vehicle proceeding in the same direction or when preparing for a left turn at an intersection or into a private road or driveway. If a vehicle is being driven at a speed less than the normal speed of traffic moving in the same direction at such time, and is not being driven in the right-hand lane for traffic or as close as practicable to the right-hand edge or curb, it shall constitute evidence that the driver is operating the vehicle in violation of this section."

In plain English, this law means if you're poking along, you had better be in the right-hand or slow lane unless you're preparing to turn left.

The elements of the violation are:

1. You drove at a speed "less than the normal speed of traffic," and
2. You didn't drive "as close as practicable to the right-hand edge or curb."

It's bad enough to get a ticket for going too fast; to be cited for going too slow is truly rude. Too bad, but the law does say that under most circumstances you have a legal duty to move over to the right lane when other traffic is going faster than you are. And in a presumed speed limit state, where it can be considered safe and legal to exceed the speed limit, this can be true even if other traffic is proceeding slightly above the posted speed.

Of course, if you read your statute carefully, you'll likely find that there is one big exception to this move-to-the-right-if-you-are-driving-slowly requirement. As long as it is permitted, you have the right to move to the left to pass an even slower vehicle, even if doing so means you are briefly driving slower than the normal speed in that lane. For example, if you are driving 35 mph in a 45-mph zone and there is a farm tractor, an oversize motor home or some other slow vehicle in the right lane doing 20 mph, it's okay for you to be one lane to the left to pass it.

The best way to defend against this ticket is to prove:

1. In an "absolute" speed limit state (see Chapter 5 and the Appendix) you were traveling at the posted speed limit.

2. You were preparing to make a left turn (if true).

3. You were passing even slower moving traffic to the left and were prepared to return to the slow lane as soon as it was safe.

4. Your speed, although below the posted limit, was the only safe speed for that road under the conditions you were driving through, which could include rain, wind, darkness or other dangerous conditions.

5. You were only blocking the traffic behind you because in fact, it wasn't safe to go any faster.

In court, the officer must only testify that you were driving below the speed limit, or, in a "presumed" speed limit state, at a speed slower than other safe-driving traffic. It is then up to you to show a legal excuse for your action.

EXAMPLE: It's a damp, drizzly day, and you're doing 35 mph. The speed limit is 35 mph. You want to turn left in a few blocks and move into the left lane and slow down in preparation. Suddenly you see two cars coming up fast behind you, followed by a police officer. You are pulled over and get a ticket for not keeping up with traffic, while the speeders happily roar away.

Your defense will rest on two issues. First that your slower speed was based on road conditions at the time. And second that you were preparing to turn left, which meant you had to be in the left lane even though you were slowing down. Armed with a good diagram explaining the situation to the judge and your testimony that other cars were speeding, you should prevail. (See Chapter 9, Section C, for how to prepare good diagrams.)

2. Impeding Traffic

This offense is similar to driving too slowly in the left lane. The difference is that you can be charged with the offense even if you're in the curb lane or the only lane on a one-lane road.

A typical impeding traffic law says:

"No person shall drive upon a highway at such a slow speed as to impede or block the normal and reasonable movement of traffic, except when reduced speed is necessary for safe operation, because of a grade, or compliance with the law."

The elements of this violation are:

1. You drove on a highway at a speed less than the "normal and reasonable" speed of traffic.

2. Your reduced speed was not made necessary by safe operation or a grade, and

3. You were not speeding.

The success or failure of your defense will normally pivot on whether you can convince the judge that your view of events was more reasonable than that of the officer's. Your best defense is

road hog

a motorist who tells a good story. If, for example, you were carrying 12 dozen cartons of raw eggs to an Easter celebration or moving your grandmother's 100-year-old dishes over a poorly paved road, it won't hurt to work it in to your testimony.

💡 **Rough pavement can be a reason to go slowly.** Speed limits are normally posted based on an assessment of how fast it is safe to go on a particular road. Occasionally, however, conditions change for the worse after the speed limit is posted. This is particularly likely if construction or heavy wear has degraded the road surface. So if the pavement was in bad shape, make sure you document it with photographs and argue that it was unsafe to go faster than your speed.

to show that your slow speed was reasonable because of road, weather or traffic conditions. An officer trying to make this one stick will likely testify that you were driving below the speed limit and holding up a long line of frustrated, finger-gesturing, horn-honking drivers. The law will excuse your slow driving if you can show:

- You were traveling at the posted speed limit, or safely above it in a "presumed" speed-limit state, or
- You were driving slower than the posted speed, but lower speed was "necessary for safe operation" of your vehicle.

During cross-examination ask the officer, "How fast was traffic moving when I was stopped?" If he says he can't remember (but can remember that cars were trying to get past you), you should prevail if you can testify that you were driving at the speed limit while the cars trying to pass you were attempting to violate the posted limit.

But if you were driving much under the posted limit, this first defense won't work. In this situation, be prepared to testify and document—with photos or diagrams—that poor road conditions, bad weather, steep grades or sharp curves, made a higher speed unsafe. Although personal reasons normally won't help, this is one circumstance where I have occasionally seen a judge side with

3. Failing to Use "Turnouts"

A turnout is usually a patch of pavement on the right side of the road where slow drivers can pull off the road to let faster drivers go past. If you're driving slowly, and there are a whole lot of drivers behind you wanting to go faster, you normally have a legal duty to pull over and let them go by.

Here, a typical state law reads like this:

"On a two-lane highway where passing is unsafe because of traffic in the opposite direction or other conditions, a slow-moving vehicle, including a passenger vehicle, behind which five or more vehicles are formed in line, shall turn off the roadway at the nearest place designated as a turnout by signs erected by the authority having jurisdiction over the highway, or wherever sufficient area for a safe turnout exists, in order to permit the vehicles following it to proceed. As used in this section, a slow-moving vehicle is one that is proceeding at a rate of speed less than the normal flow of traffic at the particular time and place."

The elements of this violation include:

1. You were driving a "slow-moving vehicle," meaning you were driving slower "than the normal flow of traffic" at the time.
2. You were on a highway with two lanes, one in each direction.
3. There were at least five other vehicles behind yours that all slowed down because of you (this number can vary from state to state), and
4. You failed to pull over at a marked "turn-out" or other widened area to the right where you could safely pull over.

Driving slowly because of safety concerns, such as a degraded pavement, is not a defense to this charge, since you could still have used the turnout. Your only available defense is normally that, for some good reason, you were unable to safely pull over to let the other traffic past. Possible excuses for not pulling over include:

1. Another vehicle was already occupying the turnout, and there wasn't enough room for you too.
2. You were unable to pull into the turnout safely because you were pulling a trailer, trying to avoid a hole in the road because of snow or ice or for some other good reason, or
3. The road was so winding that you couldn't reasonably know how many vehicles were behind you.

← tail gator

F. Tailgating

We all hate it when someone rides our bumper. And with good reason. Driving too closely behind another vehicle really is dangerous. That's why the traffic laws of all states prohibit this conduct. Most define the violation as follows:

"The driver of a motor vehicle shall not follow another vehicle more closely than is reasonable and prudent, having due regard for the speed of such vehicle and the traffic upon, and the condition of, the roadway."

Here are the elements of this violation:

1. There was a vehicle in front of you, in the same lane, and
2. You followed more closely than reasonable, given the road, weather and traffic conditions.

The key to winning a case for tailgating is to prove that your distance behind the other car was reasonable and prudent given the circumstances at the time. The big word here is "circumstances." If you are 15 feet behind another vehicle traveling at 70 mph, your actions are not reasonable or prudent. But if traffic is creeping along at 10 mph, a distance of 15 feet behind the car in front of yours is reasonable. Now suppose traffic is proceeding at 25 mph. Is 15 feet still a reasonable and prudent distance to follow the car ahead? Probably not. The normal safety guideline is that a driver should leave one car length between his car and the car in front of his for every 10 mph. So, to be safe, a car traveling 60 mph should normally have at least six car lengths of empty space between him and the car in front of him.

Convince the judge your tailgating was temporary. Every driver has experienced situations where another car suddenly slows down, with the result that you have to quickly adjust your speed by also slowing down. In this case, an officer might see you before you have completed your adjustment, making it falsely appear you were tailgating. Clearly, if this was what happened to you, you should testify along these lines.

"I was traveling at 50 mph, according to my speedometer, with the rest of traffic. I allowed at least five car lengths of space between the front of my vehicle and the pickup truck in front of me. However, when that truck abruptly slowed to about 35 mph, for no apparent reason, the distance closed to about two car lengths. Before I could slow further, to lengthen the distance to three or four car lengths, the officer behind me pulled me over. I tried to explain to the officer that because there was no objective reason such as heavy traffic for the truck to slow down, I couldn't have anticipated it, but he wouldn't discuss what really happened."

Tailgating tickets are occasionally given when a driver rear-ends another vehicle. In this instance, the officer usually has not witnessed the accident and cannot testify that he saw you tailgating. Instead, the cop has jumped to the conclusion that the accident was caused by your tailgating. Fortunately, there are ways to defend against this type of ticket. For example, the accident might have been caused by the other driver stopping too quickly or pulling into your lane too close to your car. In short, it's your job to convince the judge in your direct testimony that there was a non-tailgating explanation. (See Chapter 9, Section D, on preparing your testimony.) And when you cross-examine the officer you'll want to establish that since he didn't see what happened he can't rule out the fact that the accident was not caused by your tailgating. Since the other driver won't be present and the cop showed up later, this is often fairly easy to do.

G. Unsafe Lane Changes

Most state laws say something like this:

"Whenever any roadway has been divided into two or more clearly marked lanes for traffic in one direction, the following rule applies: A vehicle shall be driven as nearly as practicable entirely within a single lane and shall not be moved from the lane until such movement can be made with reasonable safety."

As we saw in Section C.4 above, you can be cited for an unsafe lane change under the rule that prohibits unsafe turns, or under this more specific violation, which has the following elements:

1. The road had two or more lanes for traffic in the same direction.
2. Lane boundaries were clearly marked, and
3. You either failed to drive "as nearly as practicable" within the lane or changed lanes without regard for "reasonable safety."

Police will readily and properly pounce on a driver who weaves in and out of traffic without signaling, especially if he cuts off another car, forcing it to abruptly brake. Often the officer will watch for brake lights flashing on cars in your vicinity to determine if you are endangering others with your frequent lane changes. Your defense to this one should often be based on the fact that there can be many reasons for a driver to touch the brakes and that your lane change may have had nothing to do with it. For example, a car could have been traveling much faster than the speed limit before you pulled into its lane, causing it to brake sharply. Or a car in front of you may have braked sharply, forcing you to make a quick lane change. Since all these circumstances are difficult to see from a distance or a bad angle, you'll have a good chance to sell the judge on why your lane change was safe under the circumstances.

Establish where the officer was when you changed lanes. Most drivers are on their best behavior when a police cruiser is close. So officers end up issuing many violations that they view from a distance, meaning their ability to judge the nuances of whether particular conduct was safe or not is poor. If this was true in your case, use your chance to cross-examine the officer to ask questions like these:

"How far behind the other vehicle were you when you observed it brake?"

"After I changed lanes, you were behind the other car, weren't you? [if "yes," follow up with] At that moment, you couldn't see the distance between my car and the other car, could you?"

"I assume you weren't pacing the vehicle you claim I turned in front of?" [if "no," follow up with] "Then you don't know how fast it was going, do you?"

Then work the officer's admissions into your testimony that your conduct was safe and that the officer's conclusion that it wasn't isn't reliable.

EXAMPLE: You're driving 65 mph on the freeway in the right-hand lane. To avoid cars entering from an upcoming on-ramp, you decide to move into the center lane. Preparing to change lanes, you flick on your left turn signal and look in your rear and side view mirrors. You see another car in the middle lane, but it's about eight car-lengths back, so you make the lane change. As you do, the apparently inattentive driver of the other car speeds up, with the result that your vehicles are very close together. You are ticketed for an illegal lane change.

In court, explain that you were going at or near the speed limit, and were changing lanes to avoid a dangerous merge situation. Also, testify—if true—that just after you signaled your lane change, the other driver sped up. (Since the other driver won't be in court, only the police officer will be there to contradict you.) In short, any unsafe conditions were brought about by the other driver's unsafe conduct, not your lane change.

H. Improper Passing

Unsafe passing is dealt with in several common ways in most states. Here are the contexts in which unsafe passing is made illegal:

1. Endangering Those You Pass

The violation:
In most states, you are forbidden from *"interfering with the safe operation of any vehicle"* that you pass, and any vehicle coming from the opposite direction on a two-lane highway.

The defense:
The ticketing officer must have some evidence of your unsafe passing. You must cause an accident or nearly force another car off the road before an officer has enough evidence to write you a ticket, particularly if he did not see you pass other cars on the road. If a car approaching you had to put on their brakes and slow slightly to allow you to complete your passing attempt, this is not necessarily a violation, because the other driver may have slowed down unnecessarily. But if you force them off the road, you probably have little defense.

2. Unsafe "Blind" Passing

The violation:
This law forbids you from passing in the oncoming traffic lane when *"approaching the top of a hill or a curve, so as to create a hazard"* to vehicles that might approach from the other side.

The defense:
This law does not require that you put another driver into jeopardy to be convicted. It is sufficient that you created the possibility of a collision by attempting to pass on a blind curve or in some area where your view of the road ahead is

obscured. Your defense should be aimed at challenging the officer's recollection of how far you were from the hill or curve when you passed the other vehicle. You could argue (if true) that the car you were passing sped up suddenly, making it impossible for you to complete your maneuver before reaching a blind curve area. Remember, the officer has the burden of proving each element of the violation.

3. Passing on the Right

The laws in most states prohibit passing on the right, except under the following circumstances:

- The passed vehicle is about to turn left. (You still can't drive onto the unpaved shoulder of the road.)
- The street or road is wide enough to accommodate two lanes of traffic.

Even if passing on the right is allowed under one of the above exceptions, you must do so "under conditions permitting such movement in safety."

I. NonDUI/DWI Alcohol Related Offenses

States define alcohol related offenses in several ways and use several different laws to punish drivers and passengers who carry or use alcoholic beverages while driving. Driving Under the Influence (DUI) and Driving While Intoxicated (DWI) offenses are serious offenses outside the scope of this book and often require the assistance of an attorney. There are, however, some alcohol related violations that fall into the "infraction," or "petty" offense category covered here. These include drinking while driving (but not being legally drunk) and having an open container of alcohol in your vehicle. Even if you are not charged with DUI/DWI, some insurance companies will raise your rates or cancel your insurance

for convictions of these violations. It follows that, if you have a decent defense, there is a big incentive to fight these tickets or, if possible, have them dismissed by attending traffic school. (See Chapter 3, Section C, on attending traffic school.)

⚠ **DUI/DWI are not discussed here.** Because DUI/DWI charges are very serious and can result in jail time, hefty fines, insurance premium hikes and loss of a driver's license, they are not dealt with in this book. Often, fighting these offenses requires the assistance or at least coaching of an experienced attorney.

1. Open Container on Driver's or Passenger's Person

This is the most common alcohol related offense where the driver is not charged with DUI/DWI. Most state laws say something like this:

"No person shall have in his or her possession, while driving a motor vehicle upon a highway, any bottle, can or other receptacle, containing any alcoholic beverage that has been opened, or a seal broken, or the contents of which have been partially removed."

The elements of this violation are all of the following:

1. You drove a motor vehicle.
2. You drove on any public road or "highway." (Private roads or parking lots don't count.)
3. You kept a container, such as a bottle, can or glass on your person, which means you held it in your hand, kept it within your reach, or kept it in a pocket or purse.
4. The container held any amount of an alcoholic beverage when the officer found it, although simply the odor of an alcoholic beverage is not enough, and
5. The seal, if any, on the bottle was broken, or the container's contents were "partially removed."

You can bet, in most states, if an officer finds an open container in your vehicle, he is going to charge you with the most serious offense he can. If he rules out DUI/DWI, an "open container" violation is a way for him to cite you for a less serious offense.

This offense requires that the ticketing officer "connect" the open container to the person cited. The open container must be within the control of the driver, or within his reach. If there are open containers in the vehicle, but not close to the driver or any other passenger, the driver may still be cited for keeping an open container in the vehicle.

If you are cited for having an open container on your person, and you have no good defense, it may be worth attempting to negotiate to accept a lesser violation, like simply having an open container in your vehicle. (See Section 2, below, and Chapter 12, Section B, on how to plea-bargain.) In that way, you might be able to sell your insurance company with an "I didn't know it was there" alibi.

When a passenger has an open container in the vehicle, both that passenger, and the driver, can properly be cited: the passenger for having or drinking from an open container (see Section 3, below), and the driver for allowing an open container in the vehicle. The driver's only valid defense is that he had no reason to know the passenger had the open container. See Section 2, below.

EXAMPLE: You and your friends are on the way to the beach with a few unopened sixpacks of beer. Unbeknownst to you, one of your friends in the back seat can't wait, and quietly opens a can of beer before you get there. When an officer pulls you over for an expired registration, he notices the open beer can in the back and tickets you, the driver. Your defense is that you didn't have any reason to know your passenger made that stupid move.

2. Open Container Kept in Vehicle

Almost all states forbid driving with an "open container" of an alcoholic beverage in your vehicle. In a few states—like Texas— it is legal for a passenger, but not the driver, to drink an alcoholic beverage while the vehicle is in motion. Although having an open container is a less serious offense than drinking from one, a conviction can still seriously affect your license status or insurance.

Most state "open container" laws say something like this:

"It is unlawful for the registered owner of any motor vehicle, or the driver, if the registered owner is not then present in the vehicle, to keep in a motor vehicle when the vehicle is upon any highway, any bottle, can or other receptacle containing any alcoholic beverage that has been opened, or a seal broken, or the contents of which have been partially removed, unless the container is kept in the trunk of the vehicle, or kept in some other area of the vehicle not normally occupied by the driver or passengers if the vehicle is not equipped with a trunk. A utility compartment or glove compartment shall be deemed to be within the area occupied by the driver and passengers. This section shall not apply to the living quarters of a motor home or camper."

The elements of this offense are all of the following:

1. You were a driver or owner of a vehicle.
2. You were in the vehicle.
3. The vehicle was "upon any highway," but not necessarily driven by the registered owner.
4. There was a container, such as a bottle, can or glass somewhere in the vehicle other than the trunk. (For vehicles without trunks—such as pickups and hatchbacks, the container must be "in some area of the vehicle not normally occupied by the driver or passengers," but not in the glove compartment.)

5. The container held some amount of an alcoholic beverage when the officer found it.

6. The seal, if any, on the bottle, etc., was broken, or its contents were "partially removed," and

7. The container was not in the living quarters of a motor home or camper.

About the only real defense to this is the "mistake of fact" defense that says you didn't know the open container was in the vehicle. This might work if a passenger really did open a bottle or can without your knowledge (especially if he will come to court and say so). It may also work if you borrowed a car containing an open container that was not in plain sight, but still within your "control"—like a half-finished beer can, under the seat. (See Chapter 3, Section D.4, for more on "Mistake of Fact" defenses.)

3. Drinking in Vehicle

Every state forbids drivers—and most states forbid passengers—from drinking any alcoholic beverage in a moving motor vehicle. You can be guaranteed that a police officer will administer an alcohol test on a driver caught with an open container on his person, and will probably administer the test if he finds an open container anywhere in the passenger area.

Even if you pass that test, you are not out of the woods. Every state has a law allowing you to be charged with drinking in a vehicle, even if you pass the sobriety test. However, the officer must be able to testify that he actually saw you raise the bottle or can to your mouth and drink from it. If your breath smells of alcohol, that alone is no proof you drank while driving the vehicle, even if you were carrying an open container. After all, you could have had a drink before you got into the car. Even so, you can still be convicted, in most states, of the "lesser offense" of having an open container in your vehicle.

Myth of the Road. It is a myth that some states, like Texas, allow you to drink and drive as long as you stay below the official blood/alcohol level for intoxication.

4. Illegal Drug Use/Possession

This is a serious crime, akin to DUI/DWI. A federal law requires states to lift driver's licenses for six months after any drug conviction. Some states have refused to enact this federal requirement. But in states that have enacted such a law, you can lose your license for having drugs in your car, even if you are not charged with driving under their influence. It may make sense to check with an attorney if you are charged with this type of violation. (See Chapter 4 for how to select and work with an attorney.) ■

Chapter

8

First Steps to Fight Your Ticket

Master, master, come quick! Here's a fish caught up in the net like a working man's rights in the law.

—Shakespeare

A. So You've Decided to Fight

If you are reading this chapter, it should mean you have already:

1. Looked up and studied your ticket and the law you are charged with violating (Chapter 2).
2. If you are eligible, at least considered the possibility of wiping out the ticket by attending traffic school (Chapter 3).
3. Considered the consequences of pleading guilty on your driving record and insurance premiums (Chapter 3).
4. Found what you think is a defense with a reasonable chance of success (Chapters 5, 6 and 7).

There is no question that a determined person with a good defense can achieve great success in traffic court. And with the information you'll find here, your chances of prevailing should greatly increase.

B. Taking the First Steps

Before you show up in traffic court for your trial, there are some things you *must* do, and more you *should* do. In the rest of this chapter, we will review how basic traffic court procedure works and coach you on how to increase your chances of success.

1. Contacting the Court for Information

The date by which you must pay the fine or ask to appear in court should be printed on your ticket. For obvious reasons, paying up is usually made very easy. But if you want to fight, you may need to call the court to find out exactly what you need to do. Be prepared for frustration. Many courts have automatic phone systems from hell (that is, designed not to answer even one of your sensible questions). Persevere—or stop by the court clerk's office before the drop dead date and you should find a live person who can help.

Courts on the Internet

In many courts, information is also available through a Web page on the Internet. We list informative Websites in our Appendix. You can normally find court Websites using an Internet "search engine" such as Netscape or Microsoft's Explorer. Type in the name of the court you are trying to find (e.g. "Los Angeles Municipal Court") and a list will appear that should include a Website for the court you are looking for.

The Internet is not perfect, though, so you will probably get many references to things you are not interested in. If you cannot find the proper Web page in five minutes of searching, it is best to call the court to see if they have a Web address. If they do, you can type that address into your Web browser and go to the Web page. (Also, be sure to check the Appendix, which lists a number of good Websites.) Or you can go to: http://ncsc.dni.us/court/sites/courts. htm#state, the Website for the National Center for State Courts, which has very useful links to many state, county and local courts.

Currently, most Web pages simply give you information. But soon, they will allow you to help move your case along online to schedule appearances. In addition to the Internet, an increasing number of courts use public "kiosks" located in the court clerk's office and at convenient community locations where you can pay your fine by credit card, sign up for traffic school or notify the court of your intention to contest your ticket.

If you do speak to a live clerk, either by phone or by trekking to the courthouse, you'll want to have your ticket in hand to ask for the following information:

- Does the date on my ticket indicate my court date, or just the date by which I have to say whether I plan to contest my ticket?
- What additional steps must I take to fight my ticket?
- Is it possible to obtain an extension of time in which to decide whether I want to contest the ticket or schedule a trial date?
- Am I eligible for traffic school?

2. Deciding How to Plead

After you get basic information about your ticket and your options, you'll have to decide on a course of action. In most states, if for any reason you won't go to traffic school, you'll normally have four options:

- **Pay the fine** (called "forfeiting bail" in many places, the equivalent of pleading guilty).
- Plead "**Guilty With an Explanation**."
- Plead "**Nolo Contendere**."
- Plead "**Not Guilty**" (often this can be done at the clerk's office without entering a formal plea).

Do your homework. Before going to the court clerk's office or a court kiosk you'll want to do the research necessary to decide whether you'll contest your ticket. Often this will save you a return trip to the courthouse.

Now let's look at each of these options in more detail.

a. Paying the Fine (Forfeiting Bail)

If you decide to pay the fine (equivalent to entering a guilty plea), this fact will appear on your driving record. If your record is otherwise spotless, a single violation should not affect your driving privileges or insurance premiums. But it's also true that you never know if you'll get another moving violation a week after (unless, of course, you switch to public transit, your bike, feet or stay at home). Then, of course, you would be in greater jeopardy of an insurance premium increase and—if you get several more tickets—a possible license suspension. That's why we believe, if you aren't eligible for traffic school (see Chapter 3, Section C) but have a decent defense, it often makes sense to assert it.

Courts make it easy to pay the fine in most cases. They almost universally allow you to do so by mail or through the court clerk's office. Rarely will you be required to appear in court and admit your guilt. Traffic offenses where a formal guilty plea may be required in some states include driving more than 20 mph over the speed limit, reckless driving and alcohol-related violations, like driving with an open alcoholic beverage container. If you have been in an accident related to the ticket, read the sidebar, "If You Were Involved in an Accident."

If You Were Involved in an Accident

In most states, if you pay the ticket to the court clerk without appearing before a judge (most courts allow this except for the most serious violations), you do not subject yourself to civil liability as you would if you entered a guilty plea in court. But check with your insurance company or a lawyer to make sure (see Chapter 3, Section B).

If for any reason you are required to appear in court to enter a plea and have absolutely no defense, plead "nolo contendere." This special plea, available in most states, is equivalent to a guilty plea as far as your ticket is concerned, but can't be used against you if you are later slapped with a civil damage lawsuit from someone else involved in the accident (see Section c below).

However, if you are found guilty after trial in some states, this may result in the other party winning any lawsuit against you based on the accident. This is a legally complex issue, so you should seek a lawyer's advice before going to trial for a ticket arising out of an accident.

b. Plead Guilty With an Explanation

If you did it and have no decent defense, there is no need to go to court and plead guilty, as was common in times past. Just pay the fine (forfeit bail) and the deed is done. But one exception to this rule occurs in areas where you are allowed to enter a "guilty-with-an-explanation" plea. As the name suggests, this involves pleading guilty, but telling the judge a good enough story that she may reduce or even suspend the fine. Even where allowed, this is rarely a good approach. Even if a sympathetic judge reduces or "suspends" the fine, the offense still goes on your driving record and your insurance rates may rise. People who do not want to go to the trouble of preparing a good

defense, but who want to take a shot at tugging at the judge's heartstrings, sometimes try this approach. It's far better to plead not guilty and take your best shot at trying to convince the judge you are not guilty. Also, the officer may not show up in court, which often results in the case against you being dismissed.

c. Plead Nolo Contendere

A plea of Nolo Contendere (pronounced "no-lo con-tend-er-ray") literally means: "I do not choose to contest the charge." While rarely necessary, this plea makes sense if you have been in an accident and, for some reason, you must enter a formal plea in court (can't just forfeit bail at the clerk's office). Because a Nolo Contendere plea only admits that you are not contesting the facts stated in the criminal charge (in this case, the ticket), it cannot be used as an admission of guilt in other cases. By contrast, a guilty plea can often be used against you in another lawsuit. All of this can be critical if you face the possibility of a civil lawsuit for damages because of a claim that you damaged property or caused injury or death to another person.

What if a judge balks at your Nolo plea? Some judges hate Nolo Contendere pleas. They figure you are either guilty or not guilty. If your judge resists allowing you to enter a Nolo Contendere plea, tell her that there was an auto accident—if true, of course. This should change her mind. If the judge still says no, plead not guilty. This will give you a chance to discuss strategy with your insurance company and, if the situation is serious, a lawyer.

d. The Not Guilty Plea

Under our legal system, it is always your legal right to plead not guilty. This is true whether you think you are guilty or not. In many places, you can plead "not guilty" by mail or telephone or by using a traffic court kiosk. In almost all others, this can be done at the court clerk's window. In either case, you may be required to post a fee—often called bail—which you get returned if you win. In a very few rural areas, to enter a "not guilty" plea you must appear before a judge at a brief court proceeding called an "arraignment" (see discussion below).

3. Should You Insist on an Arraignment?

Many courts have completely abolished the arraignment procedure by which you enter your plea in front of a judge. But in other courts, you do have the right to insist on entering your plea in court (although you may not be told about it unless you ask). Here are a few reasons why you might want to do this:

- At arraignment you can ask about your right to obtain—or "discover," in legal jargon—the evidence the officer will present against you at trial. (See Section C, below, for other ways to discover evidence.)
- This is often when and where you can ask for a jury trial, if your state is one that allows it for ordinary traffic violations. (If you are not allowed arraignment in your state, be sure to ask the court clerk how to ask for a jury trial, if you are allowed one. See the Appendix.)
- This is where you can plead Nolo Contendere to a violation arising out of an accident. (Normally this is necessary only if the accident makes you ineligible to forfeit bail. See sidebar above).

4. What Happens at Arraignment

If you have decided not to be arraigned, you may skip to the next section, "Using Discovery to Build Your Case."

Arraignments are used by the court to inform you of what you are charged with, as well as outlining your basic legal rights—including the right to an attorney, to cross-examine the officer, to call witnesses to testify for you and, in some states, to request a jury trial. (See the Appendix for whether your state allows trial by jury.)

At an arraignment, the judge will usually address traffic defendants in a group, informing them of their rights, which include:

- The right to a trial at which the State has the burden of proving you guilty beyond a reasonable doubt. (If you are charged with exceeding a "presumed" speed limit, the state must show "beyond a reasonable doubt" that you exceeded the speed limit. After that, you have the burden of proving that your speed was safe.)
- The right to see, hear and cross-examine the prosecution's witnesses (usually just the ticketing officer)
- The right to call or "subpoena" witnesses to testify for you
- If the offense is punishable by a jail sentence—as with drunk or reckless driving—the right to a court-appointed lawyer
- The right to a jury trial if your state allows one for traffic offenses (see Appendix).

If you plead guilty or no contest, the judge will probably ask whether you understand your rights. If you say you do, you will not be able to complain later.

Beware of tricky judges. To save court time a judge may try to confuse you into changing your mind if you request a jury trial. The judge may tell you, "I recommend that you choose (or accept) a court trial." In the parlance of lawyers and judges "court trial" means a trial before a judge, not a jury. So if a judge tries to push for a "court" trial in a state where you have a right to a jury, insist you want a jury trial by saying, *"No, Your Honor, I want a jury trial."*

a. Entering a "Not Guilty" Plea at Arraignment

If you request an arraignment, the judge will ask you how you plead. Answer "not guilty." At the same time you should specifically request the officer's presence at your trial (in some states you may waive this right without knowing it unless you insist on it to the clerk or at arraignment) and demand a jury trial. (Check the Appendix to see if your state allows jury trials and read Chapter 3 to see if it is the best choice for your case.)

Don't be talked out of your right to a jury trial. Assuming you do the homework necessary to cope with a far more complicated courtroom situation, your chances of winning are almost always better in front of a jury than before a judge. The reasons are simple. Judges tend to side with police officers; jurors are more likely to feel they have been treated unfairly in traffic court and may side with you.

Another reason to press for a jury trial is because it makes a simple traffic case more expensive and time consuming. It may cause the prosecutor to dismiss it (especially likely if the prosecution's case really is weak). Another possibility is that the prosecutor may offer you an opportunity to plead to a reduced charge or attend traffic school, if it is otherwise not an option. (See Chapter 12, Section B, on negotiating for a lesser sentence.) In short, even if the judge tries to dissuade you from trying your case in front of a jury, there can be good reasons to insist on it.

In some states, you may be asked at your arraignment whether you have been convicted previously of any traffic offenses. Occasionally, higher fines are imposed on repeat traffic law offenders. Never lie. If you do have prior offenses (sometimes called "priors") it is best to fess up or, if they are in other states or might be hard to find, say, "I deny the validity of any prior convictions." This is acceptable language in the court system even if, in fact, you have forfeited bail or been convicted of one or more prior traffic offenses. All you are saying is that it is up to the prosecution to find and present evidence of any prior traffic offenses.

b. Understand Speedy Trial Rules

The Sixth Amendment to the United States Constitution guarantees "a speedy and public trial" in all criminal cases, but fails to say exactly what "speedy" means. Many states do. For example, California requires that a case be dismissed if not brought to trial within 45 days of entering a not guilty plea before a judge.

Especially where your state's speedy trial deadline is short, harried traffic court judges are likely to ask you to waive your right to a speedy trial. Often this is done at an arraignment or if you make a motion to discover the officer's notes. Typically, the judge will say something like, *"Do you waive time for trial?"* or even *"Do you waive time?"*

If you enter a not guilty plea at a clerk's office in California and some other states, he will insist that you sign a form giving up your right to a speedy trial in exchange for the convenience of skipping a formal arraignment (going to court and pleading not guilty). In other places, you may have a choice as to whether you wish to waive time. So if you are asked to "waive time," politely ask the clerk if you have the option of refusing without having to go through with an arraignment. If so, you will almost always want to say "no." Here's why. In busy courthouses, your trial will probably be scheduled towards the end of the time allowed by the law. This means if the officer does not appear for the trial and the judge does not dismiss the ticket (something he may, but is not required, to do), he will have to reschedule your trial with the officer present before the "speedy trial" deadline. This may be impossible. In that case, you win.

Research your state's speedy trial laws. The quickest and easiest way to find your state's speedy trial laws is to go to a law library and ask the librarian to direct you to them. If you do it on your own, you should be able to locate them in your state constitution or, perhaps, in a more specific statute dealing with speedy trial rules for various crimes. (See Chapter 2, Sections B and C, for how to research the law.) You should look for them in your state's "Criminal Code," "Judicial Code" or "Rules of Criminal Procedure."

If you can get to the Internet with a computer, and your state has a Website that allows you to search the statutes by words or phrases (see the Appendix), start by typing the phrase "speedy trial" in quotes in the search engine.

c. Consider Delaying the Arraignment and/or Trial

Be prepared to negotiate for a convenient trial date. If the judge proposes a date on which you have a conflict, speak right up and tell him why it is inconvenient. He will very likely set a later date. But be careful not to accept a date that is past the number of days allowed in your state to conduct a speedy trial, since by doing so you would probably give up ("waive") your right to a speedy trial.

Sometimes it pays to delay. Instead of proceeding right to trial—or even entering a guilty plea, if that's what you eventually plan to do—you may want to put things off for several weeks or months. For example, you may be able to delay the trial date until after a time when any new points from a conviction would cause the state to suspend your license. This would be a good idea if you have points on your record that would expire during the delay. Often it's possible to get a delay by going to the court clerk a few days before the appearance deadline listed on your ticket and asking for an extension. In many

courts, the clerk will give you at least one delay without much coaxing. Then, if you can come up with a great excuse as to why you can't appear on the second date, you may be able to coax the clerk to extend it again.

When you finally have to show up in court, you can take another shot at postponing the matter even more, if necessary, by explaining to the judge that you do not want to enter a plea until you "have time to consult with a lawyer." Especially if yours is a garden-variety ticket, the judge may become impatient, but will often allow at least one short continuance (delay) for you to look for a lawyer.

When you are near the deadline given by the judge, again, you may want to try to prevail on the clerk or judge to give you one more extension. At this point, though—unless you can come up with a doctor's verification of a serious illness or some other very convincing reason—you are likely to run into a stone wall. But if you really do need a few more weeks, it never hurts to keep whining.

The cop won't show up if he is on vacation. Occasionally, you can find out or guess when an officer will be on vacation. I've even known people who simply call up and ask to be given this information. If you can convince the judge to set your trial date during this period, the chances go way up that the officer won't be present, with the result that your case may be dismissed.

5. Trial by Declaration or Affidavit

In nine states (most notably California and Florida —see the Appendix for the others), you have the option of presenting your defense in writing, rather than personally appearing at a trial. Typically, you make your testimony in a "declaration" where you swear you are telling the truth. You do this by adding this phrase at the end of your signed statement: "I declare under penalty of perjury that the foregoing is true and correct. Executed on [date] at [city and state])." Some courts may require you to have your statement notarized instead of, or in addition to, swearing it is true (precise rules will be available from the court clerk).

This procedure is called "trial by declaration" or "trial by affidavit." Even in states that don't have laws allowing this procedure, some courts will permit it anyway. Check with your court clerk, if you think you might want to use this option.

One obvious advantage of opting for a trial by declaration is that you don't have to appear in court for a trial, a big help if you got your ticket far from home and don't relish driving a hundred or more miles to testify. Another advantage is that you can take time to draft a convincing, well-thought-out defense, which may convince a judge better than the oral testimony of an inexperienced, nervous defendant.

But there is a big downside of not appearing in front of the judge—you give up your right to present your defense in person, to get the case dismissed if the officer doesn't show at trial and to cross-examine the officer if he does show up. For example, you'll never hear what the officer

says and won't have a chance to poke holes in a weak presentation. Many courts also require the officer to present specific written testimony when you opt for this procedure—without giving you the opportunity to see the officer's statement before you prepare yours. But in some states, you do have a right to request a copy of the officer's notes (see Section C below), before you submit your written statement to the court.

If trial by declaration is available (see Appendix), and you think you might want to opt for it, contact the court clerk to ask about the procedure. Some courts require that you use their forms to print or type your statement. Some courts require you to pay the fine in advance, in the event you're convicted; others don't. Every court has a policy that your statement be submitted within a certain time period.

Before submitting your defense, be sure to read Chapters 5 and 6, or Chapter 7 on traffic violations, as well as Chapter 9 on preparing your case for trial, to get an idea of the types of defenses that can work and that won't work. Keep in mind that if you have any witnesses whose testimony you think may be helpful, you can also present their declarations or affidavits, in addition to yours. Here is a sample declaration:

October 1, 2001
123 Innocent Drive
Rough and Ready, California

Traffic Court Clerk
Municipal Court of Alameda County
Oakland-Piedmont-Emeryville District
661 Washington Street, Second Floor
Oakland, CA 94607

CERTIFIED MAIL, RETURN RECEIPT REQUESTED

Re: People v. Lenny D. Leadfoot, Municipal Court No. A036912-B

Traffic Citation - Oakland Police Dept. No. 99-O-12345

Declaration of Defendant Lenny D. Leadfoot in Support of Trial by Written Declaration

Dear Clerk:

As allowed under state law/local practice, I enclose a check for $123 bail, plead not guilty to the above-referenced charge, and submit the following declaration:

On September 20, 2001, at approximately 10:30 a.m., I was driving my 1986 Honda Civic, License No. 3JXS505, west on Breezy Boulevard, a four-lane divided highway, between Drag Boulevard and Zoom Street. I was in the right-hand lane. The weather was clear and dry. There was no traffic in my direction other than a large panel truck (visible in my side view mirror) in the left lane, several car lengths behind me. The truck overtook and passed my vehicle shortly before I crossed the Zoom Street intersection. As that occurred, I wondered whether I was driving too slowly, and noticed that my speedometer indicated I was going 34 mph. The posted speed limit was 35 mph.

Officer Stickler of the Oakland Police Department stopped me approximately two blocks past Zoom Street. He informed me that he had determined my speed on his hand-held radar unit to be 49 mph. He said that he had read my speed at the Breezy Boulevard–Drag Boulevard intersection from the intersection at Zoom Street, which a street map will show is 500 feet away. Officer Stickler responded to several of my questions by stating that the radar beam width was "about six degrees," and that his unit had been "calibrated recently with this little knob," pointing to the "calibrate" position on the controls of the unit. He said he hadn't used a tuning fork, and that he didn't have one in his possession. He also indicated that his unit was capable of reading speeds of both oncoming and receding traffic. Traffic was heavy in the opposite direction at the time, but not in my direction.

I believe that there exists a reasonable doubt as to the accuracy of Officer Stickler's radar reading. As can be seen from the diagram below, a six-degree beam width at 500 feet will indiscriminately read speeds of vehicles across a width of 55 feet, all four lanes of traffic.

The radar unit may therefore have been reading both speeds of traffic in my direction (including a truck target much larger and more likely to reflect radar beams than my small Honda Civic) and the heavy traffic in the other direction. This being so, it is doubtful that the speed he recorded was mine.

Also enclosed is the declaration of Wilhelmina D. Witness.

I declare under penalty of perjury that the foregoing is true and correct. Executed on October 2, 2001, at Rough and Ready, California.

Lenny D. Leadfoot

Lenny D. Leadfoot

Now, here's the attached declaration of witness Wilhelmina Witness:

Re: People v. Lenny D. Leadfoot,

Municipal Court No. A036912-B
Dept. No. 99-O-12345
Declaration of Wilhelmina D. Witness for Trial by Written Declaration

I, Wilhelmina Witness, declare:

On September 20, 2001, at approximately 10:30 a.m., I was riding as a passenger in an automobile driven by Lenny D. Leadfoot. Mr. Leadfoot was relaxed and not driving very fast for conditions. There were no other cars on the road in our direction of travel that I could see, other than a large truck that passed us on the left shortly before we crossed the Zoom Street intersection. We were talking as we drove westbound on Breezy Boulevard in Oakland. As we drove past Zoom Street, Mr. Leadfoot said that a police officer was pulling us over. I was surprised because I didn't know why we were being pulled over. We drove to the side of the road and waited for the officer. I asked Mr. Leadfoot why we were being pulled over, and he said he did not know.

The officer approached the driver side of the car and spoke to Mr. Leadfoot. He told Mr. Leadfoot he was driving 49 mph in a 35-mph zone. I was surprised because I didn't think that we were going that fast. I think this because, when Mr. Leadfoot suddenly said, "Looks like an officer's behind me with his red lights on, I better pull over to let him pass," I looked over at the speedometer, just before he slowed to pull over, and it read about 35 mph.

I declare under penalty of perjury that the foregoing is true and correct. Executed on October 2, 2001, at Rough and Ready, California.

Wilhelmina D. Witness
Wilhelmina D. Witness

Within a few weeks after submitting your written declaration (or affidavit, if required), you should receive a notice in the mail with the judge's verdict. If the notice says you were found not guilty, any fine ("bail") that you prepaid should be refunded to you.

C. Using "Discovery" to Build Your Case

In any fight, it is best to know your opponent's strategy. Fortunately, you often have the legal right to do this (called "discovery"). In many states you have the right to demand access to the officer's notes made at or soon after your ticket was issued. You also have the right to demand access to other information, like instruction manuals on the use of equipment that was used to clock your speed. (See Chapters 5 and 6 for information on what types of equipment are used to catch speeders and Chapter 10 on how to challenge the use of the equipment. You must check with your local court clerk to confirm you have the right to demand discovery in your state.) This information can be a huge help when cross-examining the officer and presenting your own case at trial.

To discover the officer's notes, you must make a specific written request for the disclosure of all notes or documents relevant to your case. If you have an arraignment, you may be able to do this there. But if, as is far more common, you plead not guilty and post bail without an arraignment, you'll need to make your request promptly by mail. Send your discovery request to both the police agency that ticketed you and to the local prosecuting agency. The request should be printed or typed on 8½" by 11" paper and look like this:

IN THE
MUNICIPAL COURT OF CALIFORNIA
COUNTY OF LOS ANGELES
VAN NUYS BRANCH

THE PEOPLE/STATE OF THE
CALIFORNIA,
Plaintiff,

Vs.

DANIELLE DEFENDANT,
Defendant.

REQUEST FOR DISCOVERY

Court Docket No. _A-1234567_
Citation Number: _99-HK-1234_
Date Issued: _4/15/2001_
Police Agency: _Los Angeles Police Dept._
Citing Officer: _Smith_   Badge No. _LA-1234_
Prosecuting Agency: _Los Angeles City Attorney_

TO THE ABOVE-NAMED POLICE AND PROSECUTING AGENCY:

1. The above-named defendant hereby requests that you provide, to the defendant whose address is indicated below, copies of any and all relevant written or recorded statements of witnesses, including any statements, diagrams, or drawings made by the citing officer on any piece of paper—including the reverse of his/her copy of the citation—or other medium of information storage.

2. The following are names and addresses of defense witnesses, other than defendant, who will testify at trial:
   ( ) None.
   (X) The following: _Jane Doe, 345 Main St., Van Nuys, CA 90012_
        _(818) 555-5678_

3. The following copies of notes made by defendant immediately after the ticket was issued and recorded statements of witnesses are attached:
   ( ) None.
   (X) See attached.

DATED: _May 17, 2001_

Danielle Defendant

DANIELLE DEFENDANT
12345 Market Street
Los Angeles, CA 90010
Tel: (213) 555-1234

1. If Your Discovery Request Is Ignored

Because so few defendants ask to see the evidence against them, many police, prosecutors, and even some judges, believe this "discovery right" is not available in traffic court. Accordingly, even though your discovery request is probably proper in your state, you may find it's ignored. If so, you'll need to persist in making this request, reiterating that you believe access to the officer's notes is critical to presenting your defense.

If you get no response to your discovery request within three weeks, you will need to go to court and make a "pre-trial motion" to ask the judge to order the police to release the notes to you. Lawyers call this a "motion to compel discovery" or dismiss the case. Your best bet is to call or visit the court clerk to schedule this motion before your scheduled trial date. Failing this, it may be possible to have your motion to compel discovery considered on the day of your trial. (See the next section for how to do this.)

Assuming a pretrial hearing to consider your discovery request is scheduled, be prepared to show the judge a copy of your written discovery request. Then ask him to formally order the prosecution or police agency to provide a copy of the officer's notes. Be sure to ask the judge to order that this be done prior to any scheduled trial date, so you have enough time to use them to prepare.

If your discovery request has still been ignored when your trial date rolls around, you may want to ask the judge to dismiss your case. Here is sample language that, of course, will need to be adjusted to fit your facts:

"Your honor, the prosecution has failed to provide the discovery I properly requested (and, if true, "that you ordered"). I move to dismiss the case on account of the prosecution's failure to provide discovery. Here is a copy of the written request I made a month ago for the officer's notes. I sent them to the prosecutor and police agency, and they both ignored me. I have not waived my right to a speedy trial, and I shouldn't have to. I can't properly prepare for trial even if the notes are produced now. As a result, I request that the charges against me be dismissed."

If the following requirements are met, you may get your case dismissed at this point:

- You are entitled to discovery under state law.
- Your state has a speedy-trial law entitling you to trial within a certain period and you haven't given up the right to a speedy trial.
- Postponing the trial to allow the prosecution to get the notes for you would require you to give up your right to a trial within the "speedy trial" time allowed.
- You made your request for "discovery" promptly (and within any time limit).

If the judge won't dismiss your case, renew your request right then that you be given a chance to examine the officer's notes. The judge should at least be willing to give you a few minutes to do this.

The Reason Cops Have Perfect Memories

Have you ever wondered what the officer who just ticketed you is doing, sitting in his patrol car after writing you up? He is probably writing notes—something on the back of your ticket—with details of why he ticketed you and what the conditions were at the time. Just before trial, he will typically review his notes, and sometimes refer to them while testifying. With courtroom experience, an officer can often glance down at his notes every few seconds, rattling off a narrative that sounds like he was recounting something that happened yesterday. But because the officer probably won't remember much about what happened and doesn't want to be tripped up fabricating a detail, most officers will depart very little from their notes. In short, if you can discover the officer's notes, you can expect his testimony will stick pretty close to this script.

2. What to Do With the Officer's Notes

If you receive a copy of the officer's notes, you'll want to study them carefully. It's possible that these notes may cause you to re-evaluate your defense strategy, when you know what the officer is going to say at trial. Here are some things to look for:

- **Detail.** If the officer's notes don't say much, she probably won't have much to say at trial, unless you gave her a reason to remember your specific case (another big reason why it's never wise to behave like an idiot when you are pulled over). On the other hand, the more detailed her notes (such as a fact-specific statement convincingly laying out what you did), the better she'll probably sound at trial.

- **What the Notes Don't Say.** If the notes lack key details, you may be able to challenge

the officer's memory. Look to see if the notes:

1. Mention which lane you were in.
2. Say exactly how the officer recorded your speed, if you were cited for speeding. (For example, if pacing was used, how far the officer paced you before stopping your vehicle.)
3. Have detailed specific information about road and weather conditions and other nearby vehicles. For example, if you were cited for an unsafe turn across traffic, the notes should detail the exact traffic situation justifying the officer's judgment call. (See Chapter 7 for a variety of situations.)
4. Report where the officer was when she observed you.

- **Diagrams.** Police will often make a diagram on the ticket, especially with violations that occur at intersections, like running a stop sign or stoplight, unsafe turns or failure to yield. If the officer does a careful job of including significant details, she will probably look well prepared in court. If not, you have a better chance to raise a reasonable doubt as to your guilt by demonstrating through cross-examination that the officer can't honestly remember what happened.

- **Driver statements.** Most officers will note any admissions made by the driver on pulling him or her over ("Said she was going 70, asked for a break."), sometimes quoting them directly. ("Yes, I ran the stop sign, but my daughter's pet iguana was sick and I had to get her to the vet.") Of course, you are far better off if there are no such admissions written down.

Deciphering police notes. Some officers write their notes in easy-to-read narrative detail; others use abbreviations, which are sometimes hard to decipher. Here are hints that may help you decipher police slang:

- S/V = "subject vehicle" (your car, truck or motorcycle)
- D or (△) = "defendant" (you)
- Est. = Police officer visually estimated your speed
- R or r = "radar" unit, sometimes also followed by the radar unit serial number
- Cops usually list how far they paced you or measured your speed using a VASCAR system in tenths of a mile (e.g., "0.3" means one-third of a mile and "1.5" means a mile and a half). (See Chapter 6, Section B.3.)

- BUMP = "bumper pace." The officer is recording how long he kept a constant distance between your rear bumper and his front bumper to read your speed on his speedometer.
- Traffic lanes are often abbreviated. For example, "lane No. 1" might appear as "Ln. 1" or "L 1" or just "#1." Lanes are counted from the center of the road (median), with lane No. 1 being the first lane and the lane to its immediate right being lane 2. ∎

Chapter

9

Preparing for Trial—Your Case

The penalty for laughing in the courtroom is six months in jail. If it were not for this penalty, the jury would never hear the evidence.

—*H.L. Mencken*

In this chapter we tell you how to prepare for your day in court, including:

- Preparing your evidence
- Outlining and practicing your testimony
- Helping your witnesses prepare their testimony.

Some people think they can beat a ticket by simply showing up in court and telling a terrific story to the judge or jury. They couldn't be more wrong. In theory you are innocent until proven guilty. In truth, unless your presentation includes evidence or testimony that convinces the judge that you are not guilty, he will usually side with the police officer. Juries—in the states where they are allowed—tend to be more friendly towards the driver, but convincing one that there is a reasonable doubt as to your guilt can be an uphill battle.

This chapter will show you how to prepare your case so that you have a decent chance of walking out of the courtroom as a winner. We do this by explaining how to best organize and present your testimony and your evidence. And we also focus on how to prepare and present any eyewitnesses to your best advantage. But first, let's focus on what you must do if you need more time to prepare.

What Is Reasonable Doubt?

To be convicted of a traffic violation in most states, you must be found guilty beyond a "reasonable doubt." The legal definition goes like this: "Reasonable doubt is not a mere possible or imaginary doubt, but that state of the evidence where you do not have an abiding conviction, to a moral certainty, of the truth of the charge."

Now that's as clear as mud, isn't it? Here is a real-life example of reasonable doubt that may help: John is tried for murder and all the jurors vote "guilty" except Jake, who holds out for a not guilty verdict. The jury is hung. A local citizen later confronts Jake, saying, "How could you say John didn't do it?" "I didn't say John didn't do it, I'm just not sure that he did," Jake replies.

A. Asking for a "Continuance" (Postponement)

If you got a particularly unfair ticket, you may feel like running down to court to clear your good name. But there are several reasons why a more measured response makes sense. You may actually want to delay your day in court. Here are some reasons why:

- You need more time to prepare.
- You or a key witness will be out of town.
- You know the officer will be on vacation in a few months and you want to improve your chances that he won't show up to testify.
- You need to delay the time of your possible conviction in order to keep from accumulating too many "points" on your driving record over a specific period.

To delay your trial, make your written request at least a week (more if possible) in advance of the trial date. Send copies of your request to the police officer's department and any prosecuting official. Most continuances made on the day of trial will be denied, but usually at least one delay will be granted if it is made several weeks before the trial date. Be aware, though, that by asking for a continuance beyond the last day allowed for trial under any speedy-trial law, you give up that right. You can't later complain that you were denied a speedy trial because you yourself asked for a trial date after the speedy-trial law deadline.

Here is an example of a request for a postponement:

---

123 Parker St.
Berkeley, CA 94710

Jan. 1, 2001

Clerk, Municipal Court
Berkeley-Albany Judicial District
2120 Grove Street
Berkeley, California

Re: People vs. Safespeed, #A-123456

Trial Date: Jan. 15, 2001

Dear Sir or Madam:

I am scheduled to appear for trial in the above matter on Jan. 15, 2001. Unfortunately, I will be out of town on that date due to my employer's insistence that I attend a two-week seminar in New York between Jan. 1 and Jan. 20, 2001. I therefore request that trial be continued to Jan. 25, 2001. Please inform me as to whether the continuance will be granted and when my trial will occur.

Sincerely,

Sam Safespeed
Sam Safespeed

cc: Officer G. Growlski
      Berkeley Police Department

If you don't receive a reply before the scheduled trial date (or before you leave town), call or visit the court clerk. If the continuance hasn't been granted (or if dealing with the clerks proves fruitless), it is best, if possible, to appear in person on the trial date to see if your request has been granted. Be as prepared as you can to go to trial that day, even though you plan to ask again for a continuance. If you have a good reason and you show proof that you tried to contact the police and prosecutor in advance of the trial, your request should be granted. If you are really going to be out of town, write the judge directly, by priority mail or fax. Refer to your earlier request and ask for an urgent postponement.

Occasionally, because of an officer's scheduled vacation or other anticipated absence, the prosecutor or officer will ask the court to postpone your trial date, notifying you by mail or phone. Be sure to check if the court has actually granted the request. If not, your best approach is to show up in court on the trial date and object to the delay. This allows you to argue that you have gone through considerable trouble to come to court for trial, and it is unfair to make you return at a later date.

If it appears that the court is going to delay your trial, you should check out your state "speedy-trial" rules. (See Chapter 2 on researching the law.) If the court has postponed the trial until after that date, you should bring this up at the new trial date and ask that the case be dismissed. You can say, *"Your Honor, I move to dismiss under the speedy-trial rule, as the case was continued, beyond the last date allowed for trial, without my consent."*

B. Gathering Your Notes and Research

Start your trial preparation by writing down everything you can remember about your traffic violation. It's best to do this as soon as possible after the incident, while your memory is still fresh. You may also want to go back and photograph or diagram the scene from different angles and locations, if explaining to the judge or jury the exact location of vehicles, signals or other physical objects will be relevant to your case.

Remember, as discussed in Chapter 2, it's important to compare the facts of what happened to you to all legal elements of the traffic violation you are charged with. Or put another way, as you recollect the details of what happened, do so with an eye to convincing the judge that the prosecution has failed to prove you committed one or more of the necessary elements. As part of doing this, it may be helpful to write down each element of the violation on one column on a page and compare it with the actual circumstances of your violation to see if your actions failed to meet every aspect of the charge against you.

Here is an example:

Elements of Violation	My Actions
1. Driving a vehicle	1. Yes, I was
2. On a highway	2. Yes
3. Made a U-turn	3. Yes
4. In a residence district	4. No. There were only two residences on the entire block, which was just outside of town. Residence District is defined as 15 or more residences over a quarter of a mile. Went back and counted. Only 7 residences one-half-mile back from U-turn, only 10 residences one-half-mile ahead.
5. Traffic approaching within 200 feet, either direction	5. No. My rearview mirror showed no traffic behind. Approaching car was 15 to 20 car lengths (225 to 300 feet) ahead.

C. Diagrams, Maps and Pictures

Diagrams or enlarged maps of the place where you got the ticket are often useful to help the judge understand what happened. That's why so many officers include them in their notes and show them to the judge at trial. And that's also why you'll be better equipped to illustrate inaccuracies in the officer's testimony by preparing a diagram of your own.

Here are some common situations where diagrams are a big help:

- In radar or laser speed cases, they can help illustrate how the radar or laser beam might have intercepted targets other than your vehicle. (See Chapter 6, Sections B.4 and B.5.)
- Where pacing was used to give you a speeding ticket, a diagram may illustrate where the officer was when he first saw you and where you both were when he stopped your car. This can show that the officer was closing in on you and thus could never have accurately measured your speed. (See Chapter 6, Section B.1.)
- In defending against traffic-signal and stop-sign violations you may be able to show the officer would have been unable to accurately see the charged violation from the location where he was watching. (See Chapter 7, Sections A and B.)
- For turning violations, you can show how far away oncoming or cross traffic was from your vehicle when you made your turn. (See Chapter 7, Section C.)
- With tickets stemming from an accident, you want to show how your driving was safe under the circumstances and that the accident was caused by the other driver. (See Chapter 7 for a variety of "moving violation" defenses and Chapter 5, Section D, for details on accidents caused by speeding.)

A good diagram should be reasonably detailed. Thus for an intersection, it should normally include the location of stop signs or signals, dividers or traffic islands, crosswalks, limit lines and the location of parked vehicles. In addition, it should indicate the approximate widths of the streets and traffic lanes. With speeding violations, where the officer paced you over a long stretch, the diagram should show any intersections, nearby buildings and other principle landmarks and, of course, should indicate the distance between where you first saw the officer and where she stopped you.

How to prepare a diagram. Never try to draw your diagram in court. The result is sure to be time consuming and klutzy. Instead, carefully prepare it beforehand. Use a large piece of thick white paper and several thick felt-tip pens. Use black or dark blue to denote roadways and intersections and other colors for vehicles and traffic signals. If you are artistically challenged, have a more talented friend help.

1. How to Use Your Diagram and Maps in Court

You'll obviously want to refer to your diagram in court as part of presenting your testimony. To do this, inform the judge that you have a visual aid that you would like to use when you testify.

EXAMPLE: How to testify with a diagram:

You made a left turn at a stoplight and were stopped and charged with running a red light in order to make the turn. You claim you entered the intersection when the arrow light was turning from green to yellow. In court, you testify as follows:

"As I approached the intersection and got into the left-turn lane, I saw a green-arrow signal, which changed to yellow just as I crossed the final line of the crosswalk at the entrance to the intersection. As I made the turn, I saw the officer's car behind two other cars. I proceeded because the light was yellow in my direction and because a car was right on my tail, making a quick stop unsafe. I have a diagram of the intersection. I made it last week just after I went back to the intersection. May I please show it to the court?"

At this point, if a prosecutor is present, you show it to her (otherwise to the cop). Then hand it to the court clerk (who may mark it Exhibit #1 before handing it to the judge). If the courtroom has an easel or blackboard, place your diagram there, facing the judge or jury. If not, find a place to prop it up so that it can be seen clearly. (The judge or clerk will probably help by telling you how to do this.)

Your testimony should continue something like this:

"Your honor, my car is shown on this diagram in green. The dotted green arrow shows my path as I completed the turn. The officer's vehicle is indicated in red. The roadway is outlined in black, and its curvature is shown,

indicating that if the officer had been 100 feet behind me as he testified, he would not have been able to see my vehicle around the curve. The road is marked to scale, as I've confirmed with a photocopy of that portion of a city map, which I'd like to have marked as Exhibit #2 and present to the court. At this time, I ask that evidence....."

2. How to Use Your Photographs in Court

In addition to diagrams, you may want to use photographs. Photos are best used to show conditions like:

- Obscured traffic signs or signals
- The view from where the cop was sitting when she claimed to have seen your vehicle
- Road obstructions such as curves and hills, or buildings that restrict visibility
- Road width and straightness to show that an over-the-limit speed was safe, if you're charged with violating a "presumed" speed limit (See Chapter 5, Section C).

Have key photos enlarged. It's hard to look at 3x5 photos, especially in a courtroom where you are trying to explain why the photo helps establish your case. Far better to present 8x10 enlargements that the judge can see without a magnifying glass.

There are some things photos don't show well, including situations where road and traffic conditions rapidly change, so that what happened when you were ticketed can't really be replicated. It also rarely helps to show the judge photos of an accident scene taken after the vehicles have been moved. You must personally take any photograph you intend to use in traffic court or, if someone else is the photographer, have that person come to court with you. This is because you—or the photographer—must testify where and when the picture was taken.

To refer to a photo and show it to the judge, formal trial court rules require you to have it marked as an exhibit and formally introduced into evidence. But in most traffic courts, judges will simply look at your photo without the need for a lot of gobbledygook. Here's an example of what to say (if the judge is not a stickler for formality, leave out the part about marking it for identification):

"Your Honor, I would ask that this photograph be marked for identification as Exhibit #1." (Show it to the prosecutor or officer, then hand it to the clerk, who will mark the exhibit). *"I took this picture along Main Street, at the same place where the officer indicated, in his notes—and just now testified to—that he was parked when he says he saw me fail to stop at the stop sign on Market Street at its intersection with Main. I took it just two weeks after he issued me the citation, at the same time, 4:45 p.m., during the same rush-hour conditions. I believe it accurately shows the impaired visibility the officer had of traffic coming in my direction, and it shows why he couldn't have had a very clear view of where he claims I ran the stop sign. I request that this Exhibit #1 be introduced into evidence."*

D. Preparing Your Testimony

Defendants who know what to say and when to say it are far more likely to win than are defendants who stand up and hope to tell a convincing story. In short, if you've come this far, you want to be well prepared. One big key to doing this is to carefully practice your presentation.

Why You Should Always Testify

Although you're not required to testify, it's almost always a good idea. Judges won't admit it, but they generally assume that a defendant who tries to claim that the prosecutor hasn't proven her case, while at the same time asserting the Fifth Amendment right to silence, must be guilty. Or put another way, if you think you will be proven guilty by answering questions on the witness stand, it usually makes sense for you to go to traffic school. Even if the only reason you went to court was the hope the officer would not show up (but he did), you'll almost always do better by explaining your version of what happened as clearly, honestly and forcefully as you can than you will by clamming up.

How to practice your testimony. After you have practiced making your presentation enough times that you are getting pretty good, have a tough-minded friend or family member play the part of the judge. Ask them to try to poke holes in your case by occasionally interrupting your presentation with questions (many judges do this). Do this several times until you feel comfortable answering questions about your version of what happened and the evidence you present to back it up. When you are done, ask your skeptical friend for a verdict. If your friend convicts you, the judge is likely to do so. Keep practicing until you convince your volunteer judge that you are innocent.

One good approach to presenting traffic court testimony is to outline the key points you want to make on a file card well in advance of your court date (leave space between entries for later additions). Be sure your testimony establishes an adequate defense to the violation (for example, it clearly demonstrates you didn't commit at least one key element of the violation). Use your notes as you practice making your presentation. (It's fine to glance at your outline, but it is a mistake to simply read it.) Then in court, after you cross-examine the officer and learn new facts, quickly add to or edit your outline This way, when it's finally your turn to testify, you should be prepared to tell a smooth and well thought-out story.

For those who have never previously appeared in traffic court, it is a great idea to drop by and watch a few cases. Sure, this takes a couple of hours, but you are almost sure to learn more than enough to make this a wise use of the time. There is not enough space to provide sample testimony for every possible violation, but the following examples provide a road map to preparing your testimony, no matter what charge you face.

1. Exceeding Maximum Speed Limits

In states with an "absolute" speed limit, you should focus your testimony preparation on arguing that you were not speeding *at all*. (See Chapter 5, Section B, and the Appendix section for your state.) If you simply say you were going 38 mph and the officer testifies it was really 48 mph, the judge will almost always choose to believe the cop's version. However, there are some good defenses you can mount that could even the odds a little. In preparing your testimony, you should consider the following approaches:

- *"The officer didn't keep a constant distance between our vehicles when he 'paced' me. I could see him in my rearview mirror bearing down on me fast. It took him just a few seconds to close from about half a mile back to being right behind me, which is when he activated his lights. In fact, after glancing at my speedometer and seeing that I was going at the speed limit, I was convinced the officer was speeding to an emergency farther down the road. When I realized he was after me, I was genuinely surprised."*

- *"There was other traffic in my direction in front (or back) of me. The officer's wide radar beam could have hit the other traffic at the distance he was from me. Some of this other traffic was going faster."*

- *"The road wasn't straight. Visibility was poor due to curves and hills. He could not have seen me for the time necessary to determine if I was speeding, which I was not."*

- *"There were other vehicles similar to mine on the road at the time. One, the same make and color as mine, passed me. After the officer rounded the curve, he pulled me over by mistake."*

Here is an example of how you might prepare your testimony in an "absolute" speeding case:

"When the officer stopped me for speeding, it was 5:15 p.m. I had just left work to go home. I wasn't in a hurry. I drive Highway 123 home every day and I know the speed limit's 55 mph. Just before Officer Kwota pulled me over, I had slowed going around a curve because I needed to move from the left to right lane to prepare to turn right on Market Street. I had to pause for a moment because another red 1995 Chevy Blazer, almost identical to mine, passed me in the right lane at a high rate of speed and exited at Market Street. By this time, I had slowed to about 35 mph because I was still trying to move over to the right. At this point, I saw Officer Kwota's car come around the curve in the right lane. I was going to wait to allow him to proceed past me before getting in the right lane, but, to my surprise, he got into the left lane behind me and turned on his emergency lights. After I pulled over, the officer asked me if I knew why he had stopped me, and I said, 'No, I think you stopped the wrong car.' I told him that

a similar looking car had sped past me just after coming around a curve. He then asked me if I knew how fast I was going, and, not knowing where and when he was referring to, I said, 'somewhere between 35 and 50 mph'."

Notice how the testimony in these sections is specific and detailed. The more detail and specifics, the more convincing your testimony—a lot more convincing than simply saying, "I wasn't speeding, man. I was doing 50. I was cool."

2. Exceeding "Presumed" Speed Limits

When you're charged with violating a "presumed" speed, you have a much better shot at winning. (See Chapter 5, Section C, and the Appendix for states that use this system.) Here you should focus your testimony preparation on arguing that you were not speeding, but, even if you were, it was only a few miles over the limit in a situation where this was safe. But always start by understanding that unless it was obvious you were over the limit, your best approach is to admit nothing and make the prosecution prove it. (Assuming it's true, you can simply testify that you were going at or below the limit.)

If you really were going slightly over the limit, you should consider making as many of the following points as fit your situation:

"Even if I was going slightly faster than 30 mph, it was safe to do so because:

- *"There was very little vehicle or pedestrian traffic on the road."* This is a particularly good argument if you can truthfully tell the judge you were ticketed at 6:00 a.m or some other time when traffic is known to be light.
- *"There was little or no other traffic in my lane, in my direction"* (or in both directions) *"for at least a half mile."*
- *"There was no cross traffic or uncontrolled intersections."*
- *"There were several lanes in each direction and there was no one else even in my lane."*
- *"Even if I did exceed the speed limit, it was by less than 5 mph."*
- *"The road in question has an artificially low speed limit."* (Here, a picture of a wide, straight two-lane road with no traffic but a 25-mph limit might be convincing).
- *"The weather was clear (no rain, fog, hail, etc.)."*
- *"The road was dry."*
- *"The road was well lighted by regularly spaced street lamps."*
- *"There were no sharp curves, hills, dips or other such 'natural' road defect requiring a slower speed."*

Here is one example of how you might prepare your testimony against charges of speeding with a "presumed" speeding violation:

"I'm sure I didn't exceed the speed limit, but even if I did, it must have been by a small amount. Certainly by the time I saw Officer Ticketem and checked my speedometer I was going right at the 35 mph limit. But even assuming I was going a little faster a few minutes before, it was very safe to do so. Please let me explain. I was in the left of two lanes in my direction, there was no traffic ahead in my direction—except for one vehicle that suddenly passed me on the right. The road is 4-lane divided highway, two lanes in each direction, and it was straight, and slightly downhill in

my direction, so that I could see ahead for about a half mile. The next intersection, with Market Street, was about a quarter of a mile ahead, I could see the green light, and there was no cross-traffic waiting at the intersection. There were no pedestrians either. It was 6:45 p.m. in July, and most people were home eating dinner. It was still daylight, the weather was clear and the road was dry. In fact, it was the kind of situation where even going 45 or 50 mph would have been safe, even though I wasn't going nearly that fast."

3. Running a Stoplight

When you're accused of running a red light, the issue is usually whether your vehicle entered the intersection after the light changed from yellow to red. To be guilty, the front bumper of your vehicle must have passed into the cross street after the light changed (see Chapter 7, Section B). In preparing your testimony, consider the following approaches:

- *"I was driving at (or below) the speed limit."*
- *"I was only several car lengths from the intersection when the green light turned yellow."*

Both of these defenses are based on the idea that the yellow light must last long enough for a car traveling at the speed limit to make it through the intersection before the light turns red. If you testify you were a few car-lengths from the signal when the light turned yellow, you are, in effect, saying that you must have entered the intersection when the light was yellow, since you were so close.

- *"I looked up at the light and noted that it hadn't yet changed to red as my car entered the intersection."* (A diagram might be very useful.)
- *"I didn't think I could safely stop the car because I feared being rear-ended by someone tailgating me."*
- *"I proceeded through the yellow light cautiously."*

Here is one example of how you might prepare your testimony against charges of running a stoplight:

"I was driving at the speed limit, 35 mph on Warren Street. I know this because I looked down at my speedometer just as I began slowing to prepare to turn at the intersection with Maple Street. The green light changed to yellow as I was only about two car-lengths in front of the entrance to the intersection. So, I continued and the light was still yellow as my car crossed over the crosswalk and entered the intersection. As is my habit, I glanced up at the traffic signal overhead—which continued to stay yellow until it passed out of sight over the top of my windshield. At all times the cross-traffic heading in both directions on Maple Street was stopped, so my turn did not create a dangerous situation."

Be as specific as possible. Go back to the scene and attempt to determine the exact distance you were from the light when it changed from green to yellow (for example, maybe the car in front of you just turned into a gas station), the duration of the yellow light, and your car's speed. With the help of a diagram, based on the facts you present, you could argue that you only could have entered the intersection while the light was still yellow. If you show you were 100 feet away from the intersection at a gas station entrance—going 35 mph when the light turned from green to yellow—you can figure out how many feet-per-second you were traveling and prove you were well into the intersection before the light turned yellow. (See Chapter 6, Section B.3.)

E. Preparing Your Witnesses

You have the right to present witnesses who were present and observed the situation that caused you to be ticketed. This will usually be someone who was in the car with you, but could be a pedestrian or the driver of another vehicle. But before you ask a potential witness to testify for you, you'll obviously want to be sure he agrees with your version of what happened.

1. Organizing Witness Testimony

If you have more than one witness, write down all their names. Then write a description of what each will say and how their testimony will help your case. Decide in what order they should testify to present a logical sequence of events.

Don't let a witness bend the truth. Occasionally a friendly witness will volunteer to stretch the truth on your behalf. Even though the crime of perjury is rarely prosecuted in traffic cases, lying is a bad idea. Aside from the moral implications of lying, a skilled prosecutor can expose even one small lie and it will usually destroy the credibility of everything else your witness says, even if much of it is true.

Witnesses who are organized and prepared are far more convincing than those who are neither. Start by acquainting your witness with the various legal elements of the case and the strategy of your defense. Her testimony should support one or more key aspects of it. Just as you did when you prepared your own testimony, have someone pretend to be the judge and have your witness practice her testimony several times. Incidentally, helping your witness prepare in this way is completely legal and routine. Every lawyer rehearses witnesses. In case the prosecutor asks your witness whether she has discussed her testimony with you, she should simply be prepared to say something like this: "Yes, I was a little nervous and wanted to do a good job of telling the truth."

It is also wise to put yourself in the role of the prosecutor and ask the witness some tough cross-examining questions. We discuss how to cope with cross-examination in Section F, below. Have your witness read that section.

Explain to your witness that there's a possibility she will be asked to step outside the courtroom when you testify, in order to prevent her from adjusting her testimony to be consistent with yours. And that this is not a punishment, just a routine court procedure. (You also have the right to insist on this, should two or more prosecution witnesses testify against you.)

2. Subpoenaing Witnesses

A "subpoena" is a document that requires a witness to appear at the time and place of your trial. Failure to appear can result in arrest and jail or fine for contempt of court. If the witness was a friend or family member riding in your car, she will often agree to appear without a subpoena. But if the witness was unknown to you—like a pedestrian or another driver—you'll want to serve him with a subpoena telling him to show up at your trial. There are three common situations where you will want to "subpoena" an essential witness:

- A witness wants to testify on your behalf but needs to be excused from work or school.
- A witness whose testimony is essential to your case doesn't want to appear in court for some reason, but you are pretty sure he will testify in your favor if required to appear.
- A witness has volunteered to testify, but is unreliable and you believe he may forget to show up if not subpoenaed.

At your request, the court clerk must issue a subpoena in a traffic case. Rules and procedures as to how this is done and who may serve the subpoena vary from place to place. Be sure to ask the court clerk how a subpoena is to be prepared and served.

It's usually a mistake to subpoena a hostile witness. As a general rule, it's a mistake to subpoena a person who is totally opposed to the idea of appearing in court. A person who is dragged to court against his will is likely to be so mad he could mold his testimony in such a way as to hurt your case. There is a big exception to this rule—where you can't win without the person's testimony and you believe there is some chance he'll tell the truth under oath, it makes sense to risk serving a subpoena on a hostile witness who won't show up voluntarily.

Be aware of distance rules. A witness can't be required to attend court if he lives out of state. In some areas, even a witness who lives in the state can't be compelled to travel over a certain distance to the courthouse, usually 50-100 miles.

F. Preparing for the Prosecution's Cross Examination

If a prosecutor is present at your trial, she gets a chance to cross-examine you and any other person who testifies on your behalf. If a prosecutor is not present, sometimes the judge will ask the officer if he wants to cross-examine. Most officers will decline. In this situation, the judge may ask a few questions on his own.

As you probably know, the purpose of cross-examination is to poke holes in your story and the testimony of your witnesses. In case you or your witnesses have to respond to cross-examination, keep the following things in mind:

- Keep Your Cool—don't respond in an evasive, hostile or argumentative manner.
- It's often wise to keep your answers to non-damaging questions short. The reason is so that you don't end up unnecessarily volunteering information that turns out to hurt your case.
- Although you can be told to answer "yes" or "no" to a question, you have the right to fully explain any answer you give. It can be a good idea to do this if the prosecutor asks you a seemingly damaging question. For

example, if you are asked how fast were you going and you truthfully reply 30 mph in a "presumed speed" area where the speed limit was 25 mph, you would want to add that because no cars were on the road it was safe to do so. If the prosecution tries to cut you off in the middle of your explanation, turn to the judge and say, *"I believe I have the right to explain as part of my answer. May I continue?"*

- Tell the truth. Obvious as this may sound, many people think they can get away with "stretching the truth." The last thing you'll want is for a skilled prosecutor to expose a lie (or even get you to retract a minor point). This is likely to happen when you are less than truthful in response to a question to which the prosecutor already knows—and can prove—the answer.

- If you don't know, say so. Many people are so afraid to admit ignorance they trip themselves up, often needlessly. If your witness was talking and didn't notice whether two cars turned ahead of you on a yellow light (but can say you crossed the limit line when it was still yellow), make sure she knows it's okay to respond "I don't know" when she does not. ■

Preparing for Trial—The Officer's Testimony and Cross-Examination

Litigant: A person about to give up his skin for the hope of retaining his bones.

—Ambrose Bierce

Usually the prosecution's case consists solely of the testimony of the ticketing police officer. That testimony will usually sound, in part, something like this:

"I was parked observing traffic, when I observed the defendant enter the intersection at Maple and Pearl Streets, heading south on Maple after the light had turned red. There was heavy traffic at the time and several cars had to apply their brakes to avoid an accident. The road was also wet from a rain storm earlier in the day."

You should listen closely to what the officer says and focus on ways to challenge her testimony. Depending on what the officer says, you may be able to:

- Make a legal objection that results in the officer's testimony being excluded from your trial.
- Successfully ask the officer questions (called cross-examination) to cast doubt on the officer's version of the facts.

A. When and How to Object to Testimony

Few people have the legal knowledge to raise picky technical objections. Fortunately, in most traffic trials, you don't need it. In fact, raising lots of objections in traffic court can quickly become counterproductive, as it's more likely to raise the hackles of the judge than to help you win your case.

Objecting to testimony is a tactical decision. Always ask yourself: "How likely am I to succeed?" As part of doing this, you should also consider how damaging the testimony is to your case. For example, if the officer is providing background

detail about the weather or road conditions that has little to do with whether you committed a particular violation, you gain little by objecting— even if your objection is technically correct.

But a few well-placed objections can serve a major purpose. That's because the testifying police officer probably expects you to be unprepared and nervous and she is likely to be over-confident. (After all, she has probably testified many times before.) If you are able to surprise her with even a few valid objections, you may well throw her off balance and weaken her testimony.

Here are three valid tactical objections that might help you disconcert the officer.

1. Officer Reading From Notes

Immediately after issuing your citation, most police officers will note what happened on the back of their copy. They do this so that later, if there is a trial, they can remember what happened. But in most states it is technically improper for the officer to simply read directly from her notes (or from any other document) while testifying in court, unless she first follows several important procedural steps (lawyers call this "laying a proper foundation.") The officer must first testify that:

- She can't remember all the details of the violation.
- She recorded them shortly after issuing the citation.
- She needs to refer to them to refresh her memory.

Because most people who get tickets never object to note reading, most officers don't know how to follow these technical procedural steps (called "laying the proper evidentiary foundation"). This gives you a golden opportunity to toss a stick into the cop's spokes by saying: "Objection, Your Honor. The witness is clearly reading from notes which are hearsay and should be excluded from the trial." In all likelihood the judge will simply tell the officer to lay the proper foundation as outlined above and, if she succeeds (sometimes with coaching from the judge), proceed with her testimony, using the notes.

In addition to asking the officer to follow proper procedures to admit this type of hearsay into evidence, the judge should direct the officer to let you read the notes. (You may have to politely ask.) Sit down and carefully do just that. But when you finish, don't hand them back if the officer still hasn't created the proper legal foundation for using them along the lines set out above. Then when the judge asks you to return them, politely renew your "hearsay" objection and ask that the officer testify based on her "independent re-collection"—that is, without looking at her notes. Even if the judge rules that the officer can use her notes, you have won two important things:

- You have gotten to read the officer's notes, if you had been denied that right before trial. (See Chapter 8, Section C, on how to demand the right to do this prior to trial.)
- You can claim in your closing argument that the officer has a poor memory for events and can't really contradict any evidence you present, which should, of course, raise a reasonable doubt as to your guilt.

Object if the judge "coaches" the officer. Sometimes a judge will try to help a befuddled officer lay a proper foundation for getting around the hearsay rule and using the notes. If so, you may want to politely renew your objection by saying, "Objection, Your Honor; with all due respect, it appears as though the court is helping the officer testify by asking leading questions. I again ask the court to simply instruct the witness to testify from memory or lay a proper foundation for the use of this written material."

At this point, the judge will either allow your objection (require that the officer lay a proper foundation or not use her notes) or overrule it. Either way, you have made your point and it's time to move on.

2. Assuming Facts Not in Evidence

Another common improper ploy that officers use while testifying is to say something like: "I saw the defendant's vehicle go through the stop sign [or commit other dastardly acts]...." Here the officer is basically tying you (the "defendant") to what she observed by looking at a vehicle, which may or may not have been yours. This type of objection would be important if your defense rested on the officer identifying the wrong vehicle.

The proper way for the officer to testify is for her to say that she observed "a vehicle" (rather than "the defendant's vehicle") commit a violation, and that she then pulled over that vehicle and identified you as the driver, usually by asking you to produce your driver's license. When, however, you allow the officer to shortcut the process by testifying that she observed "the defendant's" vehicle, you've allowed her to improperly establish that you were the driver of the wayward vehicle that she says she saw.

Making an objection in this situation is sensible if:

- There is some reasonable question as to whether the vehicle the officer initially saw was really the one you were driving. This is often the case if for any reason the officer lost sight of the supposedly offending vehicle between observing the "violation" and making the stop.
- You simply want to fluster the officer a bit, and bring her down from her lofty, self-assured perch.

In many situations, making this objection is not frivolous. There may really be some doubt about whether the offending vehicle the officer observed was yours, especially if the officer saw it from a distance, or in poor light. For example, when an officer on the freeway first sees a speeding vehicle, it is often a half mile or more away (and at night she may really see no more than the offending vehicle's tail lamps). And if the offending vehicle is small—a compact car or a motorcycle—the officer may have periodically lost sight of it behind a bigger vehicle. This of course raises the possibility that the ticketed vehicle was the wrong one. Similarly, if there is a curve in the road, a hill or even heavy traffic, the cop may have lost sight of the offending car and stopped the wrong one.

In objecting to the officer's "assuming facts not in evidence" or "lack of personal knowledge," you say something like this:

"Objection, Your Honor. This testimony assumes facts the officer hasn't testified to. There is no evidence before this court as to who owned or was driving the vehicle that this officer claims to have seen. The officer could not possibly have personal knowledge of the identity of the owner of a vehicle she merely sees traveling on the road. I move that her testimony not be considered." (Lawyers would ask that it be "stricken," but you may be better off sticking to plain English.)

Here the judge will probably do one of two things: "Sustain" (grant) your objection and then "strike" (disregard) the officer's testimony (by often saying something like, *"So stricken. Continue, Officer Jones"*). Or the judge will ask the officer to "rephrase" her testimony (sometimes coaching her to say that she first saw the offending vehicle and then identified you).

3. Hearsay Evidence

In most states when an officer, or any witness, testifies to something she didn't personally observe, the law calls this "hearsay." (As we saw in Section 1, above, reading from notes is one type of hearsay.) Such testimony is generally not allowed, provided you make an objection. If a prosecutor's question calls for hearsay (*"And what did Officer Smith tell you, Officer Jones?"*), you should quickly interject with, *"Objection, Your Honor, the question calls for hearsay."* If the officer blurts out hearsay to a proper question before you have a chance to register your objection

(Q: *"How fast was the defendant driving?"* A: *"Officer Smith told me it was 75 miles an hour."*), your objection should be, *"Objection, Your Honor, that's hearsay, which I move be eliminated (stricken) from the record."*

Unfortunately, there are a number of exceptions to the hearsay rule, which allow certain types of hearsay to be considered by a judge or jury. Probably the most common in traffic court allows an officer to testify to any statements you made, which would tend to prove your guilt. (Q: *"Do you know why I stopped you?"* A: *"Because I was going 80."*)

Although it doesn't make sense to engage in an in-depth study of the rules of evidence just to go to traffic court, it can be a good idea to be prepared to object to two of the most common situations in which hearsay crops us:

- **When an accident occurs.** Here you should object if the officer—who probably didn't witness the accident—attempts to testify to what another person involved in the accident, or an eyewitness, told him. Again, the rule is the officer can only testify to what she saw, not what she heard from other people.

- **For speeding citations involving a plane.** You'll definitely want to object if the officer in the patrol car attempts to testify as to what an officer in an aircraft said your speed was. The ground officer must testify as to what she did and saw, not what the airplane officer told her. (See Chapter 6, Section B.2., for more on how to fight tickets involving airplanes.)

EXAMPLE: Your vehicle collides with another at an intersection controlled by stop signs at all four entrances. You tell the officer you entered the intersection first, and that the other driver ignored the stop sign. But based on the statements of the other driver and a bystander, the officer concludes you were at fault for failing to yield to the vehicle to your right. You contest the ticket and go to trial. In court, the officer appears, but neither the other driver nor passenger is present. When the officer testifies that the driver and passenger said about the accident, you should immediately say, *"Objection, Your Honor, that's hearsay. It should not be considered."* The judge should agree with your objection by saying, *"sustained"* which means the testimony is disallowed. Of course, a prosecutor can subpoena the people who witnessed the accident, allowing them to testify directly. But busy prosecutors often neglect to do this for traffic court cases, or the witnesses don't appear.

B. How to Cross-Examine the Officer

Preparation is the key to successfully questioning (cross-examining) the officer—with an eye towards raising a reasonable doubt as to your guilt. You can ask almost anything you want, so long as the answer you're seeking is in some way relevant to your effort to prove you didn't commit a particular element of the violation or to some other valid defense. Develop your cross-examination step-by-step, beginning with the least important background questions and ending with the ones that go to the heart of your defense.

Don't go fishing. If you don't have a specific reason to ask a particular question, don't ask it. Unfocused questions rarely result in answers that will help your case and they commonly give the officer a chance to repeat damaging facts likely to convict you. Also be sure your questions do not include an admission of guilt, such as, *"Where were you when I ran the stop sign?"* Instead, they should always be non-committal, such as, *"Where were you when you claim I ran the stop sign?"*

Below are the types of questions you'll want to ask in trials involving common traffic violations. If your situation is not covered, use what you learn here to develop a set of your own questions designed to show how the officer could have been mistaken in her observations.

Make a double-spaced list of questions you intend to use and bring it with you to trial. Then, depending on the officer's testimony earlier in your trial, pencil in necessary additions and changes. But remember, even after you ask a question, you'll want to retain as much mental flexibility as possible. That's because your next question should often be keyed to the officer's response. For example, if the officer's answer is evasive, be prepared to bear down with more specific questions until you either get the answer you want or force the officer to lie.

The best way to cross-examine is to ask specific—not open-ended—questions. For example, avoid questions such as, *"What happened then?"* or *"Why did you stop me, anyway?"* The officer could seriously tarnish your defense by replying, *"Because you broke the law."* Far better to ask questions such as, "Isn't it true that there was a large hedge between your location and mine?" and *"Isn't it true you stopped me because of a radio report from an aircraft, and didn't determine my car's speed yourself?"*

Your goal in cross-examination is to show the judge or jury:

- The officer's powers of observation were not perfect.

- One or more legal elements of the particular offense are missing. (See Chapter 2 for more on elements of the offense.)
- The existence of a defense, such as "mistake-of-fact" where you didn't know the stop sign was there until too late because the sign was obscured by trees (see Chapter 3, Section D).
- The officer was doing several things at once.
- The officer may have lost sight of your car between the time she observed the offense and the time she pulled you over.

Of course, you may occasionally get an unexpected answer. If you do, you'll have to rely on your broad understanding of the facts to decide whether to ask more detailed questions or quickly switch to the next line of questions.

Never argue with the officer. It is almost always a mistake to adopt an antagonistic stance towards the officer. And it never makes sense to try to argue with him. Even if the cop answers a question untruthfully, or gives a ridiculous answer, it's your job to try to expose his fabrication by politely asking more direct questions, not by saying, *"That's just not true"* or *"How could you tell such a whopper."*

> EXAMPLE:
> **Your Question:** *"Officer, how far were you from my vehicle when you initially took your radar reading?"*
> **Officer's Answer:** *"500 feet."*
> **Your Bad Response:** *"Officer, you know darn well that the radar beam width at that distance can't differentiate between vehicles in adjacent lanes. This whole deal is a sham."* (This is an argument, and isn't allowed during the cross-examination phase.)
> **Your Good Response:** (in the form of a second question): *"Officer, you previously testified that your radar unit has a beam width of six degrees. Isn't it true that at 500 feet from your radar unit this means the beam will be over 100 feet across?"*

Your Good Follow Up: *"On the road where I was ticketed, aren't the individual lanes much narrower than 50 feet?"*

Where and How to Cross Examine

Courts differ somewhat as to how you are expected to conduct your cross-examination, especially in traffic cases. If there is a lectern podium in the courtroom, you may be asked to pose your questions from there. Or you may be expected to ask them from your place at the counsel table where you have been sitting. It makes little difference as long as you stand up (the best way to keep you on your toes). But never walk up to where the officer is sitting unless you want to ask him to refer to a diagram, chart, or notes. If so, some judges will expect you to first ask, *"Your Honor, may I approach the witness?"*

1. Coping With an Officer's Non-Responsive Answer

If you succeed in asking the officer a good, pointed question—one to which a truthful answer might prove damaging to the prosecution—there is a good chance she'll try to avoid answering by either changing the subject or saying she can't remember. This is where you need to bear down by asking more specific questions—if the officer is truly putting road blocks in your way, ask the judge to order her to answer your question.

EXAMPLE: You are challenging a motorcycle officer's ability to see what happened by attempting to show that because he was not wearing any goggles or other eye protection while "pacing" your vehicle at a high rate of speed, the wind, blowing into his unprotected eyes obscured his vision. Later you'll make the point in final argument that he may have lost sight of the vehicle committing the offense, before pulling over your similar-looking car. (See Chapter 11, Section B, and Chapter 12, Section D.6, for more on closing arguments.)

Your Question:

"Isn't it true, officer, that you were not wearing any eye protection while you were riding your motorcycle on the day in question?"

The Officer's Non-responsive Answer:

"Well, I could see very well and the windshield on my motorcycle...."

At this point you want to interrupt and say:

"Objection, your honor; Officer Growlski's answer is not responsive to my question. I ask that the witness be instructed to answer the question I asked."

Another frequent annoyance occurs when, after an officer answers your question, she starts to give an unrelated speech about how bad your driving was. This can be unnerving and damaging to your case. Fortunately, it is also highly improper. You may say, *"Your honor, I ask the court to instruct the witness to confine her answers to my questions."*

2. Testing the Officer's Power of Observation

The basis for nearly every traffic prosecution lies in the officer's perceptions. Put bluntly, if you can establish both that the officer can't see more than 100 feet and that your vehicle was 200 feet from where she was sitting when the "violation" occurred, you should win without breaking a sweat. But it's not just the officer's hearing or eyesight that are issues. Since she is probably testifying many months after ticketing you (and has likely handed out hundreds of tickets in the intervening time),

her memory of what happened—or lack thereof—can often be a big issue at trial. The more you can establish she doesn't remember where, why and how she stopped you, the more doubt you raise as to the accuracy of her testimony and the more likely it is that judge or jury will find a reasonable doubt as to your guilt.

Following is a list of some of the types of general questions you might want to ask in order to test the officer's knowledge of the location and conditions where she observed you. Review these sample questions before trial, and leave out those that would be irrelevant in your case. Also, be prepared to leave out any questions that the officer answered in her initial testimony.

Keep it interesting or you'll put the judge to sleep. Your questions should always be designed to quickly get at key issues. If you seem to be getting nowhere with a particular line of questioning, move on to better questions before the judge or jurors nod off.

3. Sample Questions

Your first questions should often be designed to get the officer to admit she was doing a number of other things besides observing you (starting her car, driving her car, talking on the radio, and so on). The more tasks the cop admits to performing, the more doubt you may be able to cast in your final argument as to how clearly she was able to see what you were doing.

1. *"Where were you located when you first saw my vehicle?"*
2. *"Where was my vehicle when you first saw it?"*
3. *"Was your car (or motorcycle) parked or moving at the time?"*

If parked:

4. *"Was your engine idling, or was it off?"* (If idling, you can later argue that she was already intent on stopping someone regardless of whether she saw a violation or not.)

If the engine was off:

5. *"What did you do to start your vehicle?"*

6. *"Did you turn on your lights?"*

7. *"Did you use your two-way radio?"* (These questions are aimed at showing the police officer was too busy doing other things to watch you for more than a second before deciding you were speeding.)

8. *"Did you start your engine just before you saw the alleged violation, or while it was occurring?"* (If just before, you can argue in your closing statement that she made up her mind to stop you before she saw any violation. If during, she might have been too busy starting the engine to observe things very well.)

If moving:

9. *"In which lane were you traveling?"*

10. *"In which direction were you going?"*

11. *"How fast were you driving?"* (Leave this one out for speeding violations. You don't want the cop to say she had to go 90 mph to catch you.)

12. *"Did you have a clear view of the traffic on the road when you claim you observed the violation?"*

13. *"Was there any other traffic on the road other than your vehicle and mine?"*

If other traffic: (Your goal here is to ask questions regarding the number and types of other vehicles on the road and their movements. The less she remembers, the better your later argument will be that she can't remember much of what happened that day. On the other hand, if she describes other vehicles in great detail, you may be able to later claim that she may not have observed your car accurately, since she was so busy watching everything else.)

14. *"Could you describe the vehicles in front of your vehicle?"*

15. *"Could you describe the vehicles on either side of you?"*

16. *"How fast was the flow of traffic?"*

If slower than your vehicle, ask:

17. *"Did you see my vehicle passing any others?"*

Use the cop's answers to frame further questions. Here is an example of how you should use the cop's answers to frame subsequent questions. If she says you passed other vehicles, ask her for specifics (type of vehicle, color, make). She probably won't remember. If she says other traffic was slower than you, but also has said you weren't passing other vehicles, she's contradicting herself and you'll want to point this out in your closing argument. If she says she was traveling at the same speed as, or faster than your vehicle, your over-the-limit (but under-65) speed might have been safe, and therefore legal in "presumed" speed law states. (See Chapter 5, Section C, on presumed speed laws.) Follow up with questions on this point, such as those listed below. If she says there was no other traffic, again, your over-the-limit speed might be considered to have been safe under the circumstances in presumed speed law states. (See Appendix for the laws in your state.)

If you're charged with violating a presumed speed limit or, in an absolute speed limit state, driving under the limit but too fast for conditions, you can ask:

18. *"Do you consider yourself to have fairly well-developed powers of observation and memory for details concerning weather, and road conditions?"*

Then, ask the officer about every possible detail and hazard on the road, leaving out all hazards that were really there. This way her answers will make it seem like the roadway was pretty safe, or that she can't remember all the details. Road conditions you'll want to ask about can include:

- **Highway width.** *"Officer, isn't it true that there were two lanes in each direction?"*
- **Divider strips or islands.** *"Isn't it also true that there were divider islands present, so as to separate opposite directions of traffic? Isn't it true that this island minimizes the possibility of a collision with traffic in the opposite direction?"*

- **Sharp curves.** *"Isn't it true there were no sharp curves over the area you say you determined my speed?"*
- **Dips or hills.** *"Isn't it true there were no dips or hills over the area you say you determined my speed?"*
- **Railroad crossings.** *"There were no railroad crossings either, were there?"*
- **Road repairs in progress.** *"There were no road repairs in progress, were there?"*
- **Obstructions on the road.** *"There weren't any other obstructions in the road, were there?"*
- **Soft shoulders.**
- **Spilled liquids.**
- **Pedestrians, bicyclists or animals in the road.** *"There were no pedestrians present, were there?"* (If she answers *"yes,"* ask her to describe where they were and what they looked like. If it's not in her notes, she likely won't recall.)

Soft shoulders

![lightbulb] **If the officer repeatedly says he can't remember.** The more the officer says he can't remember, the better, since you can later use his poor memory to cast doubt on the accuracy of his

testimony about your violation when you make your final argument. In this connection it is often a good idea to ask questions you know the officer won't be able to answer. The best way to prepare to do this is to look at his notes beforehand. (See Chapter 8, Section C, on "discovery.")

4. Cross-Examination Questions for Specific Violations

The remainder of your cross-examination of the officer should be directed at undermining her testimony on the specific elements of the offense you are charged with, or getting her to admit circumstances justifying your violation. (See Chapter 3, Sections D, E and F, for a review of the principal legal theories to beat a ticket.)

It follows that these cross-examination questions depend greatly on the violation charged. For example, in radar speeding cases, you might want to bring out the officer's lack of familiarity with her radar unit. But where you were cited for speeding after an officer paced your vehicle with hers, it would make no sense to make this inquiry.

![lightbulb] **Don't read the questions out of this book.** Ask questions that really apply to your case. Hopefully you'll be able to fine-tune some of the ones you find here, but, if necessary, be prepared to start from scratch. For example, don't ask the officer about high-voltage power lines affecting radar readings unless you really can show there were nearby high-voltage lines.

a. Speed Violations in General

The following questions deal with how the officer measured your speed. (See Chapter 6 for more on measuring speeds.) The officer will undoubtedly testify as to the method she used. It will then be up to you to cast doubt on the accuracy of her claims through cross-examination.

i. Visual Speed Estimation

If the officer estimated your speed only through visual observation, without pacing your vehicle using radar, laser or VASCAR, ask questions like these:

1. *"Over what distance did you see my vehicle travel?"* (If the officer says it was short—or you can introduce evidence such as the location of a hill, curve or traffic lights proving it was short—you can later argue she couldn't have arrived at an accurate speed estimate. See Chapter 9.)

2. *"Did my speed change after you observed me?"* (If she says you slowed down after you apparently saw her car, you can later argue that the original high estimate was good only over a tiny distance and, therefore, inherently unreliable. If she says your speed suddenly went up or down, ask her to explain exactly where. Few officers have that good a memory, a fact you may be able to use in your final argument to cast doubt on the accuracy of the officer's other observations. (See Chapter 11, Section B, and Chapter 12, Section D.6, for more on how to make a closing argument.))

3. *"Was my vehicle traveling toward you, away from you or across your line of vision?"* (If accurate, you can say in closing argument that it is more difficult for the officer to estimate the speed of vehicles moving in a more or less direct line toward or away from her than if vehicles are traveling across her field of vision. Of course, before you cross-examine on this issue, you should introduce evidence during the presentation of your case on this point.)

4. *"Have you ever participated in controlled tests where you were asked to estimate vehicle speeds?"* (Most officers will say no— a point you can bring up on your closing argument. If the officer says she has participated in such tests, ask whether she always guessed the exact speed correctly. If she says *"yes,"* she's obviously lying—no one is that good; if she says *"no,"* you can later point out that she admitted how difficult it is to estimate correctly.)

ii. Speed Estimated by Pacing Your Car

If the officer's estimate of your speed was based on her looking at her own speedometer while following or "pacing" you, the following questions are usually helpful. (Also see Chapter 6, where we discuss possible defenses to tickets based on pacing.)

1. *"Over what distance did you follow my vehicle at a steady rate of speed?"* (The shorter the distance, the better your argument that she made an inaccurate reading.)

2. *"Was the distance between your car and mine always constant?"* (If she says *"yes,"* she's obviously mistaken, since eventually she almost surely had to close in on you to pull you over. What she wants to say is that the distance was the same over the entire time you were being paced, at which point she sped up to stop you.)

If she seems to deny that at some point she speeded up, follow up with questions like these:

3. *"Did you observe your speedometer while you were following me?"*

4. *"How many times did you observe it?"*

If she says she was watching it almost constantly, follow up with questions like these:

"When pacing at a constant speed is it important that you watch the subject vehicle continuously?"

If she says *"no,"* you can follow up with a question like this:

5. *"If you don't watch a vehicle continuously during pacing isn't it possible to lose track of the car you are pacing and focus on a similar looking vehicle?"* (If the officer continues to deny the need to look at the vehicle continuously, move on and attack her methods in your closing statement. See Chapter 6, Section B.1., on "pacing" for more on how pacing works.)

6. *"Was there other traffic?"* (Ask only if there was.)

7. *"Which lanes were the other vehicles in?"*

8. *"Can you describe any of the other vehicles?"*

9. *"Were you paying attention to the other traffic in order to drive safely?"*

10. *"How often did you observe my vehicle?"*

If she testifies that she was watching her speedometer carefully and testifies in detail to other traffic on the road (she may do this to try to impress the judge), follow up with:

11. *"So you were watching my vehicle, other traffic and your speedometer all at the same time?"* (If she says no, she was mostly watching your vehicle, ask, *"And you were watching other traffic too, correct?"* Then, during your closing argument, you can argue that she was mostly watching your car and others, without much time to glance down at her speedometer.)

12. *"How far behind my vehicle were you while you were pacing it?"*

If she was pacing from more than a few hundred feet back, ask:

13. *"Do you agree that the ability to pace depends on good depth perception, so that you can follow at a constant distance?"*

14. *Do you also agree that the farther away an object is, the more difficult it is to pace it?"* (If she says no, ask her which is more accurate—a pace at 100 feet, or a mile behind.)

15. *"Have you recently participated in controlled tests where you paced a vehicle a known speed from (whatever distance she claims to have paced you)?"* (The answer will almost always be *"no."*)

If at night:

16. *"Officer, you paced my vehicle at night [or dusk], correct?"*

17. *"Would you agree it's harder to keep a constant distance, in order to conduct an accurate pace, at night than in the daytime?"*

She should agree. If not, continue with questions like this:

18. *"Isn't it harder to accurately pace at night when you can see only two taillights, as opposed to driving in the day when you can see the whole car body?"*

In attacking the accuracy of her speedometer, you can ask:

19. *"How long before you cited me was the speedometer in your patrol car (or motorcycle) last calibrated?"* (If the officer tries to simply say, "it was accurate," she's bluffing and you'll want to ask her to please answer your question. If a speedometer hasn't been calibrated recently this is definitely a fact you'll want to use as part of your final argument; see Chapter 6, Section B.1.)

20. *"Did you bring a record of the most recent speedometer calibration with you today?"* (She almost never will.)

21. *"Are you aware that speedometer accuracy is affected by tire circumference?"* (She will probably say *"yes."*)

22. *"Are you also aware that tire circumference is affected by tire pressure and wear?"* (Again, she will probably agree.)

23. *"Then isn't it fair to say that speedometer accuracy is affected by tire pressure and wear?"* (She may try to hem and haw, but eventually should concede the point if you repeat the question.)

If she just doesn't seem to get it, ask this next question:

24. *"If you had such tires on your car, the odometer would erroneously read high, correct?"*

25. *"Were your tires' pressures checked when your speedometer was calibrated?"* (Probably not.)

26. *"Were they checked on the day you cited me?"* (Probably not.)

27. *"Are you aware that a tire's air pressure depends on its temperature?"*

28. *"Have the tires on your patrol car been rotated, or have any of them been changed*

since the last speedometer calibration?" (See Chapter 6, Section B.3b, for more on tire-wear and pressure problems.)

iii. Speed Estimated From Aircraft

Airplane tickets and your possible defenses to them are discussed in Chapter 6. Objecting to hearsay testimony in this type of case is discussed in Chapter 10, Section A.

As discussed in more detail in Chapter 6, there are two ways for the officer to determine your speed from an aircraft:

- By timing the passage of the vehicle between two markers on the roadway
- By using ground markers and a stopwatch to determine how fast the aircraft is going and then using the aircraft to "pace" the vehicle below.

Depending on which method is used, your cross-examination should normally attempt to cast doubt on:

- The accuracy of the timing method the aircraft officer used to time the passage of your vehicle—or the aircraft—across two highway markings. (See Chapter 6, Section B.2.)
- The ground officer's knowledge of the distance between highway markings. (Remember, if this is based on what she was told by the airplane officer it is "hearsay" evidence to which you should object. (See Section A above.)
- The accurate identification of your vehicle by the aircraft officer.
- The ground officer's proper identification of your vehicle from the aircraft officer's description.
- The accuracy of the timing of passage of either the vehicle (method 1 above) or the aircraft (method 2 above) across the two highway markings.

These questions for the aircraft officer apply regardless of which method was used to measure your speed:

1. *"Officer Aircop, you used a stopwatch or other timing device to time the passage of the aircraft or vehicle between the two highway markings, correct?"*

2. *"Isn't it true that you timed the passage of the aircraft/vehicle [depending on which method was used] over a fixed distance?"* (The answer will always be *"yes."*)

3. *"Did you actually measure the distance between the highway markings on the ground?"* (The answer will be *"no,"* at which point you should ask the judge to "strike" his previous testimony. Simply say, *"Your Honor, I move to strike the officer's testimony as to the speed of the vehicle, since it was based on a distance-divided-by-time that was not within this officer's personal knowledge."* If the judge strikes the testimony, you have won your case, as there is no other evidence of your speeding. If the judge refuses, you must, regretfully, move on.

4. *"Did you watch my vehicle that whole time without looking away?"*

If she says *"yes,"* ask:

5. *"Did you have a stopwatch and a log to read my speed?"*

If she answers *"yes,"* ask:

6. *"Didn't you look down at them and write log entries?"*

If *"yes,"* ask:

(The point you want to make in the next two questions is that the officer is doing many things, including looking at a stopwatch and log, and watching many cars, so she can easily lose sight of a particular car.)

7. *"Did you report other vehicles for speeding at or near that time?"*

8. *"How many cars were you monitoring?"*

9. *"Over what distance did you time my vehicle?"* If she says she timed your vehicle over a short distance, like 0.1 or 0.2 mile, ask:

10. *"Officer Aircop, could you state again the time it took my vehicle to travel between the two markings?"* (Be prepared to use the

formula in the sidebar "Converting Miles Per Hour to Feet Per Second" (in Chapter 6, Section B.3) to calculate the speed you would have been going, based on the answer to this question. For example, if the officer says the two markings were an eighth of a mile apart (one eighth of 5,280 feet, or 660 feet), the time to cross the marks would be 660 feet divided by 110 feet per second, or 6.0 seconds.)

Then ask:

11. *"If because of normal reaction time, you didn't start the stopwatch until a half a second after my vehicle passed over the first mark, the true time my car passed between the two points would have been [example— 6.5] seconds, correct? Incidentally, I have a calculator if you would like to check the calculation."*

    "And at [example—one eighth of a mile or 660 feet] and [example—6.5] seconds, the true speed would have been [example—660 feet/6.5 seconds = 102 feet per second or 69] mph, correct?"

Ask this question only where the officer determined the aircraft speed by using the markings, then "paced" your vehicle with the aircraft.

💡 **Use the officer's notes before trial to help you do the math.** If you have been able to obtain the officer's notes before you go to trial (see Chapter 8, Section C), you'll know the distance between the road markings and can do the math in advance. Simply do the calculation: speed (feet per second) = distance (feet)/time (seconds), then divide that result (in feet per second) by 1.47 to calculate what the officer should say the elapsed time was. Then, see if you can use a slightly longer time based on the officer's likely reaction time to compute a substantially slower speed.

12. *"And isn't it true that you determined your aircraft's speed this way before you finally determined my vehicle's speed?"*

13. *"How much time passed between the time you calibrated the speed of the aircraft and the time you paced my vehicle?"*

14. *"If a headwind had slowed the aircraft after you timed its passage between the highway markings, wouldn't you have had to again fly between the markers to determine your slower speed relative to the ground?"*

15. *"Did you do that?"*

16. *"Are you certain the wind speed did not change during this time?"*

17. *"To determine the aircraft speed, what reference point on the aircraft did you use to check the aircraft passage over each line?"* (Usually it will be a wing or wing strut.)

18. *"How far was that object from you?"* (Usually a few feet.)

19. *"If you had moved your head forward or backward while observing your reference point passing the first or second marker, the elapsed time on your stopwatch would be incorrect, isn't that so?"* (If she denies this, ask her to hold up a pencil at arm's length against a distant object in the courtroom about 20-30 feet away. Then ask her to move her head one foot forward or back while holding the pen steady. Finally, ask if the pen doesn't seem to line up a few feet off. The shorter the distance between the two reference points on the highway, the more significant this type error is—over long distances it won't affect the reading of your speed enough to matter.)

Additional questions to ask the air officer, which can be used with either speed measuring method:

20. *"When you identified what you say was my vehicle, you didn't read a license plate, did you?"* (This can't be done from 500 feet in the air.)

21. *"You didn't radio down the make or model of vehicle did you?"* (Only ask this if the air officer's log doesn't mention this. It often won't, since they often can't tell this from 500 feet up either.)

If there was other traffic:

22. *"Were there other vehicles on the highway?"*

If she answers *"yes,"* ask:

23. *"Could you describe the other vehicles by make or color?"* (If she can't describe the make and model of your vehicle or other vehicles, you can question her memory in your final argument and raise the possibility that she stopped the wrong one.)

24. *"Did you report other vehicles for speeding, along with mine?"* (If the officer answers *"yes,"* you can argue that her attention was divided among several vehicles, opening up the possibility that she was confused and mixed up your safe speed with another car's speeding).

Questions for the Ground Officer (can be used with either speed measuring method):

Only ask these questions if Officer Aircop says she radioed Officer Groundcop.

25. *"Officer Groundcop, isn't it true you were first alerted to my vehicle only because of the radio report from Officer Aircop?"*

If she says *"yes,"* and the ground officer in the patrol car didn't testify she paced you after hearing the report from the air officer, ask:

26. *"So then, your knowledge of the vehicle's speed was based solely on the radio report, correct?"* (If she says *"yes,"* you should ask the judge to "strike" her testimony because it is based on "hearsay," what the air patrol officer told her through the radio. Even if the judge denies your request, you should argue in your closing statement that the officer who actually ticketed you was acting on second-hand information, which is inherently unreliable.)

iv. Speed Estimated by VASCAR

VASCAR tickets and your possible defense to them are discussed in Chapter 6, Section B.3.

If the officer used VASCAR to determine your speed, your goal in asking questions is to show:

- She may have had reaction-time error after your car passed the first point, clocking too short a time and thus too high a speed
- She may have had difficulty seeing the stop or start point, thereby mistiming when you passed one or both.
- There may have been an odometer error due to low tire pressure or tire tread wear, which can produce a false reading. (The VASCAR unit is calibrated to the vehicle's odometer.)
- In the moving mode, the officer might have operated the unit incorrectly when faced with the necessity of pressing the buttons four different times while monitoring traffic. (Again, see Chapter 6 for an explanation of how an officer uses VASCAR in a moving vehicle.)

All VASCAR Modes

Ask these questions to cast doubt on whether the officer pushed the buttons at precisely the right times.

1. *"How far apart were the two points between which you measured my vehicle's passage?"*

2. *"How many seconds did you clock my vehicle passing between the two points?"* (If the two points were less than 500 feet apart, the time should be 5-10 seconds depending on the speed and exact distance, and a reaction time error can be significant.)

If the officer's answer is in this range, ask the next questions. If the time is 10 seconds or longer, skip to question 11.

3. *"Could the length of time it took you to press the time or distance switches, have been a factor in measuring my speed?"* (The officer will probably say *"no,"* explaining that she didn't react to your car passing points as she pressed the switches, but instead correctly anticipated when it passed the markers, thereby getting your speed correct.)

If so, ask:

4. *"But if, when I passed the first reference point, you hadn't anticipated perfectly, but instead reacted after my car passed the point, the time you measured would actually be a little too short, correct?"* (The answer should be *"yes."*)

If she won't admit this is true, follow up with:

5. *"Well, assume that if, when I passed the first point, you reacted and then pushed the 'time' switch half a second later, wouldn't my time be erroneously low?"* [If she finally conceded the point, follow up with:]

6. *"And this would mean the speed you recorded would be erroneously high, right?"*

Run the numbers. Use your calculator to do some quick math. For example, if the distance between the markers was 200 feet and the time the officer measured was 3 seconds, that would work out to 200 feet/3 seconds = 67 feet per second. Divide this by 1.47 to get 45.4 mph. It follows that if the officer reacted half (0.5) a second late, your true time of passage between the reference points was really 3.5 seconds, and your speed 200/3.5 = 57 feet per second. Again, divided by 1.47, your real speed was 38.8 mph. Assuming the speed limit is 40, you can plausibly argue you weren't speeding.

7. *"Assume you had reacted rather than anticipating, and your reaction time when I passed the first point took half a second. Now you testified that you measured my time between the two points as [example— 3.0] seconds. So isn't it true that the true time of passage would have been closer to [example—3.5] seconds?"*

8. *"At [example—200 feet] and [example—3.5] seconds, that's an average speed of [example —57.1] feet per second, correct?"* (If she says she can't do the math in her head, offer to let her use your calculator).

9. *"And you divide feet-per-second by 1.47 to get miles-per-hour, correct?"* (If she admits

this, ask the next question. If not, skip to a new line of questions exploring how this number is derived on your final argument.)

10. *"And 57.1 feet per second, divided by 1.47 works out to 38.9 mph, doesn't it?"* (Obviously, this should be adjusted to your situation.)

Stationary VASCAR

Here your prime goal is to question the officer's ability to accurately observe when your vehicle passed a distant point.

11. *"Officer, how far from the two reference points were you located?"* (She'll almost surely say she was closer to one point than to the other.)

If she admits to being more than several hundred feet from one of the points, but much closer to the other, ask:

12. *"So, isn't it true that it was easier for you to hit the 'time' switch when my vehicle passed over the nearer point?"*

If she refuses to give you a clear answer, follow up with:

13. *"Is it easier for you to hit the 'time' switch at the proper second when a car is 50 feet away than when one is half a mile away?"* (Assuming she says 50 feet away, ask question 12 again.)

14. *"Have you recently taken part in controlled tests of your ability to judge when a car has passed over a point hundreds of feet away?"* (Most likely not.)

15. *"Isn't it also true that if you misjudged when my car passed the distant point, that would result in your time measurement being incorrect?"*

16. *"And that, in turn, would mean that the speed your VASCAR device recorded was incorrect, right?"*

Quit while you're ahead. If the officer surprises you by conceding a big favorable point, it's often best to quit this line of questions. Later you can refer to the officer's admission as part of your final statement to argue that there is reasonable doubt as to your guilt. If instead you follow up with more questions on the point you've already won, the officer may qualify or withdraw his admission. For example, he might say that while the VASCAR speed reading may have been wrong, it would make no real difference since you were going so much faster than the limit.

Moving VASCAR—The Officer coming from the same direction

Here you want to focus on the fact the officer must execute four Time/Distance switch clicks in a short time, something that isn't easy to do.

17. *"Officer, to use VASCAR while your vehicle is moving, you have to press the 'time' switch twice, and the 'distance' switch twice, correct?"* (She should say *"yes."*)

18. *"And that's a total of four operations, correct?"*

19. *"And if you had improperly pressed the 'distance' switch at exactly the point where your car passed beginning and end points, that would result in an error, correct?"*

20. *"And the same is true with respect to judging my vehicle passing the two points when you had to push the 'time' switch twice, correct?"*

21. *"And if you did these four operations in the wrong order, wouldn't that also result in a major error?"*

22. *"And you had to do all four things accurately, over a period of just how many seconds?"* (This is a little bit of a trick question. You hope she'll refer to the time it took you to pass between two points, rather than the longer time it took her to click the time switch twice as you passed the two points, then pause and hit the distance switch as she passed over each point.)

If she falls into your trap, follow up with any of the applicable questions below:

Moving VASCAR—Officer coming from the opposite direction

The use of VASCAR in these circumstances is particularly tricky. Study Chapter 6, Section B.3, on VASCAR to understand why this is true before setting out to cross-examine the officer. The point is that the big possibility for operator error opens great opportunities for your cross-examination. Here are some questions designed to show the judge how difficult it is for an officer to properly use VASCAR in this way. This will definitely be a point you'll want to hit hard on final argument.

23. *"Now you say you saw my car coming from the opposite direction, picked out a reference point, and clicked 'time,' correct?"*

If *"yes,"* ask:

24. *"Had you had experience using that reference point before?"* (Probably not, since she picked it quickly because it was near you as she was coming from the opposite direction.)

25. *"And when our cars were opposite you clicked 'time' again as you simultaneously clicked 'distance?'"*

26. *"Did you do this with one hand down, while also looking at my car? Or did you look at the VASCAR machine?"*

27. *"And then you clicked 'distance' again when you reached the second marker?"*

28. *"Again, did you do this with one hand down, while also looking at my car, or did you look at the VASCAR machine?"*

29. *"Between the time you saw my car pass the reference point from the other direction and the time you passed it, did you take your eyes off that reference point?"* (If the officer gets a little confused with all this, it's fine.) If she admits she did take her eyes off the mark, you may be able to argue—in your closing statement—that her distance determination could be incorrect because she refocused on a wrong reference point after looking away from the first point.

VASCAR—Moving mode, and stationary mode—odometer used to measure distance

30. *"Now, officer, you measured the distance between the two reference points by clicking your 'distance' switch twice as you drove between them, correct?"*

31. *"And your VASCAR unit is connected to your car's odometer cable to allow for you to do this?"*

32. *"Then the accuracy of the measured distance, and hence speed, depends on your odometer's accuracy, correct?"*

33. *"If you switched to smaller tires after your odometer was calibrated, there would be more revolutions of the odometer cable for the same distance, and hence an erroneously high distance and speed, correct?"*

34. *"Isn't it true that to be accurate the VASCAR unit's odometer module must be calibrated every so often against a pre-measured distance?"*

35. *"When was this VASCAR unit last calibrated in this way?"* (If it's been a long time since the VASCAR unit was calibrated for odometer accuracy, you should argue in your closing statement that the "distance" reading, and hence the calculated speed, is suspect.)

36. *"Isn't it also true that if your tires were very worn, or if your tire pressure was too low, your tire circumference would be slightly smaller?"*

37. *"And that would result in your recording an erroneously high distance and speed, correct?"*

38. *"When did you last check the tire pressure in your vehicle?"* (Again, if she doesn't know or it's been a considerable time, you can later argue the VASCAR reading may have been wrong.)

v. Speed Estimated by Radar

If the officer used radar to measure your speed, use some or all of these questions. Your goal is to show:

- She doesn't really know how radar works.
- She was not careful about maintaining her unit's accuracy.
- The speed she measured may not have been your vehicle's.

For more on radar, please read Chapter 6, Section B.4.

Only ask these questions if the officer did not show you the radar readout at the time you were stopped.

1. *"Does your radar unit have a control that allows you to 'lock in' the targeted vehicle's speed onto the readout?"*

If *"yes"*:

2. *"Did you show your unit's speed to me when you stopped me?"* (Assuming the answer is *"no,"* claim in your final argument that because she could easily have shown you your speed, there must be some reason she chose not to.)

3. *"Could you please describe briefly how speed-determining radar works?"* (If she can't do this—or gets it wrong—consider using this admission as part of your final argument.)

4. *"Isn't it true that delicate and sensitive electronic measurement instruments such*

as radar units must be calibrated often to make sure they're accurate?"

5. *"Did you calibrate your unit immediately before and after you measured my claimed speed?"*

If *"no,"* use this point in your final argument. If *"yes,"* ask:

6. *"How exactly did you calibrate the unit?"*

If she says she turned on the unit's "calibrate" switch:

7. *"You mean, you didn't use a tuning fork?"*

8. *"Doesn't the radar unit's manufacturer recommend calibration with a tuning fork?"*

9. *"Isn't a tuning fork certified as accurate by a testing laboratory a better way to check the unit's accuracy than using the unit's own internal electronics, which may be faulty?"*

If she says she used a tuning fork:

10. *"What was the certified speed for the tuning fork you used?"*

If it's much different from the speed she says she clocked you at—for example, 25 mph, but your car clocked at 60 mph—follow up with:

11. *"Isn't it true that tuning-fork-checked accuracy at one speed is not a guarantee of accuracy at a different speed?"*

12. *"When was the tuning fork itself last calibrated by an independent testing laboratory?"*

13. *"Do you have a certificate of accuracy for this particular tuning fork?"*

No matter what calibration method was used:

14. *"Has your radar unit ever malfunctioned in any way?"*

If she says *"no,"* ask:

15. *"Then it's never been repaired, or taken to the shop, as far as you know?"*

If she says it hasn't, ask:

16. *"You mean, not even for routine maintenance?"*

17. *"What's the maximum range, in thousands of feet, of your radar unit?"*

18. *"What is the beam width of your radar unit in degrees?"* (Don't settle for an answer in

"lanes." As discussed in detail in Chapter 6, Section B.4, the beam width will get wider the farther the unit is from your vehicle, and you want to emphasize this point. If she doesn't know the beam width in degrees, ask her how much wider the beam gets for each thousand feet distance from the radar unit. Be prepared to quickly calculate the beam width at the maximum range, so you can follow up with the next question.

19. *"So then, at the maximum range, where you can still determine a target's speed, the width of the beam is about* [calculate here] *feet, isn't it?"*

20. *"Isn't that much wider than one lane of traffic?"*

21. *"Isn't this wide enough to reflect beams from other nearby vehicles or even a low-flying aircraft or nearby trains?"* (Obviously, only use this last part if you were cited near railroad tracks or an airport.)

22. *"When you aim your radar unit at a nearby object, your unit's antenna will pick up signals reflected from other more distant sources, won't it?"* (She may say *"yes,"* but that the unit is made to track the strongest reflected signal.)

If so, follow up with:

23. *"Did you know that a more distant, but larger, vehicle may reflect a stronger signal than a smaller nearby vehicle?"*

Only ask the next four questions if it was windy the day when you were cited:

24. *"Have you ever obtained what turned out to be a false speed reading by incorrectly aiming a radar unit, for example, at another vehicle or a tree blown by the wind?"*

25. *"And if those surfaces are in motion, they can cause a false reading on a radar unit, can't they?"*

26. *"Isn't it true that windblown tree limbs or even leaves can sometimes reflect radar signals to generate a false reading?"*

27. *"Even blowing dust or rain can sometimes do this, can't they?"*

28. *"Do you know what a harmonic frequency is?"*

29. *"Are you aware that harmonic frequencies of nearby radio transmissions, for example from CB sets, can cause false radar readings?"*

30. *"Did you know that electrical interference from nearby power lines or transformers or even high-voltage neon lights can generate false radar readings?"*

31. *"When you estimated my vehicle's speed, were you first observing my vehicle with your eyes or using your radar unit?"*

If the officer was looking at your vehicle:

32. *"So, then, you had already assumed I was exceeding the speed limit before you took a radar reading?"*

If the officer was looking at the radar unit:

33. *"So, you had already formed an opinion of my speed before looking up at my vehicle?"*

34. *"Could a completely untrained person use your radar unit accurately?"* (The answer should always be *"no."*)

35. *"Could you please describe the training you've had in the use of radar?"* (Most officers will try to pretend the salesman's two-hour pep talk they probably received on how to use a particular radar unit was an intense "seminar.")

36. *"How long ago were you given this training?"*

37. *"How long did the training last?"*

38. *"Was this training conducted by a salesperson for the radar-device company?"*

39. *"Did you have supervised 'hands-on' instruction out on the road?"*

40. *"Have you participated in any tests where you used radar to measure a vehicle's speed, then were told the correct speed?"* (Almost never; if she says *"yes,"* try to get her to give precise details.)

vi. Speed Estimated Using Laser

For more on lasers read Chapter 6, Section B.5.

In your cross-examination of an officer who used a laser gun to estimate your speed, you want to bring out the following points:

- The officer doesn't really know how laser works.
- The laser unit might not have been aimed and used correctly.

1. *"Officer, how does laser work?"* (This is harder to describe than radar, and the officer may not do a good job.)

2. *"Isn't it true that the laser unit works by measuring distances, using the speed of light and the time it takes a reflected beam to return, between the laser unit and the target vehicle?"* (The officer will probably agree that it sounds right.)

3. *"How many distance measurements does it make in a second?"* (She probably won't know.)

4. *"Isn't it true that the laser unit emits three separate light beams? And that each beam hits a different spot on the target vehicle?"*

5. *"And isn't it also true that when you aim the laser unit to get an accurate reading, you must aim it at the same part of the target vehicle during the entire time of the measurement?"*

6. *"Isn't it also true that if, over the measurement period, you first aim it at the passenger area, then move the gun slightly so the beams hit the hood, that at least part of your measurement will take into account the five or so feet difference between those two points?"* If she admits this, you can later argue in your closing statement that this caused an error. (See Chapters 11 and 12 on closing arguments.)

7. *"Have you read the instruction manual for this unit?"*

If *"yes,"* ask:

8. *"Doesn't it refer to this type of possible error?"*

If the cop seems confused, follow up with:

9. *"Was it possible you made this type error?"*

10. *"Was there other traffic in my direction?"* (Ask only if there was—a point you can

make in your testimony if she doesn't admit it.)

11. *"Isn't it also true that if one of the three beams reflected off a vehicle near mine, going at a different speed, and another beam reflected off my vehicle, your laser gun would have produced an incorrect result?"*

12. *"And isn't it possible, if you're, say, a quarter of a mile away, and an adjacent car going in my direction passed me, that one of the three beams might have hit my car, with the others hitting the second car?"*

Especially if she says this is unlikely, follow up with:

13. *"But isn't it true that the possibility of this type of error is also mentioned in your instruction manual?"*

b. "Presumed" Speed Limit Questions

In Chapter 5 we discuss "presumed" speed limits in detail. See your state sheet in the Appendix to see if your state uses the "presumed" speed limit system.

In preparing your cross-examination questions, start by thinking of the actual road, traffic and weather conditions when you were cited. Then use this information to edit and fine-tune the following questions. For example, if it was raining or foggy, the less said about the weather, the better. Also, don't ask about traffic conditions if traffic was fairly heavy (unless you believe you can use this information to cast doubt on whether the cop stopped the right car). Similarly, it usually makes sense to ask next about highway conditions if you were ticketed on a two-lane winding, hilly road.

Here are some sample questions:

If the traffic was light:

1. *"Was there a lot of traffic in my direction?"*
2. *"How many vehicles were there in my lane?"*
3. *"How many were behind me?"*

4. *"How many were in front of me?"*
5. *"What was the average distance between vehicles?"*

The point of many of the following questions is to establish, in a "presumed" speed area, that it was safer to exceed the limit in order to keep up with the flow of traffic around you.

6. *"Was I ticketed at rush hour?"*
7. *"Was most of the traffic going at about the same speed you say I was going?"*
8. *"Did you see my vehicle pass any others?"* (Don't ask if you did pass other vehicles.)

If she says *"yes,"* follow up with:

9. *"Could you describe the vehicles I passed?"* (She probably can't—a fact you may be able to use later in your final argument to cast doubts on the accuracy of her testimony.)

Then, only if she says you weren't passing other cars, ask:

10. *"So then, it's true that I was going slower, or at least at the same speed as the other traffic?"*

Ask all the following questions that fit in an effort to show that even if you did slightly exceed the speed limit, it was safe to do so.

If there was no rain:

11. *"Was the road pavement dry?"*

If there was no fog or rain:

12. *"Was the visibility good?"*

If it was a clear day:

13. *"Was the sun shining? Were clouds obscuring it?"*

If you were cited at night but visibility was good:

14. *"Are there street lights along this stretch of road?"*
15. *"Were the lights on?"*

If the road had at least two lanes in your direction:

16. *"How many lanes did the road have in my direction?"*

If the road was divided by a median or barrier:

17. *"Did the road have a divider or barrier down the middle?"*

If there were no intersections near where you were cited:

18. *"Were there any intersections nearby?"*

If there were intersections but all were controlled by stoplights:

19. *"Were there any uncontrolled intersections nearby?"*

If there were no blind curves:

20. *"Were there any sharp turns in the roadway?"*

If the road was flat:

21. *"Were there any hills obscuring the view from the roadway?"*

If there were no pedestrians:

22. *"How many pedestrians were in the area?"*

23. *"Were any pedestrians crossing the road? Trying to cross?"*

Don't forget to make these points in your testimony. If the road, traffic and weather conditions really were good, the above line of cross-examination questions should help your case. But remember, the best time to convince the judge that you really were driving safely is when you present your testimony along these lines. (See Chapter 9.) But if you can get the officer to agree that traffic was light and road conditions were good, you'll certainly want to refer to her statements in your final argument as part of your claim that the officer agreed with your description of conditions. (See Chapters 11 and 12, for final argument suggestions.)

c. Running a Stoplight

See Chapter 7, Section B. to review the most common defenses to traffic light violations.

The defense to this one is usually fairly straightforward. Since it's legal to enter an intersection on a yellow light, the main job of cross-examination is to cast doubt on whether the officer accurately observed that the traffic light was red when the front of your car drove across the "limit line" or cross street.

1. *"Did you see my vehicle at the time the green light first turned to yellow?"* (If she says she didn't, then she could have seen you only a few seconds before she says you ran the red light, creating at least doubt as to her ability to see something happen so fast.)

2. *"For how many seconds does the yellow light stay on?"*

If she says she doesn't know how long the yellow light was lit, follow up with:

3. *"Can you estimate how long the yellow light was lit?"* (If she still won't volunteer an answer, you can contend in your final argument that her powers of observation weren't that good.)

Questions related to your speed:

Only ask if you weren't speeding, and if the ticket itself and the officer's notes are silent about this point. The point here is to show that if you were going the speed limit, the duration of the yellow light was too short to allow you to come to a complete stop before the yellow light turned to red. Believe it or not, traffic signals are not all timed to allow a proper stop given the speed limit (see sidebar).

4. *"In your opinion, was I traveling at or near the speed limit?"*

5. *"What was that speed limit?"*

6. *"How many feet from the intersection was my vehicle when the green light turned yellow?"*

7. *"What is the normal stopping distance at that speed limit?"*

Speed and Distance: How to Do the Math

Once the officer testifies as to your speed and location when the light turned yellow, you will want to make a quick calculation with a pocket calculator. Multiply the speed in miles per hour by the number 1.47, giving your speed in feet-per-second. Next, divide this number into the number of feet she said you were from the intersection when the light turned yellow. This will give you the number of seconds you had to enter the intersection before the light turned red. If this number is less than the number of seconds the yellow light was on (based on your timing or the officer's estimate) then you would have entered the intersection while the light was still yellow. You can introduce your timing test during your own testimony and refer to it in closing arguments.

If the officer was on the cross street (at right angles to the one you were on), she probably assumed that when she saw the red light change to green, the yellow light had changed to red in your direction. If this seems to be the case, ask:

8. *"Could you see the color of the light facing me from your location?"* (If she says *"yes,"* stop here.)

But if she says *"no,"* ask:

9. *"Why do you say I entered the intersection on a red light if you couldn't see my light?"* (She will undoubtedly say because her light went green.)

10. *"You mean you assumed my light turned from yellow to red at exactly that time?"* (She will most likely answer *"yes."*)

11. *"Did you promptly examine the signal to determine whether the light in my direction was properly synchronized so as to turn red when the one in your direction turned green?"* (Very few officers check the lights for synchronization. If the officer did not,

you can contend in your final argument that it sheds doubt as to whether the light was really red when you entered the intersection. This argument is helped if you also establish that the officer was not in a good position to see exactly when you entered the intersection. If you have established this, you should hit this point hard in your closing arguments. (See Chapter 7, Section B, on strategies for beating red-light tickets.)

If the officer was at an angle that would have made it difficult to observe, you might ask this:

12. *"Isn't it true that you couldn't see the color of the signal facing me from where you were?"*

d. Running a Stop Sign

See Chapter 7, Section A, for more discussion on stop-sign defenses.

Defending this type of case almost always comes down to a choice between your claim that you stopped and the officer's assertion that you didn't. Here there are commonly only two defenses aimed at raising reasonable doubt:

- Whether you came to a complete stop behind the "limit line" or the imaginary line at the corner where a painted line would go
- Whether there was a regulation stop sign controlling traffic in your direction.

Your questions of the officer will depend on where she observed you. If she testified she was on a cross street, or on the other side of the intersection, not at the entrance to the intersection, ask:

1. *"When you observed my vehicle, were there other vehicles in front of you?"*

2. *"How many?"*

3. *"Can you describe them?"* (Unless her notes indicate, she probably won't remember the number of vehicles in front, or their descriptions.)

4. *"How far down the street could you see?"*

⚠ **Don't cross-examine when a stop sign is hidden.** As noted in Chapter 7, Section A, you can sometimes defend a stop-sign charge by claiming the sign was obscured. If that is your claim, it's probably best not to cross-examine the officer. That's because she will probably say she saw the sign clearly. Better to simply tell your story—backed up by a diagram and, if possible, a witness—when it's your turn.

e. Illegal Turns

Illegal turn defenses are discussed in Chapter 7, Section C.

Here we look at a few questions you might ask when ticketed for an unsafe turn. Whether a particular driver is really guilty beyond a reasonable doubt of making an unsafe turn is usually a subjective judgment, unless there is a clearly visible sign absolutely prohibiting the turn. Therefore, you should ask the same sorts of questions you would ask for speeding in a presumed speed law area (see Subsection b above) in order to show that under real world conditions your turn was done safely. The following questions should be helpful.

If the turn was at an intersection:

1. *"Was the intersection controlled by a traffic signal?"*
2. *"Did you see the color of the signal when I entered the intersection?"* (Unless the officer was directly behind you, she could not have seen the signal.)
3. *"Did I come to a complete stop in the intersection before turning?"* (Ask only if you did—it tends to show you were being careful.)
4. *"How many feet was the oncoming vehicle from me when I made the left turn?"*
5. *"How fast was the oncoming traffic moving?"*

Based on the answers to 4 and 5, the time you had, in seconds, to make the turn before being hit by the oncoming traffic is equal to: Distance of oncoming vehicle from yours in feet divided by 1.47 multiplied by the speed of oncoming traffic in miles-per-hour. If this works out to five seconds or more, you can later argue that there was plenty of time for you to turn safely.

6. *"Was my turn signal flashing?"* (Ask only if it was.)
7. *"For how long?"*
8. *"Did any vehicle blow its horn in response to my turn?"* (Ask only if none did.)
9. *"Did the oncoming vehicle slow down, in your opinion, because of my turn?"* (She will almost always answer *"yes."*)
10. *"Did that vehicle screech its tires?"* (Ask only if it didn't.)

If the cop says *"no,"* you should ask:

11. *"Could the oncoming vehicle have slowed down because the driver was waving me to turn?"*
12. *"Isn't it true that many safe drivers slow down at intersections out of general caution, whether or not someone up ahead is turning?"* ∎

Trial Before a Judge (No Jury)

We must remember, too, that we have to make judges out of men, and that by being made judges their prejudices are not diminished and their intelligence is not increased.

—*Robert J. Ingersoll*

A. Introduction

In most of the 50 states you do not have the right to a jury trial in a traffic ticket case, which means a judge alone decides whether or not you are guilty. In the others, you can insist on a jury trial. (See Appendix for the jury trial rules in your state.) When only a judge is present, traffic violation trials tend to be fairly informal—certainly more so than the trials for serious crimes portrayed in movies or on TV. Informality is particularly likely to be the order of the day when the only witness for the state is the police officer and no prosecutor is present. (This is common in many states.) However, if a prosecutor is present, her legal training will almost guarantee that some traditional court-room formalities will be observed. Here we provide you an overview of what is likely to happen with and without a prosecutor.

States That Are Really Informal

A few states—including Florida, Massachusetts, Michigan, Oregon and Washington—have completely "decriminalized" traffic offenses, technically making them "civil" not "criminal" infractions. You may still fight your tickets in court in these states. But you lack some important rights. In Massachusetts, Washington and the District of Columbia, for example, you may not have the right to insist on the ticketing officer being present. You can be found guilty, "responsible" or "liable," even if you raise a reasonable doubt about your guilt. In short, to make a finding of guilt in these states the judge only need to conclude that 50.01% of the evidence points to you having committed the violation for which you were ticketed. (See sidebar, "What Does 50.01% Really Mean?" in Chapter 3.)

In the states where you have a choice, you should almost never opt for an "informal hearing" in which you give up your right to have the officer present. By insisting on the officer's presence, you get the advantage of being able to challenge the officer's statements in court. And you also gain the very real possibility that the officer will not show up to testify against you, which means the case will most likely be dismissed.

1. Understanding the Courtroom

Traffic court trials are generally conducted in courtrooms that look much like those on television. In addition to the judge, a clerk and a bailiff will normally be present. The clerk sits at a table immediately in front of the judge's elevated bench, or slightly off to the side. Her job is to keep the judge supplied with necessary files and papers and to make sure that proceedings flow

A Typical Courtroom

smoothly. Depending on the state, there may also be a court reporter present who keeps a word-by-word record of proceedings.

Be a little early for your trial (it can take a few minutes to find the right courtroom, which in some states is called a "department"). Once you arrive, tell the court clerk or bailiff you are present, then take a seat in the spectator section.

Courtrooms are divided about two-thirds of the way toward the front by a sort of wooden fence known as "the bar." The judge, court personnel, lawyers and you (after your case is called) use the area in front of the bar. The public, including you and other people waiting for their cases to be heard, are seated in the main body of the room. When the judge or clerk reads (calls) the name of your case, you may cross through the bar into the area where the judge sits. When you come forward, you sit at one of two long tables, known as the counsel tables, facing the judge.

In courtrooms that follow an informal approach, your witnesses should accompany you to the counsel table. At more formal trials they remain behind the bar (as does the officer) and testify at the witness stand only when their names are called. If you watch a few cases before yours, you'll quickly see how things are being handled. In some courtrooms, you and any witnesses will be asked to raise your right hand and swear to tell the truth before the judge arrives. In a few, you or your witnesses will only be sworn in just before testifying.

Be polite and respectful. Be polite (but not obsequious) to all court personnel—most especially the judge. This may be tough to do if you have a genuine beef with the legal system and feel truculent or angry. But realize that if you express your anger or truculence, the judge is very likely to hold it against you. Judges are used to "lawyerly attitudes," which means they want you to be able to separate your emotion from the facts of the case. Again, it should help you to do this if you realize judges often decide against people who make a scene or have a hostile attitude. No matter how informal a courtroom, all judges, when spoken to, expect to be called *"Your Honor."*

2. Traffic Trials Without a Prosecutor

In many states, it's common for traffic-court trials to be handled without the presence of an assistant district attorney or other prosecuting attorney. After the clerk calls the case, the police officer simply presents his testimony as to why he thinks you are guilty. Then you have a chance to cross-examine before presenting your defense.

With no prosecutor present, the judge normally will allow the officer to tell his side of the story in narrative form, perhaps interrupting to ask a few questions. You should then have an opportunity to ask the officer relevant questions—called cross-examination. As discussed in Chapter 10, you should normally be prepared to cross-examine the officer.

What to do if the judge tries to get you to waive cross-examination. Some judges may not tell you that you have the right to cross-examine or recommend that you just skip this stage and present your defense. But as discussed in Chapter 10, in most states they must let you cross-examine if you insist. It is usually wise to do so, since getting the officer to appear unsure of what happened or to admit he can't remember key facts is one important way to create a reasonable doubt as to your guilt.

After you question the officer, you get to present your side of the dispute and present the testimony of any of your witnesses. At any time during either presentation or after you are both done, the judge may ask questions. Finally, the judge will announce his verdict of guilty or not guilty. If he finds you guilty, he will usually pronounce sentence (the fine) right away.

The judge is boss: be prepared for anything. While this chapter outlines the usual ways a traffic case works, understand that judges have a great deal of leeway in running their own courtroom. Some judges won't listen patiently to your well-prepared and practiced presentation. Instead, they will insist on questioning you, the officer and all witnesses. And, as noted above, a judge may even try to rebuff your attempts to cross-examine the officer, ask questions of your own witnesses or make a final statement.

It will greatly help you understand what is expected (and modify your presentation accordingly) if you can watch a few cases in the courtroom of the judge who will hear your case. And it should also help if, in advance, you make a concise list of the points of your defense that you feel must be made during the trial. Then, if the judge derails your presentation, you can glance at your list and say something like this: *"Your honor, I have prepared a few points that I think are crucial to my case and would like to be allowed to present them to you."* Most judges will slow down and grant you this polite request.

3. Trials Handled by a Prosecutor

In some courts, a prosecutor (normally a lawyer from the district, county or city attorney's office) will present the State's case. As mentioned, this is likely to result in a more formal courtroom proceeding. In addition to each side presenting its own testimony and having a chance to cross-examine witnesses, this can mean that a formal opening and closing statement will be made. (We discuss these in Sections B.3 and B.11, below.) In theory, you have the right to make an opening statement before the officer testifies, and a closing statement after all evidence is presented, but if no jury or prosecutor are present, many judges will try to save time by pressuring you to waive these procedures. To find out in advance if a prosecutor will be handling the case, you can try to ask court personnel or actually go to the courtroom where

traffic cases are held and see what the standard procedure is.

B. Trial Procedure

This section takes you step-by-step through a traffic court trial, with information on your options at the various stages of the proceedings. For simplicity's sake, throughout this section the term "prosecutor" and "the prosecution" will be used to refer to whoever is doing the prosecuting against you, whether it is the police officer, an assistant district attorney or other prosecuting attorney.

1. Clerk Calls the Case

Your trial begins when the clerk calls your case, usually by saying, "State [or "People"] vs. [your name]." Assuming you and your witnesses have already been sworn in, you should now come to the front of the courtroom and sit at one of two tables (usually the one farthest away from the jury box). Whether you stand or sit when making your presentation (and often where you do so) depends largely on the courtroom's architecture and the preference of the judge. Most courtrooms have a traditional witness box next to the judge's bench where you and any witnesses—including the officer—may be asked to testify. However, many traffic-court judges prefer that you and your witnesses tell your story from behind your table, while the officer does the same from the adjacent table. To ask questions during cross-examination, you simply turn slightly to face each other (but do not leave your table).

To start the proceeding, the clerk (or the judge) may then recite the bare facts of the case. He may say something like, *"Mr. Loo, you are charged with a violation of Section 1180 of the Vehicle and Traffic Law of the State of New York, by driving 48 mph in a 35-mph zone on the 400 block of Main Street in Sun City."*

2. Last Minute Motions

Before the prosecution begins its case, you may want to make one or more requests of the judge. These are called "motions" and, depending on the facts of your case, might include:

- Requesting a continuance if you need more time. (See Chapter 8, Section B.4, for tactical reasons to delay your trial.)
- Requesting dismissal of the charges for failure of the prosecution to disclose the officer's notes as per your written request. (See Chapter 8, Section C, on discovery.)
- Requesting the judge to order the prosecution to provide you a copy of the officer's notes so you can better prepare for trial. (See Chapter 8, Section C.)
- Requesting dismissal, if the prosecution has taken too long to bring the case to trial. (See Chapter 8, Section B.4, on speedy trial rules.)

To make a motion, stand up as soon as the judge stops speaking and say, *"Your Honor, I would like to make the following motion."* Then, depending on the motion, you continue along these lines: *"I move to dismiss this case based on the fact that the prosecution has completely ignored my written request to discover the officer's notes. I have here a copy of that request made on January 15, 2001."*

Below we cover other situations where you may wish to make a motion.

a. If Officer Fails to Show Up (Lack of Prosecution)

One of the cornerstones of the American legal system is that you have the right to confront your accusers and cross-examine them when you are charged with a criminal offense, even if it is minor. If the officer fails to show, you should point out to the judge that this right has been denied and your case should be dismissed. (Lawyers call this a "dismissal for lack of prosecution.") Make sure the judge knows how inconvenienced you have been by the officer's failure to show up.

Here is an example of what you can say (adjusting the facts to fit your circumstances, of course):

"Your Honor, I move that this case be dismissed. I am ready to proceed to trial. I've subpoenaed two witnesses, both of whom are present. We have each taken the morning off work, at substantial expense, to defend against this. I received no advance notice from anyone that the case would not proceed. Certainly if I failed to show up and the officer was present, I wouldn't be entitled to a last-minute postponement. So I respectfully ask that the court dismiss this case for lack of prosecution and in the interest of justice."

Requests to dismiss under these circumstances are often granted. The judge will normally deny your request only if the officer has communicated to the court some really good reasons for his failure to show up and for not notifying you in advance. Acceptable excuses might include law enforcement or medical emergencies. Unacceptable excuses include planned events like vacations and previously scheduled training or medical leave—reasons for which you could have been notified well in advance.

b. Excluding Multiple Witnesses

Occasionally the prosecution will have more than one witness. This is usually true in aircraft patrol situations, since one officer must testify to clocking your vehicle from the air, the other to pulling you over and identifying you on the ground. This can also occur when two police officers were present at the time you were cited. In addition, if you were involved in an accident, other drivers or bystanders —in addition to the officer—may be asked to testify against you.

You never want to allow two or more prosecution witnesses to be in the courtroom at the same time during the trial, since doing so allows them an easy opportunity to coordinate their stories and present the same version of the facts. By contrast, if each officer or other prosecution witness testifies outside the presence of the others, you have the opportunity to exploit likely inconsistencies in their individual versions of events. To do this, say, *"Your Honor, I request that multiple witnesses be excluded from the courtroom."* Such a request is not impolite or hostile and will be routinely granted. (If your motion is granted, it will also mean any witnesses you have must also wait outside.)

c. Requesting a Continuance

If you feel a delay (continuance) would work in your favor (See Chapter 8, Section B.4, on how a continuance can help you) you have a final opportunity to ask for it just before trial actually starts. For example, a continuance might be needed if you've subpoenaed an essential witness who has not shown up. If you have subpoenaed a witness to produce certain documents—called a subpoena "duces tecum"—and the documents have not arrived, you may also want to ask for a delay.

But don't ask for a continuance until you see if the ticketing officer has arrived. Obviously, if the officer is not present, you'll want to ask for a dismissal (see Section 2a, above).

3. Opening Statements

Before testimony is presented, both the prosecution and the defense have the right to make an opening statement briefly reviewing the violation and saying how they intend to prove each element of the case. It's important to realize that in doing this, neither you nor the prosecutor needs to prove anything. The point is to simply lay the groundwork for the officer (or maybe other witnesses as well) to testify later.

a. The Prosecution's Statement

Some prosecutors make an opening statement, but most are sensitive to the judge's desire for a quick trial and waive the opening statement, since their facts will come out during the testimony of the ticketing officer. When just the police officer shows up and there is no prosecutor, it's even rarer for an opening statement to be made. That's because most officers realize their role is to present evidence, not to act as an advocate for a guilty verdict or suggest to the judge how to view the testimony.

If a prosecutor chooses to make an opening statement, it may sound like this:

"Your Honor, the People (or State) will show, through the testimony of Officer Tim Ticketem of the Dayton Police Department, that the defendant, Sam Safespeed, was driving a red 1997 Corvette on Walnut Street, where posted speed limit signs indicate the speed limit to be 35 miles per hour. It will also show that Officer Ticketem, relying on his radar speed detection device, determined Mr. Safespeed drove in excess of 50 miles per hour and he visually confirmed for over half a mile that Mr. Safespeed was weaving in and out of traffic."

b. Your Opening Statement

You also have the legal right to give an opening statement before any prosecution testimony or to "reserve" the right to make it until just before your defense begins. In many courts, the judge will assume you don't want to make an opening statement and simply ask the prosecutor or police officer to begin their presentation. At this point you will normally want to say, *"Your honor, I would like to reserve the right to make a very brief opening statement until just before I testify."*

Why reserve your opening statement? Because by waiting you have the opportunity to tailor your remarks to what you learn in the officer's testimony. Also, by not giving your statement at the beginning, you avoid revealing your strategy in advance. (A sample reserved opening statement is given in Section 7, below.)

You get an opening statement even if the prosecution waives it. Even when a prosecuting attorney does not make an opening statement or isn't even present, you still have the right to present—or reserve—an opening statement. But again, in some courtrooms you'll need to make sure the judge knows you wish to do so by politely speaking up.

4. The Prosecution's Testimony

After opening statements, the officer who cited you will explain why you are guilty of the violation you were ticketed for. In most traffic trials, he will testify by standing behind the counsel table (See courtroom diagram at the beginning of this chapter.) But in courts that prefer a more formal approach, he will testify from the witness stand.

If no prosecutor is present, the officer will recite what occurred and why he believes these facts justified issuing you a ticket. You have the right to interrupt the officer's presentation, but only if you identify a legitimate legal reason to

"object" to a particular aspect of his testimony. Of course, you should never interrupt to say, *"He's lying! That's not true!"* or something similar. Instead, you must politely say *"Objection, Your Honor,"* and then briefly explain the legal basis for your objection.

Don't object frivolously. In a trial before a judge, without a jury, there is often little to be gained by making lots of objections. The judge almost surely knows the rules of evidence far better than you do and is likely to discount any testimony or documents the officer presents that are way out of bounds.

Most objections to testimony are made on one of the following four grounds:

a. The Witness Has Not Provided Enough Detail to Show Why He Has Personal Knowledge of His Testimony

This is called failing to provide a "foundation" or "legal basis" for the testimony. For example, if a police officer refers to a diagram, he must first say how he knows the diagram is an accurate reflection of the place you were stopped and ticketed. Usually this is done when the officer testifies that he drew the diagram after writing the ticket while still looking at the scene.

If he fails to do this, you could say, *"Objection, Your Honor. The officer has not provided a proper foundation for using the diagram. He apparently has no independent recollection of the incident and should not be allowed to refresh his memory with the diagram that may not even be of the proper area."*

This objection can be useful if you believe the officer really isn't prepared to lay the proper foundation, in which case the diagram could not be used against you. But, if you are pretty sure the officer will simply explain facts and convince the judge his diagram accurately reflects the area where the ticket was given, it's a mistake to waste the judge's time with what he will likely consider to be a frivolous objection.

Object to the officer's use of notes. Watch the officer carefully during his testimony, to see if he's using notes. As discussed in Chapter 10, officers commonly testify by using notes scribbled on the back of their copy of the ticket. If the officer refreshes his memory in this way, you have a right to object on the basis he hasn't "laid the foundation" necessary to use the notes. This may discombobulate the officer who may then have to admit he can't remember much without the notes. On cross-examination, you may then want to press this point home by asking the officer about details of what happened. Assuming he can't remember, you'll have a better shot at testifying to facts that raise a reasonable doubt as to whether you are really guilty. And then in your final argument tell the judge that, based on the officer's poor recollection and your testimony, there is a reasonable doubt as to your guilt. (See Chapter 10, Section A, on when to object to testimony.)

b. The Officer Presents Evidence You Requested Well Before Trial, But Never Received

Here you can say: *"Objection, Your Honor, the officer is referring to his notes, a copy of which I requested by way of discovery several weeks ago; my written request for those notes—which I'd like to show the court is right here—was never responded to. I ask that this evidence be excluded and the officer's testimony be disallowed."*

Then, you hand a copy of your written discovery request (see Chapter 8, Section C, on discovery) to the clerk for the judge to see. If your objection is approved—or "sustained"—by the judge you should ask for a continuance to study the notes. If granted, this means the officer must come back to

court a second day (something he may be unable to do). At worst, the judge should give you the opportunity to study the notes right then—which may still be very helpful when you cross-examine the officer. For example, if they are cursory or sloppy (but the officer has already claimed he needs to refer to them to refresh his recollection), you may be able to get the cop to admit he can't recall other details not mentioned in his notes.

c. The Officer Says Something That Is Clearly Outside His Knowledge

If the cop testifies to what someone else saw or heard—called "hearsay"—you'll definitely want to object. This includes anything the officer testifies to that did not come from his direct observation. You can say, *"Objection, Your Honor, the officer's testimony as to how fast the officer in the aircraft told him my vehicle was going, is hearsay."*

The point here is to begin to discredit any information the officer doesn't know firsthand, so that later you can argue that there is reasonable doubt as to your guilt. For example, if the officer says that another driver (perhaps after an accident) said you were going 70 mph, you'll want to object. Later you'll point out that this "hearsay" evidence does not prove that you were speeding.

d. The Testimony of an Officer Assumes Facts Not in Evidence

When an officer testifies that "the defendant's vehicle" exceeded the speed limit, but he hasn't testified how he knew it was your vehicle, he's assuming a fact—that *you* drove that vehicle—which hasn't been established yet. It is important to object here, particularly if you later plan to claim he may have stopped the wrong car. You can say, *"Objection, Your Honor, the officer has so far testified only that he observed a vehicle, not that he identified me as having driven it, and his reference to 'the defendant's vehicle' therefore assumes facts not in evidence."*

If your objection is approved ("sustained"), the officer will have to go back to square one and explain exactly how he determined that you were the driver of the vehicle. He will have to describe the vehicle, how he pulled it over and how he identified you through your driver's license. Especially if he may have trouble doing this (your car was out of his sight briefly) this objection may throw him off balance (never a bad thing, since many officers are almost insultingly cocky in court) and remind him he's not out on the street where he runs the show. If the judge denies ("overrules") your objection, just let the officer continue testifying.

5. Your Cross-Examination

In Chapter 10, we provide a number of examples of good—and not so good— cross-examination questions and much information on how to prepare for cross-examination.

After the officer is finished, you get to cross-examine him. (If you have not read Chapter 10 on preparing your cross-examination, do so now.) Remember to be polite and non-argumentative. Ask him simple questions that require short and direct answers. If he gives an unexpected answer, don't argue with him. If you think he is not being completely truthful or covering up important facts, ask a more detailed question. Otherwise, just go on.

Again, as discussed in Chapter 10, it's best not to ask vague questions that give the officer a chance to tell more of his story. If, despite your pointed questions, he tries to do that anyway, politely interrupt with *"Thank you"* or *"I think you've answered my question."* If all else fails, say to the judge, *"Objection, Your Honor, the latter part of his answer is non-responsive, and I ask that it be stricken."*

6. Redirect Examination

If a prosecuting attorney handles the case, she has the chance to ask the officer more questions after you finish your cross-examination. This is called "redirect examination," and the questions asked are supposed to relate only to issues you brought up during your cross-examination.

If the prosecutor asks more questions, you too get another chance to ask more questions of the officer. Called "re-cross-examination," you must limit your questions to issues brought out by the prosecutor on redirect examination. If you start asking questions you have already asked earlier— or ask about new issues—the prosecutor will almost surely object and the judge will probably ask you to sit down.

7. Reserved Opening Statements

If, as discussed in Section 3b above, you reserved your opening statement at the beginning of the trial, you'll want to make it now, just before you give your testimony. Why make an opening statement and then immediately set about testifying to the same facts? Because it allows you to get the judge's attention focused on what you intend to prove.

What if the judge asks you to waive your opening statement? Many judges will attempt to hurry you along by suggesting that you start your testimony by explaining what happened from your point of view and go on from there. Assuming you have prepared carefully, agreeing to do this may be a good idea. Not only does it keep the judge happy, but artfully done, you can make all the same points anyway.

If you do decide to make an opening statement, it should be short and to the point. Here the idea is to outline what you intend to prove, not to testify to the detailed facts that you claim back up these points (you do this next when you testify).

Your opening statement should go more or less like this:

"Your Honor, I will show facts that I believe will demonstrate that I am not guilty. Specifically, I will rely on my own testimony, and that of my passenger, that we both ascertained my speed to be approximately 35 miles per hour on Main Street at the time I was ticketed. I did this by occasionally glancing at my speedometer as I was driving and my witness did it by checking my speed when she saw the reflection of the officer's colored lights on the windshield. I will also show my speedometer was accurate at that speed reading. Finally, I will testify to the fact that just before Officer Ticketem pulled up quickly behind me and used a radar gun, I saw a large truck pass in the 'fast' lane to my left."

8. Your Testimony

In most traffic-court trials, you will simply stand up at the counsel table, look at the judge, and present your view of what happened. But in a few courts, you'll be asked to take the witness stand. Either way, as discussed in Chapter 9, you'll want to have practiced your presentation ahead of time. It's okay to glance briefly at notes, but don't read directly from them. Here is an abbreviated version of Sam Safespeed's testimony.

"I was driving down Main Street at 35 mph, in the right-hand lane of two lanes in my direction. When I passed the speed limit sign just past Elm Street, I looked at my speedometer and it read between 32 and 35 mph. Because I was so surprised I was ticketed, later that same day I took my car to Spartan Speedo Shop and had my speedometer checked. I have proof of that certification, which says my speedometer was accurate, in this document, which I'd like to have marked and introduced as Defendant's Exhibit #1.

When I was driving, I also glanced in my rearview mirror from time to time. Just before the of-

ficer pulled me over, I looked and saw a vehicle, about a quarter mile behind, rapidly gaining on me, just as a large truck went by pretty fast in the left lane. I didn't recognize the car gaining rapidly on me from behind as a police vehicle until the officer activated his lights—which he did when he was fairly close to my rear bumper. At that point, I said to my passenger, 'Gee, Pam, there's an officer flashing his lights, maybe he's after that trucker, so I better pull over to let him pass.' I pulled over, but he stayed behind me."

At this point in the trial, you would want to refer to any diagrams, photos or other evidence supporting your case. (See Chapter 9, on preparing your case for trial.) Once you have told your story and submitted all the evidence you have, the prosecutor (if present) may cross-examine you. (See Chapter 9, Section F.) She may ask a few questions or simply waive her right to cross-examine. The judge may also ask you some questions. But if the testifying police officer tries to question you, you should politely but promptly object on the ground that he is only a witness and not licensed to practice law. Say something like this, *"Objection, Your Honor. Officer Ticketem is not a lawyer and therefore I do not believe it's proper for him to cross-examine me."* If your objection is overruled, you must answer the officer's questions.

All of your responses should be given courteously, truthfully, and as briefly as possible. Contrary to old Perry Mason episodes, you are not limited to only a *"yes"* or *"no"* answer. After all, what if the prosecutor asks you whether you knew you were speeding, in which case both "yes" and "no" are terrible answers. Far better—as is your right—to say, *"I know I wasn't speeding because I had just looked at my speedometer."*

9. Witness Testimony

Next will be your chance to present the testimony of any eyewitnesses. Depending on local court rules and customs, your witnesses will be expected to either testify in the same narrative fashion in which you testified, or you'll be expected to ask questions designed to allow the witness to explain what happened.

Here is what Pam Passenger, a passenger in Sam Safespeed's car, might say if allowed to simply explain what happened:

"Well, Your Honor, on March 15th at about 4:30 p.m., I was seated in the front passenger seat of Sam Safespeed's car. I recall just before Sam was pulled over by the officer, that we were in the right or 'slow' traffic lane. Other cars were passing us on the left, including a large truck. Suddenly, I saw colored lights reflected on Sam's windshield and immediately glanced at the speedometer, and saw that we were going 35 mph. I am quite sure I did this before Sam had a chance to slow down."

It pays to practice with your witness. It is both legal and sensible to ask your witness to practice giving her testimony. (If you don't know whether your court uses the narrative or question and answer style, practice both.) This will allow you to discuss and clear up any discrepancies in how you remember events.

The prosecutor will also have a chance to cross-examine your witnesses when each one is finished testifying.

11. Closing Statements

The final stage of your traffic court case is the closing arguments or statements. Each side has a chance to present their argument after both have presented their testimony and evidence and have been allowed to cross-examine any witnesses. This is the time when you must sum up the best arguments you have to be found not guilty. In most states, your goal is to make it clear that there is a reasonable doubt as to whether you committed the actual offense (In a few states, you must prove your innocence—see the Appendix.) If you have admitted the violation, you must explain that you had a very good legal reason for technically violating the law.

a. The Prosecution's Statement

If there is no prosecutor present, the case normally concludes after the officer's testimony and your cross-examination, unless you ask to make a final statement. In trials with a prosecuting attorney, she is allowed to summarize her case first. She will explain how the officer's testimony (and maybe some cross-examination testimony given by you or your witnesses) "proves beyond a reasonable doubt" each element of the offense and disproves any defenses you've raised. During the prosecutor's closing argument, remain calm and poker-faced. It is a mistake to express outrage, indignation, derision or any other emotion. Remember, this is just another day in the office for the judge, who won't appreciate histrionics. But do listen carefully to the prosecution's arguments so that you can respond to them in your own closing argument, which comes next.

How to Ask Your Witness Questions

It's difficult for an inexperienced person to ask just the right questions. If you feel intimidated by this process, tell the judge, *"Your Honor, I haven't attended law school and I'm unfamiliar with technical rules. May I just ask Ms. Passenger to simply tell you what she saw?"*

If you choose—or are required—to have your witnesses respond to questions, particularly if a prosecuting attorney is opposing you, here are some hints that should make things go easier:

- Be sure to ask non-leading questions, which normally begin with "what," "who," "where," "when" or "how." Leading questions—which are not allowed in court—are questions that provide the answer you are seeking. For example, it is fine to ask, *"What color was the car?"* It is not acceptable to ask, *"Was the car red?"*

- Avoid irrelevant details. For example, if you are accused of running a red light, the judge will not care that you were on your way to help your Mom take your dog, Bonzo, to the vet to be cured of a severe flea infestation.

- Don't ask questions that assume facts that the witness hasn't testified to. This is another way of saying, *"help the witness explain what happened in chronological order."* For example, don't ask, *"Did you see a truck pass my car"* before the witness says anything about a truck being present. Instead, you could first ask, *"Did you see any other vehicles traveling in my direction?"* If the witness says, *"Yes, I saw a big truck,"* then it's time to ask her what it was doing.

- Don't ask your witness to recount what she was told by someone else. That is hearsay and cannot be used at a trial. But there is one big exception: a witness can testify to what the ticketing officer said to you and what you said to the officer, if the officer testified earlier about your conversation together.

- Make a list of the few key facts to which your witness will testify. Design a question calculated to get at each fact. Arrange them in chronological order. By asking your questions in chronological order, your goal is to build a logical foundation for later ones, using the expected answers from earlier questions. For example, you might start with, *"Where were you on March 15th at 2:30 p.m.?"* Assuming the witness says *"in your car,"* it makes sense to follow up with *"Do you recall Officer Ticketem pulling me over?"* Only then is it time to ask, *"What did you observe before the officer pulled me over?"*

For example:

Q: *"On March 5th at 5:15 p.m., what were you doing?"*

A: *"I was traveling with you, in your car."*

Q: *"At that time, were you able to see which lane I was in?"*

A: *"Yes."*

Q: *"Which lane was that?"*

A: *"The right, or slow, lane."*

Q: *"Did you observe any other vehicles on the road?"*

A: *"Yes."*

Q: *"Where were they located?"* (At this point, the witness should refer to the other cars she saw and explain where they were and in which direction they were going.)

A: *"Traffic in our direction was passing on our right and I think there was traffic in the other direction."*

Q: *"Do you recall seeing anything unusual?"*

A: *"Yes, I suddenly saw colored lights reflected on your windshield."*

Q: *"What, if anything, did you do then?"*

A: *"I looked over at your speedometer to see what it said."*

Q: *"Did you look at my speedometer before or after I started slowing down to pull over?"*

A: *"I looked so quickly, I'm sure it was before."*

Q: *"How fast was I going?"*

A: *"35 mph."*

EXAMPLE: Priscilla Prosecutor sums up the evidence, saying, *"Your Honor, Officer Ticketem, an officer with 20 years of traffic enforcement experience, testified as follows. He calibrated his radar unit with a tuning fork at the beginning of his shift. While parked northbound on Main Street, he observed a blue Plymouth Voyager van traveling about 45 mph in a 35-mph-zone. Easy-to-read speed-limit signs are posted every quarter of a mile in that area. He also testified that he aimed his radar gun within seconds after the vehicle had passed him, that he heard a strong Doppler tone, and that his radar unit read a speed of 49 mph. The officer testified he never lost sight of the vehicle, pulled it over, and ticketed Sam Safespeed. The evidence shows beyond a reasonable doubt that the defendant exceeded the posted speed limit by 10 mph."*

If a police officer tries to give a closing statement, you can object on the ground that this involves the practice of law. Do this by saying something like, *"Objection, Your Honor, the officer is a witness, not a lawyer or advocate. He's here to present evidence only, not to practice law by arguing which evidence is more believable, or how this Court should apply the law to the facts."*

Do not refer to new evidence or testimony in a closing statement. If the prosecutor or officer refers to any key fact not already brought out in court testimony, promptly object by saying, *"Objection, Your Honor, no evidence was presented on that point."*

b. Your Closing Statement

When you represent yourself in court, you have two roles—witness and advocate. In your role as witness, you have already testified to what you claim happened. Now, as your own attorney, you have a chance to review and summarize the main points you made during the trial and explain to the judge why you should be found not guilty.

Making a closing argument is different than testifying. Your best approach is to act as if you were a third party, and summarize and comment on the evidence—the point, of course, is to convince the judge that there is at least a reasonable doubt as to your guilt.

Some judges—especially where no prosecutor represents the other side—will try to wrap up the case with no closing argument. Unless you are sure your case is hopeless—or the judge has all but said you have won—you'll want to politely request your right to make a final argument. With some judges, you'll need to insist by saying something like this: *"Your honor, I believe it's my right to make a brief final statement. I'll be well organized and quick, but I do want to briefly explain why I'm not guilty."*

To make an influential impression in final argument, you need to explain your position, convincingly and politely, usually in less than 15 sentences. Don't read a statement. Do outline your speech ahead of time and practice giving it several times in the days before your court date. If you have already obtained the officer's notes, study them carefully, looking for deficiencies in the evidence he cites or inconsistencies in the conclusions he draws. (See Chapter 8, Section C, on how to get the officer's notes.) You'll probably need to modify it a bit at the last minute to take into account what the officer says at trial, but this should be easy enough as long as you have a clear plan as to how to make your major points. Conclude with something like: *"And for these reasons, Your Honor, there is a reasonable doubt as to whether I committed the offense, and I therefore ask that you find me not guilty."*

Three closing argument no-nos:
- **Don't bring up new facts you or other witnesses haven't already testified to.** You are not allowed to refer to anything that was not already brought up during the trial.
- **Don't make it personal.** Never insult the ticketing officer by suggesting he is lying or

personally biased against you. It is proper to point out weaknesses in the officer's testimony—especially his failure to give convincing or thorough answers to your cross-examination questions.

- **Don't challenge the authority of the judicial system to charge you with a traffic offense or say you will ignore the court's ruling if you are found guilty.**

Your closing statement—given after the prosecution makes its closing statement—should emphasize that at least one of the elements of the offense hasn't been proven beyond a reasonable doubt. Or you can argue that you have presented some other legally sufficient defense. (See Chapter 3, Section D, on legal elements of a ticket and Chapters 5, 6 and 7 for defenses to various charges.)

To begin your closing argument, say to the judge: *"Your Honor, I would like to summarize the evidence."* Then explain how:

1. The officer's testimony failed to show that one or more of the necessary elements of the violation you are charged with was present, and/or

2. Your own testimony (and that of any other witness) has shown that you did not violate one or more elements, despite the officer's contrary testimony, and/or

3. Your testimony establishes a legally sufficient reason why you violated the statute, such as your legitimate mistake of fact or reaction to a dire emergency. (See Chapter 3, Section D.)

EXAMPLE: Sam Safespeed's Closing Argument

"Your Honor, let me quickly summarize the evidence as part of telling you why I'm not guilty. First, Officer Ticketem never really established that I violated (the code section you are charged with violating) when he relied heavily on his notes and didn't really remember what happened. When I cross-examined him, he honestly admitted:

- *That he had not calibrated the radar unit with a tuning fork at the beginning and end of his shift, as is recommended in the radar unit's operating manual.*
- *That he was over 180 feet away from my vehicle when he activated his radar unit.*

"By contrast, both Pam Passenger, my witness, and I testified that I was in the right lane, the 'slow' lane, and that there was plenty of other traffic, in both directions, including a large truck quickly pulling ahead of me in the lane to my left. In addition, the officer testified that he took at least three seconds to aim the radar unit at my vehicle, meaning that my car was about 180 feet in front of his, and receding, when he activated it. He also conceded that at that distance the radar beam was at least 30 feet wide, which is the same width as two lanes. Finally, he also reluctantly conceded that his radar unit is more sensitive to a larger target, such as a large truck, and that it's quite possible to get a false reading in a situation like this.

"Finally, Ms. Passenger and I testified that I was going about 35 mph based on looking at my speedometer, which I proved was accurate. So to sum up, I think that in this situation there really is a reasonable doubt as to whether Officer Ticketem correctly determined my vehicle's speed, and I therefore respectfully ask that you find me not guilty."

c. Prosecution's Rebuttal Statement

Since the prosecution has the burden of proving you're guilty, it gets two shots to argue its case. The second one is intended to allow a rebuttal to the things you covered in your argument. Often, the prosecutor will choose not to make a rebuttal statement. If only an officer is present, he almost never will.

12. The Verdict

After all the evidence and closing statements have been presented, the judge must either announce his verdict or take the case "under advisement" or "under submission." This means the judge wants to think about it.

If the judge takes the case "under advisement," it means you will be notified of the decision by mail. But if you are considering appealing if you lose, it's wise to call or visit the court about once a week to find out if the verdict has been filed. That's because in most places your appeal to a higher court must be made between five and 30 days from the time the judge files the verdict with the court clerk, and some court clerks don't get their paperwork in the mail on time. This can leave you with very little, or no, time in which to appeal.

If the judge finds you not guilty, you don't have to pay any fine and are entitled to a refund of any bail you may have posted.

13. The Sentence

In most places, for routine violations, judges state the amount of your fine immediately after announcing a guilty verdict. If you mounted a decent defense—but have not convinced the

judge of your innocence, the judge may reduce, or even suspend, the fine. In a few states, if you are found guilty and fined, the judge may listen to a plea (or read a letter) from you requesting that your fine be suspended or reduced based on your good driving record (or for some other convincing reason). Or, the judge may agree to your request for a payment schedule, if you cannot afford to pay the amount all at once. (Talk to the court clerk if you wish to ask for a fine reduction.)

C. Appealing for a New Trial

If you haven't convinced a judge of your innocence at trial, your chances of overturning his decision by appealing are small. Even though every state gives a person the right to appeal, the process is almost always tedious, typically involving many hours and some expense. In short, before you seriously consider appealing, think long and hard about whether the time and effort is worth the outcome.

Very broadly speaking, there are two types of appeals. One type allows only an appeal on the law—that is, an appellate court will overturn the trial court only if the trial judge made a significant legal error. Another type—called "trial de novo"— allows you a second shot at a trial. Some states use one type of appeal, other states allow the other type and a few states allow both types of appeals. It is generally easier to win when you are entitled to a new trial.

Appeal rules vary widely, so check with a court clerk. Laws governing appeals vary considerably from state to state, so start by checking your state's entry in the Appendix. Armed with this general information, it is then essential to also check with the clerk in the court where you were convicted for the specifics on your rights to a new trial. At the same time, ask the clerk how long you have to file a "notice of appeal," which starts the appeals process moving.

In most states where new trials are allowed, you will have to appear before a judge and plead your case again. There can be at least three reasons to consider this approach:

- If the judge in your first trial was a real "hanging" judge clearly biased against traffic court defendants. In this instance, you should check with the court clerk to see if judges are randomly selected or if a different court would handle your appeal. It's possible you could get a less punitive judge the second time around.

- If you really did a lousy job presenting your case the first time. If you were nervous, unprepared and railroaded by a good prosecutor or clever cop, you probably learned a lot about court procedure and how to present your case. You might want to give it a second try.

- In about a dozen states, a "de novo" trial is the first chance you have to appeal to a jury. Since it's probably fair to say juries are more friendly to defendants than judges are, you may get a better shot at acquittal the second time around in these states. (Note that in states allowing "de novo" jury trials there can be fees for the second trial, so be sure to check them out.)

But what about the majority of states (and the District of Columbia), where you are only entitled to appeal a conviction to an appellate court, claiming that the trial judge made a legal error.

Here your chances of reversing the trial judge are usually somewhere between slim and slimmer. That's because the appellate court will almost always conclude that the traffic court judge ran your trial fairly and applied the law correctly. One reason this is true is that the Appeals Court has the power to ignore minor procedural glitches (like the trial judge let the officer glance at his notes) if they conclude that the errors were not significant.

An appeal might delay or prevent a license revocation. One time when you might want to consider an appeal—even if your case is weak—is if you face the loss of your license because of the number of points that a new conviction will add to your record. If you are only a few points away from a license suspension—and some of those points are due to expire soon—the time it takes to appeal may keep you from losing your license, even if the appeals court eventually upholds your conviction.

The process of taking your case to an appellate court is also complicated and time consuming—so much so that preparing and arguing an appeal is beyond the scope of this book. But if you are truly committed to your cause you can consult a law librarian for reference books on appeals, or try to find a lawyer who shares your zeal and is willing to give you some pointers and support. ■

Jury Trials

I have never met a litigator who did not think he was winning the case right up to the moment when the guillotine came down.

— *William Baxter*

A. Introduction

➡ Check the Appendix to see if your state allows jury trials for routine traffic offenses. If the answer is no, read Chapter 11 on trials before a judge.

Defense lawyers will nearly always say that a jury trial is better for a defendant. This is true, but only if you prepare carefully to fight in a much more complicated legal arena. Not only will you need to pick a jury, but instead of just facing the arresting officer (as often happens when your trial is conducted without a jury), the State will likely send an experienced prosecutor against you, someone who knows the rules of presenting evidence. And since the judge may resent the time and trouble you are causing by insisting on a jury for a case involving a traffic ticket, he may insist on your following technical rules of evidence (something it can be hard to do without legal training or experience). So even in states that allow jury trials, many defendants will choose a trial by a judge only.

Not All States Require 12 Jurors or a Unanimous Verdict

Don't assume that because you demand a jury trial you must be convicted by the vote of 12 unanimous jurors. In traffic cases, some states provide for 8-member, 6-member or even 4-member juries. And other states allow jurors to reach a verdict on a 5-1 or 10-2 vote. Check with the court clerk for your state's rules.

However, there can be good reasons to insist on a jury trial. The biggest one: If you make a convincing presentation, a jury is probably more likely than a judge to side with you. After all, at least some people on the jury are likely to feel they have been victimized by the traffic court system. In short, if you face serious consequences from a guilty verdict—like the risk of losing your license or an astronomical increase in your insurance premiums—you should at least consider requesting a jury trial where it is available.

The format of a jury trial is similar to a formal non-jury trial described in Chapter 11 except for one huge difference: you must participate in the process of choosing a jury. In this chapter, we go through the steps of a jury trial that are different from a trial in front of a judge. Where procedures are the same, we send you back to Chapter 11, which we assume you have already read.

B. Try to Settle Your Case

Jury trials are time-consuming for you, judges, prosecutors and the police. This means once you ask for one, the system has some incentive to settle your case without going to trial. Deals can take many forms, depending on the situation. For example, if you are charged with speeding and running a stop sign, the prosecutor might offer to drop one of the charges if you plead guilty to the other. If you are trying to reduce the number of points against your license (or one ticket allows you to go to traffic school, but two don't) this can be a compromise you're willing to accept. In another case, the judge or prosecutor might be willing to offer you a chance to go to traffic school to keep your record clear.

1. The Negotiation Process

There's nothing to prevent you from approaching the prosecutor at any time to see if she is willing to make a deal to avoid a jury trial. Negotiations in jury-trial cases can take place in several locations, at a formal "pretrial" or "settlement" conference in the judge's chambers, informally by phone, or just before trial in a corner of the hallway outside the courtroom. But no matter the forum, the idea behind negotiating with the prosecutor is almost always to compromise on a better deal than you would get if you were found guilty and sentenced. It is seldom realistic to assume that you can get your case dismissed. Options that are more realistic often include:

- Allowing you to plead guilty to a less serious offense than you are charged with. For example, in some states you could accept "simple" speeding rather than exceeding the speed limit by more than 30 mph.

- Dismissal of one charge against you, in exchange for a guilty plea to another. For example, dismissing the charge that you made an unsafe lane change and failed to stop at a signal in exchange for your guilty plea to a speeding charge.

- Agreement that your sentence will not involve a high fine or license suspension. For example, in a situation where you can be fined $400 for deliberately running a red light and have your license suspended, you can bargain for an agreement to fine you $100 with no suspension.

- Approval of your attending traffic school (meaning the offense won't go on your record) where this otherwise wouldn't be an option.

Other points to remember while negotiating are:

- Be wary about agreeing to plead guilty to several offenses in exchange for the promise of a lesser fine. If you are entitled to a jury trial, you usually have more bargaining power than this. If the prosecutor won't dismiss at least one charge in exchange for pleading guilty (or nolo contendere), you may want to go to trial.

- Don't be bullied by a "hard ass" prosecutor into accepting a poor "take it or forget it" offer. No matter how much the prosecutor tries to intimidate you, if she makes one offer, she'll often be willing to eventually sweeten it up a little if you say "no."

- Never lay everything "on the table" by detailing your strategy to the prosecutor. If negotiations fail, you will have exposed your strategy to the opposition. Better to simply say you believe you can present a very strong case as to why you are not guilty. If the prosecution's case really is weak, the prosecutor will spot it and be more willing to negotiate.

- Never—repeat—never admit guilt to a prosecutor or police official before a deal is formalized. If you do, your admission can be used against you in court.

EXAMPLE: You talk to a prosecutor who says, *"Come on now—just between us—you were going 65 mph, weren't you?"* Never reply, *"Sure, but I think a jury will let me off."* If you fail to make a deal, the prosecutor can simply put himself on the stand and testify to what you said. Far better to respond, *"I don't think you can prove that"* and very briefly explain why. (But again, don't reveal the details of your defense strategy.)

Never make a deal on trial day until you see the officer. If the police officer isn't present, the judge will probably dismiss the case. Knowing that the officer isn't going to make it, the prosecutor may propose a generous settlement immediately before court. Before going further, you should just ask the prosecutor if the officer is going to be present. They are not supposed to lie about this. Or, you could ask for a few minutes to think about any deal and, if the cop still hasn't appeared, just say no.

2. How a Deal Is Made

If you and the prosecutor orally agree to a compromise settlement, the two of you will then appear before the judge. The prosecutor will request permission to dismiss or reduce one or more charges against you "in the interests of justice" and tell the judge that you intend to plead guilty to the reduced charge. Depending on your agreement, sometimes the prosecutor will go on to recommend a particular punishment.

Although the judge does not have to agree to the prosecutor's proposal to dismiss or reduce the charges, or to impose the agreed punishment, he almost always will. If for some reason he doesn't, ask to withdraw your plea and proceed to trial.

C. Selecting the Jury

Here we look at the jury-selection process, including:
- Basic jury selection procedures
- Good questions to ask potential jurors
- How to disqualify a hostile juror.

1. How Jury Selection Works

Many lawyers believe that selecting members of a jury is the single most important phase of the trial. As the defendant, this is because you want to send narrow-minded, police-oriented individuals straight home, since they will rarely vote for acquittal no matter how good a case you present. By contrast, you are hoping for jurors who are open-minded, willing to listen to both sides and at least a little skeptical of police and prosecutorial power.

But realize that in an ordinary traffic case, many judges will already be annoyed that you are insisting on a jury. It follows that they will want to complete the jury selection process expeditiously, believing that any group of fair-minded citizens is qualified to decide whether or not you rolled through a stop sign. Although, as discussed below, you'll want to protect your rights, it is almost always a big mistake to act as if your case is akin to "murder one" and to try to insist on every technical procedural right. Or put another way, if you piss a judge off seriously enough, he has many ways to all but make sure the jury finds you guilty.

Jury selection normally begins as soon as the judge calls your case and after any preliminary motions are resolved. (See Chapter 11, Section B.2, for more on motions.) Potential jurors will normally wait in a "jury assembly room" where you will not have contact with them. In a few courts, they may be milling around in the corridors or seated inside the courtroom. In the unlikely event you find yourself talking with a potential juror, do not discuss your case, since this may be seen as attempting to tamper with the jury. Casual conversation about the weather or sports is OK.

When your case is called, the first group of potential jurors will be asked to take their seats. In some courts, you will be provided with a list of the names and occupations of the potential jurors. If so, write them down on a chart that looks like the one below. Modify the chart if your jury has less than 12 members. If you don't get the names in advance, fill them in as you go along.

Use sticky paper notes. Removable sticky paper comes in handy to write jurors' names and place them in the appropriate place on your jury-seating chart. That way, if a juror is removed and replaced, you can simply peel off the old note and write a new one.

The next step is to question jurors to see if any juror is biased or may view you in a negative way. This is called "voir dire," from the French words for "to speak the truth." In many states the judge will probably elect to ask all the questions himself. Usually the judge will direct questions at the entire panel, not to individual jurors. Often

Municipal Court Jury Panel Chart													Only for offenses punishable by over 90 days in jail			
			Peremptory Challenges													
			No.	1	2	3	4	5	6	7	8	9	10			
Date	Case No.	People of State of Calif.	Plaintiff													
		vs.	Defendnt													
1	2	3	4			5			6							
7	8	9	10			11			12							

this will consist of only a few perfunctory questions relating to occupation, spouse's occupation, previous experience with the criminal justice system, and possible acquaintance with police officers and attorneys. For example, a judge might ask:

- *"Do any of you know any of the parties to this case, specifically Sam Safespeed, Pam Passenger or Officer Ticketem?"*
- *"Do any of you work for the police, the district attorney's office or any other law enforcement agency?"*
- *"Do any of you have relatives or close friends who work in law enforcement or in a district attorney's office?"*
- *"Does anyone on the jury panel know of any reason why he or she can't render an impartial decision in this case?"*

If a potential juror reveals a possibly significant prejudice that could bias him against you, the judge will probably quickly excuse that particular juror "for cause" without you even having to say anything (see Section 3a, below). When the judge is done, he may allow you and the prosecutor to ask a few additional questions designed to ferret out a juror's prejudice or bias. (A sample list is shown in Section 2 below.) This lets you avoid using up your peremptory challenges (see Section 3b, below). If a judge excuses a juror, a new juror will be called to sit in the jury box. At this point, the judge may ask additional questions of these new individuals or, if these people have already been in the courtroom, simply ask if they heard the questions and if they personally know any of the parties or anyone who does.

When the judge is finished questioning the jurors, it often makes sense to indicate that you accept the jury with no need to ask more questions. Again, in a garden-variety traffic court case, you'll likely score more points by being fair and reasonable than you will by acting like Perry Mason (something you're likely not too good at anyway). That being said, there can, of course, be times when you'll want to ask jurors a few additional questions. This is particularly likely if the judge has done a half-baked job in attempting to determine if any jurors might be biased against you.

2. Questions to Ask on "Voir Dire"

Assuming you are given a chance to ask questions, don't repeat any of those the judge or prosecutor has already asked. Instead, follow up on any possibly unsatisfactory answers a particular juror already gave by asking for more detail. If you are told to ask questions directed at the whole panel, try these:

1. *"Do any of you have any objections to sitting here as jurors in a traffic-related offense case? Please raise your hand if you do."*

2. *"Do any of you object to the fact that I will be representing myself without an attorney?"*

3. *"Do any of you have trouble believing that a person is innocent until proven guilty beyond a reasonable doubt on the basis of the evidence?"*

4. *"Have any of you ever been employed as a law enforcement officer or security guard?"* (Note: Anyone with this background within the past ten years should probably be disqualified with a "peremptory" challenge—see Section 3b below—if the judge has not already excused them for "cause.")

5. *"Do any of you have any close friends or relatives who have been employed as law enforcement officers, security guards or in the district attorney's office?"* (Note: You should probably exercise "peremptory" challenges on spouses, parents, children or siblings of anyone in law enforcement— see Section 3b, below—if the judge has not already excused them for "cause.")

6. *"Are there any among you who would believe the word of a police officer, solely because she is a police officer, over my own testimony?"* (Note: Definitely exercise your "peremptory" challenge against anyone who even vaguely reeks of "bad vibes" when you ask this question.)

7. *"Do any of you believe that police officers are highly unlikely to make mistaken observations?"*

8. *"Do any of you believe a police officer always tells the entire truth?"*

9. *"Have any of you ever sat on a jury previously where the defendant was charged with the offense I'm charged with?"* (Note: If anyone answers *"yes"* to this question, follow up by asking, *"Did that jury reach a verdict?"* If they say *"yes,"* you should assume the verdict was "guilty" and exercise your "peremptory" challenge. See Section 3b, below.)

10. *"Have any of you ever been involved in an automobile accident which you believe was caused by someone breaking the law?"* (If a prospective juror answers *"yes,"* be prepared to follow up by asking him to describe the accident, when it occurred, and how he thinks the other driver violated the law. If the accident was recent, and he says the other driver violated the same law you're charged with, you may want to exercise a "peremptory" challenge to excuse this juror. See Section 3b, below.)

11. *"Are there any of you who don't drive or drive less than five thousand miles each year?"* (Note: A person who mostly takes public transit and only drives to church on

Sundays may not be as sympathetic to your technical violation as a traveling salesman who drives 20,000 miles a year and gets frequent speeding tickets.)

12. *"Are there any among you who have never been cited for a moving traffic violation?"* (Note: You probably want to disqualify any juror who's never been subjected to the indignity.)

What to do if you are unhappy with a juror's answer. If a juror says something that indicates to you that he might not be fair, be prepared to ask a follow-up question. For example, you might say, *"Mr. Jones, I noticed you seemed to nod slightly when I asked you if you had any friends or relatives who were police officers. Was that a 'yes' answer?'* Depending on the answer, you might want to ask further questions to expose a possible anti-defendant or pro-police prejudice. If you decide to excuse that particular person, either use one of your peremptory challenges or, if the juror's possible bias is obvious, ask the judge to excuse the juror for cause (see below, How to Challenge a Juror).

3. How to Challenge a Juror

There are two reasons you may want to get a particular person off the jury:

- The person exposes a clear bias against you (says he hates people who drive fast).
- You have a bad feeling about a juror for a vague, undefined reason.

Fortunately, there are also two ways to get rid of a juror you do not want.

a. Challenges for Cause

If a prospective juror strongly indicates that he can't be fair, the judge may disqualify him before you say anything. But if this doesn't occur, wait until you are given a chance to make a challenge and ask the judge to disqualify that person for cause. To do this, simply say, *"Your Honor, I respectfully challenge prospective juror Smith for cause on account of his statement that he would 'find it hard to be fair' in light of his statement that his mother was injured by someone who was speeding."*

Here are common reasons why a judge will agree to dismiss a juror for cause:

- The prospective juror, or his close friend or relative, was seriously injured by someone who committed the same type of offense you're charged with, and the juror admits he would "have a hard time" being objective.
- The prospective juror indicates he'd believe the word of a police officer over you, just because the witness was a police officer.
- The prospective juror is a close friend or relative of the officer or any other prosecution witness, or of the prosecuting attorney.
- The prospective juror learned of your case before being called to court as a juror, and has expressed some opinion about your guilt.

It pays to be polite. If you are nasty or sarcastic when you ask the judge to excuse a juror, you are likely to alienate the remaining jurors. As with most areas of life, it pays to be pleasant.

If the judge disagrees with you and refuses to remove the juror, you still have another way to get him off the panel.

b. Peremptory (Automatic) Challenges

In most states, you have the right to excuse a certain specified number of prospective jurors for any reason, or for no given reason at all. How many of these automatic or "peremptory challenges" you are allowed varies from state to state (often depending on the offense you're charged with, and on the size of the jury). With a jury of 12, it would be typical for you and the prosecutor to each have anywhere from three to ten peremptory challenges. If the jury only has six members, you might only be allowed two to five such challenges. But since this is an area where each state does things a little differently, you'll want to ask in advance what your state's rules are.

Most experienced trial lawyers believe that, when considering whether or not to challenge a juror, it's wise to respect your instincts. If you get bad vibes from someone—even if you can't explain why—you'll want to remove him from the jury. But in addition to trusting your gut, if the judge does not excuse them himself, you probably would be wise to consider exercising peremptory challenges to exclude the following types of people:

- Present and former police officers and security guards, their spouses and children
- Anyone who has ever worked in a prosecutor's office, including lawyers, paralegals and support staff
- Relatives or close friends of the above
- Anyone who has ever been involved in an accident, or had a relative involved in an accident, caused by someone who was charged with the offense you're charged with (assuming, of course, you've been able to get this information)
- People who don't drive much, or who have never received a traffic ticket
- People who, from gestures, body language, and a generally hostile attitude, obviously resent being called for jury duty
- People you feel uneasy about but don't know why
- Possibly people whose dress and/or lifestyles are very different from yours.

Again, when you exercise a peremptory challenge, be polite. Simply say something like this, *"Your Honor, the Defense would like to thank and request the court to excuse the fifth juror, Ms. Jones."*

D. Trial Procedure

After the jury is selected, the jurors will be "sworn in" by the judge or clerk. Then, the trial proceeds in much the same way as a trial before a judge. (See Chapter 11, Section B, on trial procedure).

1. Opening Statements

While opening statements are often skipped during a ticket-related trial before a judge, it is unwise to waive your opening statement when a jury is present. That's because it is very important to get the jurors on your side from the start. Remember, as discussed in Chapter 11, Section B, you have a choice to either give your opening statement after the prosecutor gives (or waives) hers, or you can reserve your opening statement until after you cross examine the officer and just before you put on your testimony. But I advise making it as soon as possible in front of a jury. That's because jurors often make up their minds as to guilt or innocence very early in the trial, often right after opening statements. If you reserve your opening statement until later, jurors who only hear from the prosecution may have already decided you are guilty before you open your mouth.

Stand up behind your counsel table and make your opening statement facing the jury. Don't try to walk around the courtroom. Just stand straight, look right at the jury members and tell them briefly what evidence you will produce to show you are innocent. It's fine to quickly glance at notes, but since you should have already practiced your statement at home with friends, you should never need to read your statement. (See Chapter 11, Section B.3 and B.7, on making your opening statement.)

💡 **Be sincere and straightforward.** The important thing to remember is that your bearing and how you make your presentation will probably have a much greater effect on a jury than it would have on a judge. Never be sarcastic or insulting, even if the arresting officer treated you poorly. Instead assume the officer, acting in good faith, simply made an honest mistake which you now wish—with the help of the jury—to correct.

2. The Prosecution's Testimony

In jury trials, the officer will always take the witness stand and testify in response to the prosecutor's questions. You have the right to object to improper questions, but in a jury trial you should save your objections for issues that really are critical. That's because jurors typically resent anyone they think is trying to hide information from them and may rule against the side that objects the most. In addition, trying to keep evidence from a jury may backfire. Even if the judge agrees with your objection, jurors are likely to guess at what was excluded and give it more importance than if you just let it pass without objection. But despite this caution, if the prosecutor treads too far over the fairness line, you'll probably wish to object. (See Chapter 10, Section A, for tips and guidelines on objecting to testimony.)

3. Your Cross-Examination

When you cross-examine the prosecution's witnesses, be courteous but firm. If the officer tries to say more than you wish her to say, promptly but politely interrupt and direct her to, *"Please answer the question, you've already had a chance to tell your story. I'd appreciate it if you wouldn't try to influence the jury any further."* Otherwise, the cross-examination should follow the approach discussed in Chapter 11 with questions gleaned from Chapter 10.

4. Your Testimony

As discussed in Section 1 above, I recommend that you make your opening statement at the beginning of the trial. But if for some reason you have not, you should definitely make it before you start your testimony. Then, with several important exceptions, your testimony in a jury trial should proceed in the same way as before a judge (see Chapter 11, Section B).

You Don't Have to Ask Yourself Questions

In a typical trial, lawyers ask the questions and witnesses answer them. But if you are acting as your own lawyer, most judges will allow you to dispense with this format and simply tell your story. If you come across a judge who insists on the question-and-answer format, you should object as follows: *"Your Honor, I just want to tell the jury what happened in my own words. I'm not a lawyer and I don't know how to ask myself questions. I assume that if I say something inappropriate, you will advise the jury to disregard it."* If after that, the judge still refuses to allow you to tell your story, you'll probably have to do your best to ask yourself pertinent questions before giving sensible answers. (Just in case this might happen, see Chapter 11, Section B.9, for tips on how to frame proper questions.) At the very least, you'll have obtained the jury's sympathy.

Be sure to look directly at the jury from time to time while you explain key points. You want the jurors to see you as an honest, law-abiding citizen who has been mistakenly accused. But don't overact. People who suck up to the jury (pretending to be always 100% honest and truthful, for example) usually get what they deserve.

A few sympathetic personal details won't hurt. You may be able to exert subtle influences on the jury by very lightly sprinkling your testimony with personal information that one or more members of the jury might identify with. Jurors tend to like and sympathize with people who help others (and aren't paid huge salaries), such as firefighters, medical personnel, teachers and people who volunteer for good causes. For example, if you were on your way to a church function to raise money for refugee relief when you were pulled over, and you suspect there are a few churchgoers in the jury, it won't hurt to casually mention that fact. But don't overplay your good-guy associations. If jurors think you are a phony—or trying to play them for fools—you're almost sure to be found guilty.

But don't reveal unpopular occupations. If you're an undertaker, lawyer, used car salesperson, bill collector or insurance salesman, you'll probably be wise to keep your occupation to yourself.

Judges often train themselves to remain totally expressionless even while listening to the most blatant nonsense. But most jurors are neither trained to do this nor particularly interested in appearing impartial. So, be alert for non-verbal signs that might suggest that one or more jurors is confused or skeptical about your testimony, and adjust your conduct accordingly. For example, when questioning a not particularly believable witness, if you see jurors frowning or snickering, you probably won't want to rely heavily on what that witness said in making your closing statement.

When your testimony is completed, and after the prosecutor has cross-examined you, it's time to present any witnesses who will testify on your behalf. (See Chapter 9, Section E, for more on preparing your witnesses for trial.)

Depending on the preferences of the judge, your witnesses will either testify in narrative fashion as you probably did, or in response to your questions. If the judge indicates that you

...on my way to church, with a carload of canned goods for needy mothers, when I saw a hurt puppy in the street, so naturally...

should question the witness, you may want to explain that because you're unfamiliar with the way such questions should be asked, you would prefer just to let your witness explain what they saw. But if the judge doesn't agree, be prepared to ask questions. (See Chapter 11, Section B.9, for the proper questioning technique.)

5. Cross-Examination by the Prosecution

When you have finished testifying, it's your time to be cross-examined by the prosecutor. Listen carefully to each question. If you don't fully understand a question, don't guess at the answer; instead, ask the prosecutor to repeat and clarify it. If you understand the question, but just don't know the answer, say so, keeping in mind that you have a right to explain your answer, even when your answer is *"I don't know"* or *"I'm not sure."* On the other hand, do not purposely avoid answering reasonably clear questions. Otherwise, the jury will think you are being evasive.

Again, be polite. Sorry to belabor this point, but if you are obnoxious or impolite to the prosecutor, it may cause jurors to decide a close case against you. Your response to cross-examination should be the same as in non-jury trials, except that during your responses you should occasionally look at the jury as you might when explaining something to a group of friends (see Chapter 11, Section B).

6. Closing Arguments

After all the evidence is presented, both you and the prosecutor will have the opportunity to present a closing argument. Making a closing argument to a jury is much more important than making one to a judge in a non-jury trial. Judges pride themselves on deciding cases based on evidence—which they have already heard—not on the arguments from the opposing sides. Jurors, on the other hand, are usually far less sure of their legal judgments and will listen more carefully to your argument as to why there is reasonable doubt as to your guilt.

a. The Prosecutor's Closing Argument

During the prosecutor's closing argument, remain calm—poker-faced if you can. Never express outrage, indignation, derision or any other emotion, no matter how much the prosecutor tortures the truth. Just listen carefully and take appropriate notes so that you can make any necessary modifications to the closing argument, which you should have already planned.

b. Your Closing Argument

Your closing argument should be designed to serve two purposes. First, you want to clearly explain how the evidence that has been presented at trial isn't sufficient to establish your guilt beyond a reasonable doubt, or actually disproves it. Second, you should rebut damaging statements made by the prosecutor in her arguments. For example, if the prosecutor says you entered an intersection when the light was already red, you'll want to discuss the fact that the officer had a lousy viewing angle and was doing something else at the time. Please refer to "Closing Statements," Chapter 11, Section B.11. Much of the information set out there applies equally when making a closing argument before a jury.

It is essential to point out to the jurors, at both the beginning and end of your brief talk, that each element of the offense must be proven "beyond a reasonable doubt." Although legally this is something between a "great" doubt and an "insignificant" doubt, it is proper to state that a "reasonable" juror who has any doubt at all about any element of the offense must find you not guilty. Since everyone considers himself or herself reasonable, you hope that any juror who has any doubt about your guilt will vote not guilty. In states that allow jury trials for traffic offenses, most still require unanimous agreement for a verdict. If only one doubting juror sides with you, the result is a "hung" jury and no conviction.

Here is an example of how your argument might begin to a jury:

"Ladies and Gentlemen, since I know that I'm innocent of the offense(s) charged, I'm contesting it/them here. Attorneys are very expensive, and so I'm defending myself. Although I have no legal training, I've presented my case as best I know how to show you why I am not guilty. But there is one thing I do know about the American legal system—and it's something you know, too—the prosecution must prove every defendant, including me, guilty of each and every element of an offense beyond a reasonable doubt. Now I want to explain exactly why the prosecutor has failed to do that in my case."

(Now, describe the elements of the offense and how, in light of the evidence presented, and based on your testimony, evidence and any witnesses, doubt as to your guilt remains. This is the most important part of your argument! See other examples in Chapter 11, Section B.11, under "Closing Statements.")

"You have heard my evidence (and the statements of my witnesses). You have also heard from the police officer. These are conflicting versions of what happened. Please do not believe the officer's powers of observation are infallible just because she's a police officer. And please do not accept uncritically what the prosecutor just said when she repeated the officer's versions of events. The point is: neither the prosecutor nor the police officer disproved any of the evidence my witnesses and I presented. Remember, if the law required you to believe law enforcement personnel are perfect, we wouldn't need trials at all! So again, please consider my side of the story—I've presented it as honestly as I can."

"When I am done speaking, the prosecutor is allowed another chance to undermine my argument. She may tell you that I have a lot to gain by being declared not guilty, and that therefore the officer's story is more believable than mine. I have no hard feelings toward the officer, and I know that part of the reason she's on the roads is to protect us from hazardous drivers, but she's not infallible, and in this particular case, she was mistaken.

"Finally, you will recall that in the beginning of this case, you each indicated you would honor my constitutional guarantee that I am not guilty until and unless the prosecution proves each element of the offense I'm charged with beyond a reasonable doubt. Indeed, in this case, the prosecution has come up far short in doing this. In retiring to the jury room, I ask you to do your duty in this regard and to enter a verdict of not guilty. Thank you."

This may seem a bit long-winded but it goes pretty fast when you're talking. Feel free to change it to suit your particular case. It's wise to practice this sort of statement a number of times before you go to court.

c. The Prosecution's Rebuttal Argument

Since the prosecution has the burden of proof, it gets two shots to argue its case to the jury. The second one is intended to allow it to rebut any points you raised in your argument. Sometimes the prosecutor won't exercise this opportunity. Other times she will make a brief final statement.

E. Preparing Jury Instructions

After you have presented your evidence, you have an opportunity to submit proposed "jury instructions" to the judge to be read to the jury. Because most judges are required to—and do— a fairly decent job of doing this for routine cases, we normally recommend that you leave it to the judge. But if the judge is particularly hostile, you may want to take a shot at doing this.

Whole books have been written on how to prepare jury instruction. It's a very specialized skill, not something we can teach you in a couple of pages. But if you're determined, start by going to a law library and, with the help of the librarian, finding the jury instruction books judges most often use in your state. Then page through the instructions that relate to traffic offenses. A judge is required to give a jury instruction at your request, if there is evidence to support it. For example, if you testified you had to speed to the hospital with your wife, who was actually giving birth, the judge is probably required to read the jury instruction on the "necessity defense" (see Chapter 3, Section D).

The standard instructions, which the judge can usually be trusted to give on his own, include explaining to jurors how they are to understand the duties of the judge and jury, and how they are expected to consider different types of evidence and how to determine the credibility of witnesses. Finally, and most importantly, the judge will explain the presumption of innocence. Often he will say something like this:

"A defendant in a criminal action is presumed to be innocent until the contrary is proved, and in case of a reasonable doubt as to whether his guilt is proven, he is entitled to a verdict of not guilty. This presumption places on the State the burden of proving him guilty beyond a reasonable doubt. Reasonable doubt is defined as follows: It is not a mere possible doubt, because everything relating to human affairs, and depending on moral evidence, is open to some possible or imaginary doubt. It is the state of the case which, after the entire comparison and consideration of the evidence, leaves the minds of the jurors in that condition, such that they cannot say they feel an abiding conviction, to a certainty, of the truth of the charge."

F. The Judge Instructs the Jury

Finally, the judge will instruct the jury from the standard instructions, plus any the judge accepted from you or the prosecutor. Then the bailiff will take the jury into the jury room to deliberate. When they come back, they will announce a verdict. If you are found guilty, the judge will set a later date for you to appear for sentencing.

G. Appeals From a Jury Verdict

If you are convicted at a jury trial, your chances of successfully appealing are very small. That's because in the vast majority of states, you do not have the right to a new ("de novo") trial (see the Appendix for your state's appeal rules). Instead, an appellate court will simply look to make sure that the trial court judge followed the law. Even then, the judge has to make a pretty big error to catch the attention of an appeals court and reverse your conviction. Given the fact that, even for those who know how to do it, the appeals process is complicated and expensive, appeals rarely make sense for traffic cases. ■

Chapter

13

Where Do We Go From Here?

Much of this book was written on the assumption that you will get a fair hearing in traffic court. To a person wrongly accused of a traffic violation he knows he didn't commit, a fair hearing is obviously very important. Unfortunately, rather than a fair process, many folks accused of traffic violations experience a sham and corrupt system that mocks justice.

Too many judges presume that a person who has received a ticket is guilty. They will too often believe the word of a police officer over an individual accused of a violation and will turn off their minds when it's the defendant's turn to tell his side of the story.

In most states, traffic court is designed primarily to find people guilty as efficiently as possible. But so what? With all the problems in the world, you may ask whether fairness in traffic court merits much attention. Just how important is a fair shake in traffic court? I believe it's very important. Traffic court is the place where the greatest number of Americans come into contact with the American justice system. Even serving on a jury is a far-distant second in terms of bringing ordinary folks to experience firsthand, and participate in, the court system. In the foreword to *The Law on Speeding and Radar,* by A.S. Manraj and P.D. Haines (Butterworths, 1985), the former attorney general of the Canadian province of Ontario, R. Roy McMurtry, states:

"Most persons who come into contact with the justice system do so in response to the alleged infraction of the laws governing the use of motor vehicles. The fairness and justice they find in the courts dealing with these matters will color their perception of the entire justice system. It is accordingly very important that the courts which administer these laws demonstrate a rigorous respect for, and a deep commitment to, the even-handed administration of justice."

What people see when they're called to court affects how they see the entire system. If they see an even-handed system presided over by a neutral judge who seriously considers testimony and arguments, they are more likely to feel that our justice system is a good one—just like we were all told in our high school civics classes. Even where the judge wrongly finds a person guilty, the trial may still have been fair, with the judge using the full force of his impartiality, fairness and intelligence. Obviously, no system of justice based on the perceptions of humans—on the road or in the courtroom—can ever be perfect. But if the basic system is perceived to be fair, everyone wins.

Of course, the reality is often otherwise. Too many times, what we see when we fight our tickets is an impersonal assembly-line court system presided over by a bored judge who assumes we're guilty and that police officers never lie or make mistakes. Not all traffic court judges are this way, but too many are. Fair and impartial judges seem to be vastly outnumbered by those who regard traffic-court trials as an annoying obstacle to the raising of revenue. The result is often that people emerge from traffic court disillusioned with the whole system of justice.

Am I exaggerating the defects of traffic court? Ask anyone who's contested a ticket for a moving violation. One reader of our California Edition says this:

"The officer's testimony is apparently accepted as the one/only/total truth and the defendant is listened to grudgingly, as only a show of compliance with the forms of the law. I watched several cases before mine. The verdict was invariably guilty, even when the defendant had witnesses and documentation, which the judge did not look at. In my case, the judge seemed to have pre-judged me. He seemed to barely listen to me, preferring to listen to a conversation between the officer and the prosecuting attorney, and he seemed to be communicating with them by means of signals. The judge refused to accept or even look at documents I wished to present as evidence. I presented various motions for dismissal, but the judge summarily dismissed them, sometimes cutting me off before I had finished the first sentence."

Another reader, before deciding whether to fight her ticket, took the time to watch a few traffic-court trials conducted by the judge before whom she would have to appear if she chose that option. These are her observations:

"I attended traffic court to observe the judge's pattern in judging traffic cases. The room was packed with angry and demoralized people. We were sternly warned that Her Honor finds people guilty in 99% of the cases. I watched several people plead their case, and they were all found guilty. Even though some had pretty good cases, their fines were all dramatically increased. In light of my visit to the court, I decided to just pay the fine, as it was clear I stood no chance of winning or having the fine reduced below the original amount."

Many folks report similar experiences, feeling that the judge only grudgingly let them say what they wanted before finding them guilty. Others have noted the smug and nonchalant attitudes of some police officers in court, who seem to know they won't lose. Many judges privately admit that they almost always believe the word of a police officer over that of someone defending himself in traffic court.

Why is traffic court so poorly run? Surely being appointed a judge doesn't instantly convert a lawyer into a rubber-stamp for police and prosecutors. But as a judge settles into office, he begins to realize just how dependent he is on police officers' groups for both financial and public support come re-election time. Police officers who appear before the same traffic-court judges again and again are generally part of an efficient political organization. You and the countless other ordinary folks brought into traffic court are not.

A judge who frequently rules against police officers is likely to wake up next election to find police-organization support and money going to his opponent, perhaps an ambitious deputy prosecutor ready to accuse the judge of being "soft on crime." Persons summoned as jurors, of course, suffer no such pressures. This is why conviction rates are much higher for judge trials than for jury trials.

The right to a trial by an impartial jury is more important than you might think. Most judges, prosecutors, and even many defense attorneys often assume that the accused person is really guilty. Their years of experience dealing with real criminals sours them into thinking that nearly everyone must be guilty, or else why would they have been accused? Although some people selected as jurors also have this attitude, it tends to be more widespread among people in the legal profession. ("The purpose of trial by jury is to prevent oppression by the Government by providing a safeguard … against the compliant, biased, or eccentric judge." *Apodaca v. Oregon*, 406 U.S. 404, 406 (1972).) Furthermore, the possibility that an accused defendant may opt for a jury trial in the face of a known "hanging judge" may itself serve as a check on such judges, where the right to a jury trial still exists.

Ordinary folks seeking even-handed justice are also faced with the systematic effort to remove from traffic court any constitutional protections that stand in the way of a more "efficient" production of revenue. Every important right mentioned in the Bill of Rights whose purpose is to protect the people from oppression by government adds a financial cost to the system. Jury trials cost money. So do public defenders. So, starting about 30 years ago, politicians and judges at all levels began a silent conspiracy to gradually eliminate procedural rights that interfered with the revenue-raising aspects of the traffic-enforcement system. Many states did this by creating a new category of crime known as the "petty" or "summary" offense or "infraction." Before that, offenses were either felonies or misdemeanors. Anyone charged with either could, and often did, respectfully request a trial by jury. The petty or summary offense, or infraction, became a new type of category for which no jury trial was allowed, even if demanded by the accused. As a trade-off, some of these states provided that no one could be imprisoned for this new category of offense. Other states didn't have to go so far. The U.S. Supreme Court helped them by ruling that there is no Sixth Amendment right to trial by jury where the maximum period of imprisonment is six months or less.

Even rights that don't cost the system very much have been ruled inapplicable to traffic matters. Thus, the Supreme Court has ruled that no police officer who stops you is required to tell you that you have a right to refuse to answer his questions, and that he can use any of your admissions against you. Hardened criminals get the benefit of "Miranda" warnings, but an alleged traffic law violator does not get the same rights. (*Bertemer v. McCarty*, 468 U.S. 420, 104 S.Ct. 3138 (1984).)

Another part of the problem is the role that tickets play in generating revenue for all sorts of purposes unrelated to promoting traffic safety. Over the years, this factor has assumed a greater importance than the quite legitimate concept of ticketing—and hopefully deterring—people who drive dangerously. If you figure that, on the average, a $100 fine is collected for each of the thirty million traffic citations handed out in our country each year, the total fines would generate approximately $3 billion. This is a very big business indeed. This amounts to an annual average of approximately $30 for every car on the road. And local and state governments, rather than using these funds to promote traffic safety, use them for all sorts of purposes, including hiring more officers to give more tickets, to generate more revenue, and so forth.

In more recent years, many states have begun adding onto each traffic fine various "assessments" and "surcharges" for many non-traffic related purposes, such as for courthouse and jail construction and the training of police officers and prison guards. Thus, an ordinary moving violation ticket that would have been $30 a few years ago now exceeds $100. This has become especially fashionable in the last few decades, as property-tax revenues dwindle, or at least stabilize.

Traffic ticket fines started to skyrocket in the late '70s and early '80s, surpassing normal rates of inflation, at about the same time folks in many states started passing ballot initiatives to limit property taxes. In essence, politicians have circumvented tax-reduction movements by imposing new taxes on top of traffic fines.

A judge who consistently applies the "reasonable-doubt" rule, and who too frequently fails to find people guilty and impose fines, is considered by the system to be shortchanging the city, or county, of revenue, badly needed to pay for what property taxes used to pay for—more courthouses and jails. Is it any wonder many traffic-court judges find traffic-court defendants guilty 90% of the time in cases where the officer does appear?

And then there are police-officer ticket quotas to make sure that enough tickets are issued to keep the flow of money coming in. All police agencies officially deny quotas for traffic violations, and they are even illegal in some states. But don't be fooled. Although public pressure has forced some police agencies to abandon formal numerical quotas, many police agencies use an unwritten quota system. One way this works is the system of police officers "performance evaluations." If a cop turns up short in the ticket race, his chances for promotion decline. In some cases, officers are suspended or even fired for "inefficiency" when they fail to produce enough tickets. As a result of performance evaluations, each officer tries hard to write at least slightly more than the average number of department tickets per month. With everyone trying to beat the average, it doesn't take a mathematical genius to see that the average is likely to increase over time. Thus, average-beating becomes an important contributing factor to the rise in the number of tickets issued each year.

Perhaps we should not get so excited about this. There are, after all, other things to worry about besides fighting an occasional traffic citation. Yes, and that's exactly how your state's politicians and judges want you to think. They gradually deprive us of our freedoms by starting, slowly and innocuously, to take away a right one at a time, hoping that most folks won't notice. The right to confront one's accuser and the right to a fair hearing before a neutral decision-maker may, in the future, be reserved only for hardened criminals.

Most of us have been led to believe that any excesses of the system can be corrected by an appeal if you lose. In about half of the states—the predominantly rural ones—you have the right to a new trial in a higher court if a judge finds you guilty. But three-quarters of the nation's population do not have this right. So for most people, appeal from an unjust verdict is simply a false hope. Appeals courts will only reverse cases on technicalities, and never on the basis that the judge should have believed you and your witnesses rather than a police officer. Appeals court judges will always rubber-stamp traffic-court judges' "findings of fact," on the basis that the trial judge, who observed the defendant, police officer and other witnesses testify, was best able to tell who was telling the truth. The rule that allows appeals courts to do this (called the "substantial evidence standard"), was originally adopted to prevent elitist English-trained judges from overturning common-sense verdicts of juries. Today, though, where the right to trial by jury has been taken away from most folks, it makes little sense and simply shields judges from any meaningful scrutiny. What it boils down to is that appeals courts won't second-guess traffic-court judges, who in turn don't want to second-guess the police officer who writes you a ticket. The driver is the only one whose conduct is second-guessed—by the officer, the judge and the appeals court.

What started out as a legitimate offshoot from the criminal justice system designed to correct the behavior of errant motorists and deter dangerous drivers, has degenerated in an assembly-line that grinds up your constitutional rights and spits out money into government coffers. Sadly, in too many places, your rights consist mostly of hoping your case will be dismissed if the officer doesn't show up for trial, or the prosecutor or judge commits a serious legal error.

In one case, two out of three appeals court judges predictably ruled that a traffic court judge could act as both judge and prosecutor (*People v. Daggett*, 206 Cal.App.3d Supp. 1 (1988) to save the county the cost of a prosecutor. The third judge disagreed, stating, "the inescapable conclusion that the court is, or at least appears to be, both the prosecutor and the court, rather than being impartial." He continued:

"The people of this country have fought hard against a police state. Their success should not be erased by elimination of an adversary trial. Actually, traffic court is one of our most important venues. To a large part of our population, this will be their only contact with the justice system. They are certainly going to wonder what happened to the impartial, blind Miss Justice and the doctrine of separation of powers."

How would a fair traffic violation scheme work? A good start would be to instruct the police to hand out citations only where there was a clear violation of the law that either resulted in rudeness to another driver (or bicyclist or pedestrian) or caused a dangerous situation. Officers now hiding behind bushes with taxpayer-paid radar, laser and VASCAR units could be instructed to look for drunk drivers instead. Secondly, the issuing of tickets should be separated from the collection of revenue for more police cars, radar units and more luxurious courthouses.

Another measure of fairness would be to allow jury trials for at least those violations that are reported to the state motor vehicles bureau and which can be used as a basis for suspending your license (but not for parking or equipment violations). How would this work? Why not the same way it does in about a dozen smaller states to this day? A person accused of a moving traffic violation would first have a non-jury trial. If he lost and was dissatisfied with the way he was treated, he could "appeal" for a new trial in a higher trial court, where he or she could request a jury trial.

But wouldn't this hopelessly tie up the courts? I don't think so. It hasn't in the states that still allow it. Jury trials are time-consuming and diffi-cult; it is for this very reason that 30 years ago, when those accused of traffic violations were allowed the option of a jury trial, few people actually opted for one. Even so, the possibility that a traffic-court defendant treated unfairly by a traffic judge may appeal for a new trial—by jury—may keep judges a little more honest. In fact, judges could be evaluated based on the number of appeals eventually won by the defen-dant, which they generated by unjustly finding people guilty. A consistently biased judge whose unfair decisions provoke an unusually high number of such appeals for trials by jury could be given a different assignment—or perhaps tossed out of office.

Having only recently celebrated the 200th anniversary of the Bill of Rights (adopted in 1791 as the first ten amendments to the U.S. Constitu-tion), let's resolve to bring the fairness and justice envisioned in it back into the traffic court process. Let's work for the recall and election defeat of judges who think the Constitution is just for vicious criminals, but not for law-abiding folks who occasionally wind up in traffic court.

Sadly, there's no sign that any state's legislators are on the right track. Many conservative legislators, congratulating each other for voting to "get government off our backs," hypocritically vote for higher taxes (disguised as "surcharges" and "assessments"), push for increased punishments and work to reduce procedural rights that insulate us from oppressive actions by the government. Moderates and liberals fare no better, trying to outdo their conservative colleagues lest they appear "soft on crime."

Pandering to the public's fear of drunk drivers, the politicians heap absurdly punitive measures on the younger generation. This includes federally-mandated legislation for one-year license suspen-sions for anyone under 21 who:

- Possesses even unopened cans or bottles of an alcoholic beverage, in, out or away from a vehicle,

- Drives with a blood alcohol level so low (0.01%) that a teenager who took a teaspoon of Nyquil cough syrup would be violating the law

- Refuses to be subjected to a test for this absurdly low amount, with a measuring de-vice so inaccurate its use isn't allowed in court.

Is the fear of a police-state an exaggeration? In 1988, the late Justice William Brennan of the U.S. Supreme Court, concerned over the approval, by other justices, of low-flying helicopter surveillance, said this:

"The Court today approved warrantless helicopter surveillance from an altitude of 400 feet.... The Fourth Amendment demands that we temper our efforts to apprehend criminals with a concern for the impact on our fundamental liberties of the methods we use. I hope it will be a matter of con-cern to my colleagues that the police surveillance methods they would sanction were among those described 40 years ago in George Orwell's dread vision of life in the 1980's: 'The black-mustachioed face gazed down from every commanding corner. There was one on the house front immediately opposite. BIG BROTHER IS WATCHING YOU, the caption said.... In the far distance a helicopter skimmed down between the roofs, hovered for an instant like a bluebottle, and darted away again with a curving flight. It was the Police Patrol, snooping into people's windows.' Nineteen Eighty-Four (1949).' Who can read this passage without a shudder, and without the instinctive reaction that it depicts life in some country other than ours? I respectively dissent." (Florida v. Riley, 488 U.S. 445, 466–467, 109 S.Ct. 1659 (1988).)

Big words for a few inconveniences and seem-ingly minor injustices on the road and in traffic court? Not really. The slow erosion of traffic-court rights is just a single symptom of the broader problem of creeping governmental oppression, just as was the seemingly minor tax on the tea the colonists threw into Boston Harbor.

Have I rambled for a long time? I guess I have. But now it's your turn. If you have any ideas and comments on how you would like to see traffic laws and court procedures changed, let me know. You can write down your thoughts and mail them to me at Nolo Press, 950 Parker Street, Berkeley, CA 94710. ■

Appendix

Traffic Court Rules for 50 States (And the District of Columbia)

Please Read This

Here we list the courts where traffic cases are heard, along with other important legal information for the 50 states and Washington, D.C. We have made it as complete as possible. But rules and laws change, so it is important to check with your local court to make sure you are working with the most up-to-date information.

We list information under the following headings:

Courts: The courts where traffic violations are normally heard. The name of the court varies from state to state and sometimes within a state. For example, in Pennsylvania, traffic cases are heard in "District Justice's Court" in most parts of the state, but in that state's largest cities they are heard in "Philadelphia Municipal Court" and "Pittsburgh City Magistrate's Court."

Informative Court Websites: More and more courts are making information available via Websites. However, few of them have useful information on traffic cases. We only list sites that we think provide useful information on traffic citations.

State Law Websites: There is a Website for almost every state, where you can view your state's laws. We list them here. We also note whether these sites are searchable by expandable tables of contents, statute section number, or a search engine allowing you to list key words (like "speed trap" or "radar," for example).

Vehicle Laws and Speed Laws: State laws relating to the operation of motor vehicles (called "Vehicle Code" in most states) are listed here, along with where you can find your state's Speed Laws. Here we also indicate whether the speed limits are "ABSOLUTE" or "PRESUMED." (See Chapter 5 for an explanation of this important distinction.)

Speed Detection: The five most common methods police use to determine your speed, as listed in Chapter 6, are pacing, aircraft, VASCAR, radar and laser. Here we list the methods allowed in your state.

Trial by Declaration: Some states allow you to present your defense in writing, without having to appear in court. (See Chapter 8, Section B.5, for more information.)

Jury Trial: Here, we indicate if your state allows jury trials for traffic violations. Among the states that do allow you a jury trial, most only allow it at a "trial de novo" after you are found guilty in a lower court.

Appeal Procedures: There are two different kinds of appeals to higher courts. In some states, you can automatically get a new trial, or "trial de novo." In other states (or in "trial de novo" states if you lose after your second trial), you can appeal only "on the law." That means your conviction is reversed only if you can convince a higher court that the traffic court judge committed a legal error. Here we list the type of appeal ("de novo" or "on the law") allowed, and the name of the court to which you appeal.

Alabama

Court(s)

District or Municipal Court

Informative Court Website(s)

None

State Law Website(s)

http://www.legalonline.state.ala.us/Search SearchText.htm (Searchable by words only)

Vehicle Laws

Code of Alabama, Title 32 (Motor Vehicles & Traffic)

Speed Laws

Above, Ch. 5A (Rules of the Road Act)

§§ 32-5A-170 to 32-5A-177 (ABSOLUTE)

Speed Detection

Pacing, aircraft, radar, laser

Trial by Declaration

No

Jury Trial

No (see below)

Appeal Procedures

On law only, to Circuit Court

Other

Jury Trial available on de novo appeal to Circuit Court only for misdemeanor with possibility of imprisonment, but not fine-only traffic violation. See §15-14-30, Rule 18.1(a), Ala.R.Crim.Proc, and *Thomas v. City of Montgomery*, 690 So.2d 546 (1997). See also *Deming v. City of Mobile*, 677 So.2d 1233 (1995).

Alaska

Court(s)

District Court

Informative Court Website(s)

None

State Law Website(s)

- http://www.touchngo.com/lglcntr/akstats/ statutes.htm
- http://www.legis.state.ak.us/cgi-bin/ folioisa.dll/stattx98

(Both searchable by expandable contents and words)

Vehicle Laws

Alaska Stats., Title 28 (Motor Vehicles)

Speed Laws

Generally enacted by municipalities when state highway speed limits (§19.10.072) don't apply. Speed limits ABSOLUTE.

Speed Detection

Pacing, aircraft, radar, laser

Trial by Declaration

No

Jury Trial

No (AS 28.40.050—"infractions")

Appeal Procedures

On law only, to Superior Court

Other

AS 29.35.230 defines traffic infractions as "civil" in nature.

Arizona

Court(s)

Municipal (City) Court, Magistrate Court, Justice Court

Informative Court Website(s)

Pima Co. Consolidated Justice Courts: http://jp.co.pima.az.us/www/envelope.html

State Law Website(s)

http://www.azleg.state.az.us/ars/ars.htm

Vehicle Laws

Ariz. Revised Stats., Title 28 (Transportation)

Speed Laws

Above, Ch. 3 (Traffic & Vehicle Regulation)

§§ 28-701 to 28-708 (PRESUMED generally, but ABSOLUTE on state/interstate highways)

Speed Detection

Pacing, aircraft, VASCAR, radar, laser

Trial by Declaration

No

Jury Trial

No

Appeal Procedures

On law only, to Superior Court

Other

Arizona classifies traffic offenses as "civil traffic violations," for which one is "responsible" (guilty) or "not responsible" (not guilty). Proof is by "preponderance of evidence," which officer still must show at trial. See ARS 28 §§ 1596-1601.

Arkansas

Court(s)

Municipal ("Little Rock Traffic Court" in Little Rock), City, Police, and Justice of the Peace Court

Informative Court Website(s)

Little Rock Traffic Court, http://www.littlerock.state.ar.us/trfcourt/

State Law Website(s)

http://www.arkleg.state.ar.us/cgi-bin.om_isapi.dll

(Searchable by expandable contents and words)

Vehicle Laws

Arkansas Code of 1987 (updated), Title 27 (Transportation), Subtitle 4 (Motor Vehicular Traffic)

Speed Laws

Above, Ch. 51 (Operation of Vehicles—Rules of the Road), Subchapter 2 (Speed Limits) §§ 27-51-201 to 27-51-214 (ABSOLUTE)

Speed Detection

Pacing, aircraft, radar, laser

Trial by Declaration

No

Jury Trial

No in first trial. Yes, on de novo appeal to Circuit Court. See *Johnston v. City of Pine Bluff*, 525 S.W.2d 76 (1975).

Appeal Procedures

To Circuit Court for trial de novo. Thereafter, on law only, to Court of Appeals (§ 16-96-507).

California

Court(s)

Superior or Municipal Court

Informative Court Website(s)

- Los Angeles County: http://www.lamuni.org/ (Best Website in the country. You can search your own citation, by court location, ticket no., and surname, for status, bail, etc.)
- Burbank: http://www.courts.org/Burbank/burbank.htm
- Citrus http://www.co.la.ca.us/courts/citrus/
- Long Beach: http://www.lbmuni.org
- Pasadena: http://www.pasadenacourt.com/
- San Francisco: http://www.ci.sf.ca.us/courts/
- Alameda County: http://www.co.alameda.ca.us/courts/[INSERT]/ NOTE: For "[INSERT]", substitute "berkeley," "fremont," "pleasanton," "oakland" or "hayward" for respective court locations
- Orange County: http://www.oc.ca.gov/[INSERT]/ NOTE: For "[INSERT]", substitute "southcourt," "harborcourt" or "north" for respective court locations
- Ventura County: http://www.ventura.org/courts/crtstraf.htm
- San Mateo County: http://www.co.sanmateo.ca.us/sanmateocourts/dome.htm NOTE: Due to recent consolidation of Municipal Courts (which handle traffic cases) with larger Superior Courts, some county sites (Santa Clara, Sacramento, Riverside, Stanislaus) give little or no info on traffic-court procedure.

State Law Website(s)

- http://www.leginfo.ca.gov/calaw.html
- http://caselaw.findlaw.com/cgi-bin/getcode.pl (Both searchable by expandable contents for each code, and by words)

Vehicle Laws

Vehicle Code (California laws are divided into separate "codes" which have no title number)

Speed Laws

Above, Div.11 (Rules of the Road, §§ 21000-23336), §§ 22348-22358.3 (PRESUMED, but ABSOLUTE as to 65-70 state highway limit and 55 on 2-lane undivided highways)

Speed Detection

Pacing, aircraft, radar, laser

Trial by Declaration

Yes; if found guilty, can request "trial de novo," or regular trial, in same court, Veh. C. § 40902.

Jury Trial

No. (Penal Code 19.6.)

Appeal Procedures

On law only, to Superior Court Appellate Division/Department

Other

Under Veh. C. §§ 40800-40808, VASCAR and aircraft timing between points (but not aircraft pacing) are illegal. For most roads, PRESUMED violations of Veh. C. 22350 (Basic Speed Law—Max. Limit of 55/65/70 not applicable), prosecution must show engineering and traffic survey justifies speed limit, when radar or laser is used.

Colorado

Court(s)

County Court or Municipal Court (municipal violations only, but many cities are allowed to enact own traffic ordinances)

Informative Court Website(s)

Denver County Court Traffic Division Website: http://infodenver.co.us/~cntycourt/webp11.htm

State Law Website(s)

http://www.intellinetusa.com/statmgr.htm (Searchable by words or statute numbers only)

Vehicle Laws

Colo. Revised Stats., Title 42 (Vehicles & Traffic)

Speed Laws

Above, Art. 4 (Regulation of Vehicles & Traffic), §§ 42-4-1101 to 42-4-1104. (PRESUMED, but ABSOLUTE as to 65/70 limits on state/interstate highways)

Speed Detection

Pacing, aircraft, VASCAR, radar, laser

Trial by Declaration

No

Jury Trial

No. (CRS § 16-10-109)

Appeal Procedures

On law only, to District Court, from Municipal Court "of record"; de novo trial from Municipal Court "not of record" to County Court; thereafter, on law only, to District Court. (§ 13-10-116)

Connecticut

Court(s)

Superior Court

Informative Court Website(s)

None

State Law Website(s)

http://www.cslnet.ctstateu.edu/statutes/index.htm (Searchable by expandable contents only)

Vehicle Laws

Conn. Gen. Stats., Title 14 (Motor Vehicles. Use of Hwy. by Vehicles. Gasolines)

Speed Laws

Above, Ch. 248 (Vehicle Highway Use), § 14-218a to 14-219. (PRESUMED, but ABSOLUTE as to 55/65/70 highway limits)

Speed Detection

Pacing, aircraft, radar, laser

Trial by Declaration

No

Jury Trial

No. (CGS § 54-82b)

Appeal Procedures

On law only, to Appellate Court (§ 54-95)

Delaware

Court(s)

Municipal Court of Wilmington, Alderman's Court, Justice of the Peace Court

Informative Court Website(s)

None

State Law Website(s)

http//www.lexislawpublishing.com/sdCGI-BIN/ (Click on "decode")

Vehicle Laws

Delaware Code, Title 21 (Motor Vehicles)

Speed Laws

Above, Part III (Operation & Equipment), Ch. 41 (Rules of the Road), Subchapter VIII (Speed Restrictions) 21 §§ 4168-4174 (ABSOLUTE)

Speed Detection

Pacing, aircraft, VASCAR, radar, laser

Trial by Declaration

No

Jury Trial

Yes

Appeal Procedures

On law only, from Municipal Court to Superior Court; from Justice of the Peace or Alderman's Court, to Court of Common Pleas for trial de novo, if penalty exceeds $100 or 30 days jail (11 § 5920); thereafter, on law only, to Superior Court.

District of Columbia (Washington, D.C.)

Court(s)

Bureau of Traffic Adjudication, of D.C. Dept. of Transportation

Informative Court Website(s)

None

State Law Website(s)

http://www.findlaw.com/11stategov/dc/laws.html (Only D.C. Municipal Regulations, not D.C. Code. No expandable contents or word search)

Vehicle Laws

D.C. Code, Title 40 (Motor Vehicles & Traffic); D.C. Municipal Regulations, Title 18 (Vehicles & Traffic), Ch. 11 (Motor Vehicle Offenses & Penalties), Ch. 22 (Moving Violations)

Speed Laws

D.C. Code, Title 40, Ch. 7 (Regulation of Traffic), § 40-712 (refers to D.C. Municipal Regulations, but they are ABSOLUTE)

Speed Detection

Pacing, radar

Trial by Declaration

No

Jury Trial

No

Appeal Procedures

On law only, to Appeals Board of Bureau of Traffic Adjudication. Thereafter, must apply for allowance of appeal, on law only, to D.C. Superior Court.

Other

- D.C. Code §§ 40-601 to 40-642 "decriminalizes" traffic offenses. Burden of proof is on District, by "clear and convincing" evidence. Officer must appear, where violation is denied (40-616(c)), but officer's presence must be specifically demanded. Non-court administrative system.

- Radar detectors are illegal in D.C.

Florida

Court(s)

County Court ("Traffic Violations Bureau")

Informative Court Website(s)

- Bay Co. Circ. Ct.: http://www.baycoclerk.com/traffic.htm
- Brevard Co. (Titusville): http://www.clerk.co.brevard.fl.us/pages/trafpg.htm
- Martin Co. (Stuart): http://www.martin.fl.us/govt/co/clerk/division/traffic.htm
- Orange/Osceola Counties: http://www.ninja.state.fl.us/trafcrt.htm

State Law Website(s)

http://www.leg.state.fl.us/citizen/documents/statutes/index.html (Searchable by expandable contents and words)

Vehicle Laws

Fla. Stats., Title XXIII (Motor Vehicles)

Speed Laws

Above, Ch. 316 (State Uniform Traffic Control) §§ 316.183-316.1895 (ABSOLUTE)

Speed Detection

Pacing, aircraft, VASCAR, radar

Trial by Declaration

Yes

Jury Trial

No

Appeal Procedures

On law only, to Circuit Court

Other

- § 316.1905—VASCAR and radar units must be tested every six months. VASCAR operator must be state-certified for evidence to be admitted. Officer must appear, if defendant insists, in VASCAR and radar cases.

- § 316.1906—Radar evidence not admissible unless operating officer completed state course. Also, visual detection required, with "clear assignment of speed to single vehicle."

- Traffic offenses classified as "civil."

Georgia

Court(s)

- Atlanta Traffic Court (City Court of Atlanta)
- Municipal Court (Columbus and Muscogee Counties)
- State Court (where no City or Municipal Court)

Informative Court Website(s)

Atlanta Traffic Court:
http://www.atlanta.org/dept/courts/citycourt/courmiss.htm

State Law Website(s)

http://www.ganet.org/services/ocode/ocgsearch.htm

(Searchable by words and statute numbers)

Vehicle Laws

Official Code of Georgia, Title 40 (Motor Vehicles & Traffic)

Speed Laws

Above, Ch. 6 (Uniform Rules of the Road) §§ 40-6-180 to 40-6-188 (ABSOLUTE)

Speed Detection

Pacing, aircraft, VASCAR, radar

Trial by Declaration

No

Jury Trial

No, at first trial. Yes, on de novo appeal to Superior Court from Atlanta Traffic Court or Municipal Court and in State Court (§ 5-3-30).

Appeal Procedures

De novo appeal to Superior Court from Atlanta Traffic Court or Municipal Court, thereafter, or from State Court, to Court of Appeals on law only.

Hawaii

Court(s)

District Court

Informative Court Website(s)

None

State Law Website(s)

None

Vehicle Laws

Hawaii Revised Stats., Title 17 (Motor & Other Vehicles)

Speed Laws

Above, Ch. 291C (Statewide Traffic Code), Part X (Speed Restrictions) §§ 291C-101 to 291C-102 (ABSOLUTE)

Speed Detection

Pacing, VASCAR, radar, laser

Trial by Declaration

Yes. (§ 291D-6(a)(2) If found guilty on declaration, can request regular trial within 30 days.

Jury Trial

No

Appeal Procedures

To Circuit Court, on law only

Other

Per §§ 291D-1 to 291D-14, traffic offenses "decriminalized," arraignments eliminated. Can deny charges by filling out ticket form and mailing to court. Officer need not appear at hearing. No prosecutor present. Case goes to regular criminal procedure, however, if offense would bring total points to 12 or more, although without the right to a Jury Trial.

Idaho

Court(s)

District Court, Magistrate Division

Informative Court Website(s)

3rd Jud. Dist. (Adams, Washington, Payette, Gem Canyon, Owyhee Counties) Dist. Ct.—Mag. Division:
http://www.webpak.net/~tca3sec/

State Law Website(s)

- http://www.idwr.state.id.us/legislat/idstat.html (Searchable only by words and section numbers)
- http://www2.state.id.us/legislat/legislat.html (Searchable on three sub-sites via contents, words, and section numbers)

Vehicle Laws

Idaho Code, Title 49 (Motor Vehicles)

Speed Laws

Above, Ch. 6 (Rules of the Road) § 49-654 (ABSOLUTE)

Speed Detection

Pacing, VASCAR, radar, laser

Trial by Declaration

No

Jury Trial

No. (Title 49, Ch. 15, § 49-1502)

Appeal Procedures

On law only, from District Court Magistrate Division to District Court (§§ 49-1504, 1-2213).

Other

Traffic offenses are "infractions" not triable by jury, per § 49-1502

Illinois

Court(s)

Circuit Court

Informative Court Website(s)

- Cook County Circ. Court: http:/www.cookcountyclerk ofcourt.org/html/divides.htm#TRAFFIC
- Monroe Co. Circ. Court: http://www.htc. net/~jacobdj/mcc/trffcfaq.htm
  (Very good site with frequently asked questions and answers)

State Law Website(s)

None

Vehicle Laws

Smith-Hurd Illinois Compiled Stats., Ch. 625 (Vehicles), Act 5 (Ill. Vehicle Code)

Speed Laws

Above, Ch. 11 (of Act 5) (Rules of the Road), Art VI (Speed Restrictions) §§ 5/11-601 to 5/11-605 (ABSOLUTE)

Speed Detection

Pacing, VASCAR, radar, laser

Trial by Declaration

No

Jury Trial

Yes

Appeal Procedures

On law only, to Appellate Court

Indiana

Court(s)

Municipal Court (Marion County), County Court, or City/Town Court

Informative Court Website(s)

None

State Law Website(s)

- http://www.law.indiana.edu/codes/in/incode.html
  (Searchable by expandable contents and keyword)
- http://www.ai.org/legislative/ic/code
  (Searchable by expandable contents only; can download Zip files in Wordperfect or Adobe Acrobat format)

Vehicle Laws

Indiana Code, Title 9 (Motor Vehicles)

Speed Laws

Above, Art. 21 (Traffic Regulation) Ch. 5 §§ 9-21-5-1 to 9-21-5-6 (ABSOLUTE)

Speed Detection

Pacing, aircraft, VASCAR, radar

Trial by Declaration

Yes

Jury Trial

Yes

Appeal Procedures

De novo appeal from City/Town Court to Circuit Court or Superior Court (§ 33-10.1-5-9), thereafter, on law, to Court of Appeals. From Municipal or County Court, appeal is on law only, to Court of Appeals (§ 35-38-4-1).

Iowa

Court(s)

District Court (Magistrate Division)

Informative Court Website(s)

None

State Law Website(s)

- http://www.legis.state.ia.us/Code.html
- http://www2.legis.state.ia.us/Code.html
  (Both searchable only by words or section numbers)

Vehicle Laws

Indiana Code, Title VIII (Transportation), Subtitle 2 (Vehicles)

Speed Laws

Above, Ch. 321 (Motor Vehicles & Laws of the Road) §§ 321.285-321.293 (ABSOLUTE)

Speed Detection

Pacing, aircraft, VASCAR, radar, laser

Trial by Declaration

No

Jury Trial

Yes

Appeal Procedures

Appeal on law only, to Iowa Supreme Court—
which will transfer to Court of Appeals.

Kansas

Court(s)

District Court

Informative Court Website(s)

Johnson County: http://www.jocoks.com/
jococourts/court_traffic.htm

State Law Website(s)

http://www.ink.org/public/statutes/statutes.html
(Searchable by words and section numbers
only. Contents not expandable)

Vehicle Laws

Kansas Stats., Ch. 8 (Automobiles & Other
Vehicles)

Speed Laws

Above, §§ 8-1557 to 8-1560 (ABSOLUTE)

Speed Detection

Pacing, aircraft, VASCAR, radar, laser

Trial by Declaration

No

Jury Trial

No. See KSA 22-3404, *City of Wichita v. Rice*,
889 P.2d 789 (1995), and *State v. Irving*, 216
Kan. 588, 533 P.2d 1225 (1975)

Appeal Procedures

On law only, to Court of Appeals

Other

Kansas classifies traffic offenses as "infractions."

Kentucky

Court(s)

District Court

Informative Court Website(s)

(Although counties of Fayette (Lexington) and
Jefferson (Louisville) have court Websites, they
are silent on traffic court issues)

State Law Website(s)

http://www.lrc.state.ky.us/krs/statrev/frontpg.htm

Vehicle Laws

Kentucky Revised Statutes, Title XVI (Motor
Vehicles)

Speed Laws

Above, Ch. 189 (Traffic Regulations [Etc.])
§ 189.390 (PRESUMED)

Speed Detection

Pacing, VASCAR, radar, laser

Trial by Declaration

No

Jury Trial

Yes. See KRS 29A-270(1) and *Crone v.
Commonwealth*, 680 S.W.2d 138 (1984)

Appeal Procedures

On law only, to Circuit Court

Louisiana

Court(s)

Traffic Court (New Orleans), Justice of the
Peace Court, or Mayor's Court

Informative Court Website(s)

Several courts have Websites, but no useful
information on traffic courts.

State Law Website(s)

None

Vehicle Laws

Louisiana Revised Stats., Title 32 (Motor
Vehicles & Transportation)

Speed Laws

Above, Ch. 1 (La. Hwy. Regulatory Act), Part IV
(Traffic Regulations), Subpart A (Speed Restrictions) §§ 32:61 to 32:64 (ABSOLUTE 55/65/70
limits, otherwise PRESUMED)

Speed Detection

Pacing, aircraft, VASCAR

Trial by Declaration

Yes

Jury Trial

No

Appeal Procedures

De novo appeal from Mayor's or Justice of the
Peace Court to District Court or Parish Court
(§ 13:1896; *State v. Fontenot*, 535 So.2d 488

[1988]); thereafter, on law only to Court of Appeal. On law only from Traffic Court of New Orleans to District Court.

Maine

Court(s)

District Court

Informative Court Website(s)

None

State Law Website(s)

http://janus.state.me.us/legis/statutes/homepage.htm

(Searchable by expandable contents, words, and section numbers)

Vehicle Laws

Maine Revised Statutes, Title 29A (Motor Vehicles)

Speed Laws

Above, Ch. 19 (Operation) § 2074 (ABSOLUTE)

Speed Detection

Pacing, aircraft, VASCAR, radar, laser

Trial by Declaration

No

Jury Trial

No, except for "Class E" crime of exceeding speed limit by 30+ mph

Appeal Procedures

On law only, to Superior Court (15 §§ 2111, 2114)

Other

Traffic offenses are classified as "civil violations."

Maryland

Court(s)

District Court

Informative Court Website(s)

Single site leading to all District Court sites: http://www.courts.state.md.us/T261 (However, most District Court sites give only hours, locations and phone numbers for traffic courts)

State Law Website(s)

http://mlis.state.md.us/cgi-win/web_statutes.exe (Searchable by section number only, among pull-down list of different titles. No table of contents)

Vehicle Laws

Code of Maryland—Transportation

Speed Laws

Above, Titles 11-27 (Vehicle Laws), Title 21 (Rules of the Road), Subtitle 8 (Speed Restrictions) §§ 21-801 to 21-803.2 (ABSOLUTE)

Speed Detection

Pacing, aircraft, VASCAR, radar, laser

Trial by Declaration

No

Jury Trial

No. *Smith v. State*, 17 Md. App. 217, 301 A.2d 54 (1972)

Appeal Procedures

To Circuit Court or Criminal Court (Baltimore) for trial de novo (§ 26-156(a)); thereafter, on law only, to Court of Special Appeals.

Massachusetts

Court(s)

District Court (Division of Trial Court of the Commonwealth) or Boston Municipal Court

Informative Court Website(s)

None

State Law Website(s)

http://www.state.ma.us/legis/laws/mgl/ (Searchable by expandable contents, words, or section numbers)

Vehicle Laws

Mass. General Laws, Part I, Title XIV (Public Ways & Works), Chs. 89 (Law of the Road), 90 (Motor Vehicles & Aircraft)

Speed Laws

Above, 90 §§ 17, 17A (ABSOLUTE 65 on interstates, PRESUMED otherwise)

Speed Detection

Pacing, VASCAR, radar, laser

Trial by Declaration

No

Jury Trial

No

Appeal Procedures

If hearing by "magistrate other than a justice," de novo appeal for trial in District Court. Thereafter, or if by justice, then on law only, to District Court Appellate Division (90C § 3).

Other

Traffic violations are "civil motor infractions." Discovery at judge's discretion, guilt by "preponderance of evidence" standard, and officer need not appear unless judge requests it. (Citation is "presumed" evidence of guilt.) See 90C§3.

Michigan

Court(s)

District Court (Traffic Violations Bureau) or Municipal Court

Informative Court Website(s)

Michigan courts have many Websites, but little information on traffic court

State Law Website(s)

None

Vehicle Laws

Mich. Stats., Title 9 (Michigan Vehicle Code)

Speed Laws

Above, §§ 9.1431 to 9.3577 (ABSOLUTE)

Speed Detection

Pacing, aircraft, VASCAR, radar, laser

Trial by Declaration

No

Jury Trial

No. *People v. Schomaker*, 116 Mich. App. 507, 323 N.W.2d 461 (1982)

Appeal Procedures

On law only, to Circuit Court

Other

Traffic offenses are "civil infractions." See MSA § 257, 741 et seq.

Minnesota

Court(s)

County Court, District Court, or Municipal Court (Hennepin and Ramsey Counties)

Informative Court Website(s)

Fillmore County Dist. Ct.:
http://www.courts.state.mn.us/districts/third/fillmore/index.htm#INFORMATION ABOUT TRAFFIC TICKETS
(Hennepin County site gives no useful traffic info, only phone number)

State Law Website(s)

http://www.leg.state.mn.us/leg/statutes.htm

Vehicle Laws

Minn. Stats., Chs. 160-174A (Transportation)

Speed Laws

Above, Ch. 169 § 169.14 (ABSOLUTE in municipalities, otherwise PRESUMED)

Speed Detection

Pacing, aircraft, VASCAR, radar, laser

Trial by Declaration

No

Jury Trial

No, not for "petty misdemeanor" traffic offenses. *Village of Vadnais Hts. v. Beardsley*, 296 Minn. 154, 207 N.W.2d 339

Appeal Procedures

On law only, to Court of Appeals.

Mississippi

Court(s)

Justice Court or County Court

Informative Court Website(s)

None

State Law Website(s)

- http://www.mscode.com/free/statutes/toc.htm (Searchable by expandable contents)
- http://www.sos.state.ms.us/MsCode/mscodeindex.html (Searchable by words or section numbers.)

Vehicle Laws

Mississippi Code, Title 63 (Motor Vehicles & Traffic Regulation)

Speed Laws

Above, Ch. 3 (Traffic Regulations & Rules of the Road) §§ 63-3-501 to 63-3-513 (ABSOLUTE)

Speed Detection

Pacing, aircraft, VASCAR, radar

Trial by Declaration

No

Jury Trial

Yes

Appeal Procedures

For de novo trial from Justice Court to County Court (§ 99-35-1); On law only, from County Court to Circuit Court.

Missouri

Court(s)

Municipal Court, Traffic Court of St Louis, or Circuit Court (Associate Division)

Informative Court Website(s)

None

State Law Website(s)

http://www.moga.state.mo.us/homestat.htm (Searchable by expandable contents, words or section numbers)

Vehicle Laws

Missouri Revised Stats., Title XIX (Motor Vehicles, Watercraft & Aviation)

Speed Laws

Above, Ch. 304 (Traffic Regulations) §§ 304.009, 304.010 (ABSOLUTE)

Speed Detection

Pacing, aircraft, radar, laser

Trial by Declaration

No

Jury Trial

Yes

Appeal Procedures

De novo from "municipal judge" or "associate circuit judge," to a circuit judge (§ 479.200); thereafter, or otherwise, on law only, to Circuit Court Appellate Division

Other

Speed over the limit by 5 mph or less is an "infraction" for which no "points" go on driving record. No right to jury trial in this situation.

Montana

Court(s)

Justice's Court, Municipal Court, or City Court

Informative Court Website(s)

None

State Law Website(s)

http://statedocs.msl.state.mt.us/cgi-bin/om_isapi.dll
(Searchable by expandable contents or words)

Vehicle Laws

Montana Code, Title 61 (Motor Vehicles)

Speed Laws

Above, Ch. 8 (Traffic Regulation), Part 3 (Vehicle Operating Requirements) §§ 61-8-303 to 61-8-314 (ABSOLUTE 55/65 (Interstates) at night and 25 in urban district, PRESUMED otherwise)

Speed Detection

Pacing, aircraft, radar

Trial by Declaration

No

Jury Trial

Yes, in Municipal Court

Appeal Procedures

To District Court, for trial de novo (with a jury, if requested) (§ 46-17-311); thereafter, on law only, to Montana Supreme Court

Other

Montana has no daytime speed limit on Interstates, the only rule being to drive at a "reasonable and prudent" speed. This law was ruled unconstitutional by the Montana Supreme Court in December 1998, and the legislature is expected to respond by imposing a daytime speed limit on Interstates.

Nebraska

Court(s)

County Court

Informative Court Website(s)

None

State Law Website(s)

http://www.unicam.state.ne.us/statutes.htm, (Searchable by expandable contents or words)

Vehicle Laws

Revised Stats. of Nebraska, Ch. 60 (Motor Vehicles)

Speed Laws

Above, Art. 6 (Rules of the Road), Sub-article (a)(Speed Restrictions); §§ 60-6, 185 to 60-6, 195 (ABSOLUTE)

Speed Detection

radar, laser

Trial by Declaration

Yes

Jury Trial

No. See §§ 24-536, 25-2705

Appeal Procedures

To District Court, for trial de novo (§ 25-1937); thereafter, on law only, to Court of Appeals

Nevada

Court(s)

Municipal Court or Justice Court

Informative Court Website(s)

Washoe County's District Court has a Website, but without any mention of traffic court or Justice Court procedures.

State Law Website(s)

http://www.leg.state.nv.us/law1.htm

Vehicle Laws

Nevada Revised Stats., Title 43 (Vehicles & Watercraft)

Speed Laws

Above, §§ 484.361 to 484.375 (ABSOLUTE)

Speed Detection

Pacing, aircraft, radar, laser

Trial by Declaration

No

Jury Trial

No

Appeal Procedures

On law only, to District Court (§ 177.015)

New Hampshire

Court(s)

District Court

Informative Court Website(s)

None

State Law Website(s)

- http://www.state.nh.us/gencourt/gencourt.htm
- http://199.92.250.14/rsa/
  (Searchable by expandable contents or words)

Vehicle Laws

N.H. Revised Stats., Title 21 (Motor Vehicles), Chs. 259-268

Speed Laws

Above, Ch. 265 (Rules of the Road) §§ 265:60 to 265.63 (ABSOLUTE 65, otherwise PRESUMED)

Speed Detection

Pacing, aircraft, radar, laser

Trial by Declaration

No

Jury Trial

No

Appeal Procedures

On law only, to Superior Court (§§ 599:1 to 599:4)

New Jersey

Court(s)

Municipal Court

Informative Court Website(s)

None

State Law Website(s)

http://www.njleg.state.nj.us/cgi-bin/
(Searchable by expandable contents or words)

Vehicle Laws

N.J. Revised Stats., Title 39 (Motor Vehicles & Traffic Regulation)

Speed Laws

Above, Ch. 4 (Traffic Regulation), Art. 12 (Speed) §§ 39:4-98 to 39:4-100 (ABSOLUTE)

Speed Detection

Pacing, aircraft, VASCAR, radar

Trial by Declaration

No

Jury Trial

No. See § 2C:1-4

Appeal Procedures

On law only, to Superior Court (Law Division)

Other

"Photo-radar" is illegal. § 39:4-103.1

New Mexico

Court(s)

Metropolitan Court (Bernalillo County) or Magistrate Court

Informative Court Website(s)

Although Bernalillo County Metropolitan Court has a Website, no traffic court information is given. Some, statewide, for Magistrate Court sites.

State Law Website(s)

http://www.lexislawpublishing.com/sdCGI-BIN/
(Click on "nmsa1978")
(Searchable by expandable contents, or words)

Vehicle Laws

N.M. Revised Stats., Ch. 66 (Motor Vehicles)

Speed Laws

Above, Art. 7 (Traffic Laws [Etc.]) §§ 66-7-301 to 66-7-304 (ABSOLUTE)

Speed Detection

Pacing, aircraft, VASCAR, radar, laser

Trial by Declaration

No

Jury Trial

No

Appeal Procedures

De novo appeal to District Court (§§ 34-8A-6, 35-13-1); thereafter, on law only, to Court of Appeals

New York

Court(s)

Criminal Court of City of New York, City Court, District Court, County Court, Town Court or Village Court

Informative Court Website(s)

None

State Law Website(s)

gopher://leginfo.lbdc.state.ny.us/
(Searchable by expandable contents only)

Vehicle Laws

McKinney's Consolidated Laws of New York, Book 62A (Vehicle & Traffic Law) [Ch. 71 of the Consolidated Laws]

Speed Laws

Above, Title VII (Rules of the Road), Art. 30 (Speed Restrictions) § 1180 (ABSOLUTE)

Speed Detection

Pacing, aircraft, VASCAR, radar, laser

Trial by Declaration

No

Jury Trial

No

Appeal Procedures

De novo trial from Town Court and Village Court, on appeal to County Court. From all other courts, appeal is on law only, to "Appellate Term" of "Supreme Court" (county-level trial courts)

North Carolina

Court(s)

District Court

Informative Court Website(s)

Master list of Dist. Ct. sites:
http://www.aoc.state.nc.us/www/public/html/trial_courts.htm
(However, the only court site that mentions traffic court is the one for Onslow County.)

State Law Website(s)

http://www.ncga.state.nc.us/html1997/statutes/statutes.html
(Searchable by expandable contents or by words)

Vehicle Laws

Gen. Stats. of N.C., Ch. 20

Speed Laws

Above, § 20-141 (ABSOLUTE)

Speed Detection

Pacing, VASCAR, radar

Trial by Declaration

No

Jury Trial

Yes

Appeal Procedures

Appeal for trial de novo from District Court magistrate to District Court judge (§ 7A-290) and from District Court to Superior Court; thereafter, on law only, to Court of Appeals

North Dakota

Court(s)

County Justice Court

Informative Court Website(s)

None

State Law Website(s)

http://www.state.nd.us/lr/statutes.html

Vehicle Laws

N.D. Century Code, Title 39 (Motor Vehicles)

Speed Laws

Above, Ch. 39-09 (Speed Restrictions) §§ 39-09-01 to 39-09-07.1 (PRESUMED (see "Other," below))

Speed Detection

Pacing, aircraft, radar, laser

Trial by Declaration

No

Jury Trial

No. See § 39.06.1-03(5)(a)

Appeal Procedures

De novo trial on appeal to District Court (§ 33-12-34, N.D. Rule Crim. Proc. 37); thereafter, on law only, to N.D. Supreme Court

Other

It is difficult to tell from §§ 39-09-01 to 39-09-07.1 whether speed limits are PRESUMED or ABSOLUTE. Speed limits are "not absolute," according to *Moe v. Kettwig*, 68 N.W.2d 853 (1955).

Ohio

Court(s)

County Court, Municipal Court or Mayor's Court

Informative Court Website(s)

None

State Law Website(s)

- http://orc.avv.com/search.htm
- http://204.89.181/cgi-bin/om_isapi.dll (Both searchable by expandable contents or words)

Vehicle Laws

Ohio Revised Code, Title 45 (Motor Vehicles [Etc.])

Speed Laws

Above, Ch. 4511 (Traffic Law, Operation of Motor Vehicles) § 4511.211 (ABSOLUTE on interstates, otherwise PRESUMED)

Speed Detection

Pacing, aircraft, VASCAR, radar, laser

Trial by Declaration

At discretion of each court

Jury Trial

No, unless jail sentence is a possible penalty

Appeal Procedures

Appeal for de novo trial from Mayor's Court to Municipal Court (§ 1905.25); from County Court or Municipal Court, appeal is on law only, to Court of Appeals

Other

Operation of a vehicle at a speed greater than the PRESUMED limit may be proper, depending on circumstances. *State v. Nedelkoff*, 263 N.E.2d 803, and *Eversole v. Seelback*, 47 OLA 583.

Oklahoma

Court(s)

Municipal Court

Informative Court Website(s)

None

State Law Website(s)

- http://www.oscn.net/quickcase.htm
- http://oklegal.onenet.net/statutes.basic.html (Both searchable by words only)

Vehicle Laws

Oklahoma Stats., Title 47 (Motor Vehicles)

Speed Laws

Above, Ch. 11 (Rules of the Road), Art. VIII (Speed Restrictions) 47 § 11-801 (ABSOLUTE as to 65/70/75 limits & school zones (25), PRESUMED otherwise)

Speed Detection

Pacing, aircraft, VASCAR, radar

Trial by Declaration

No

Jury Trial

Yes

Appeal Procedures

Appeal for de novo trial in District Court (§ 11-27-129); thereafter, on law only, to Court of Criminal Appeals

Oregon

Court(s)

City Court, Municipal Court (Salem), Justice Court or Circuit Court

Informative Court Website(s)

Marion Co. Circ. Ct.: http://marion-court.ojd.state.or.us/Violat.htm (Excellent site. "Trial by affidavit" forms can be downloaded online)

State Law Website(s)

http://landru.leg.state.or.us/ors/ (Searchable by expandable contents or words)

Vehicle Laws

Oregon Revised Stats., Chs. 801-826 (Oregon Vehicle Code)

Speed Laws

Above, Ch. 811 (Rules of the Road for Drivers) §§ 811.100-811.124 (ABSOLUTE for interstates and ocean shore, otherwise PRESUMED)

Speed Detection

Pacing, aircraft, VASCAR, radar, laser

Trial by Declaration

Yes. ORS 153.170—submission of declaration constitutes waiver of hearing

Jury Trial

No

Appeal Procedures

Appeal for trial de novo from Justice, City or Municipal Court, to Circuit Court (§§ 138.057, 153.280). From Circuit Court, appeal is on law only, to Court of Appeals

Other

1. Speed over PRESUMED limit could be lawful. *Loofburrow v. Flynn*, 262 Or. 63, 496 P.2d 220 (1972).

2. Under ORS 153.110-153.630, traffic violations are "infractions," proof by "preponderance of evidence" standard, pretrial discovery is available (see ORS 135.805-135.873), officer must appear at trial, and defendant can't be called as witness against him/herself.

Pennsylvania

Court(s)

District Justice's Court, Pittsburgh City Magistrate's Court, Philadelphia Municipal Court

Informative Court Website(s)

• Philadelphia Traffic Court:
http://courts.phila.gov/tc.htm

Several District Justices' sites exist, but without traffic court information. See:

• Dist. Ct. State College:
http://www.vicon.net/~cwp101

• Dist. Ct. 15-4-04:
http://members.aol.com/Judiciary/DistrictCourt15404.html

State Law Website(s)

http://members.aol.com/StatutesPA/
(see, "index.html")
(Searchable by expandable contents only)

Vehicle Laws

Penna. Consolidated Statutes, Title 75 (The Vehicle Code)

Speed Laws

Above, Part III, Ch. 33 (Rules of the Road in General) §§ 3361-3368 (ABSOLUTE)

Speed Detection

Pacing, aircraft, VASCAR, radar

Trial by Declaration

No

Jury Trial

No

Appeal Procedures

Appeal for trial de novo to Court of Common Pleas; thereafter, appeal is on law only, to Superior Court

Other

Radar may be used by State Police only, and cannot be used unless violator exceeds speed limit by 6 mph or more. VASCAR cannot be used unless violator exceeds speed limit by 10 mph or more. See § 3368.

Rhode Island

Court(s)

Administrative Adjudication Court

Informative Court Website(s)

None

State Law Website(s)

http://www.rilin.state.ri.us/statutes/statutes.html
(Searchable by expandable contents or words)

Vehicle Laws

General Laws of R.I., Title 31 (Motor & Other Vehicles)

Speed Laws

Above, Ch. 31-14 (Speed Restrictions) §§ 31-14-1 to 31-14-8 (PRESUMED)

Speed Detection

Pacing, aircraft, radar, laser

Trial by Declaration

No

Jury Trial

No

Appeal Procedures

Appeal on law only, to Administrative Adjudication Court's 3-member appellate panel (§ 31-43-4)

Other

In Administrative Adjudication Court, traffic violations are "civil," proof is by "preponderance of evidence" standard, "not responsible" pleas may be entered by mail, and if driver has no violations over past three years, can avail him/herself of special hearing to seek dismissal based on good driving record (§§ 31-43-1 to 31-43-17).

South Carolina

Court(s)

Magistrate Court or Municipal Court

Informative Court Website(s)

None

State Law Website(s)

http://www.lpitr.state.sc.us/code/statmast.htm (Searchable by expandable contents)

Vehicle Laws

S.C. Code of Laws, Title 56 (Motor Vehicles)

Speed Laws

Above, Ch. 5 (Uniform Act Regulating Traffic on Highways), Art. 11 (Restrictions on Speed; Racing) §§ 56-5-1510 to 56-5-1580

Speed Detection

Pacing, VASCAR, radar, laser

Trial by Declaration

No

Jury Trial

Yes

Appeal Procedures

On law only, to Circuit Court

South Dakota

Court(s)

Magistrate Court

Informative Court Website(s)

None

State Law Website(s)

http://www.state.sd.us/state/legis/lrc/statutes/ (Searchable by expandable contents or words)

Vehicle Laws

S.D. Codified Laws, Title 32 (Motor Vehicles)

Speed Laws

Above, Ch. 25 (Speed Regulation) §§ 32-25-1.1 to 32-25-21 (ABSOLUTE)

Speed Detection

Pacing, aircraft, radar, laser

Trial by Declaration

Yes

Jury Trial

No. *State v. Auen*, 342 N.W.2d 236 (1984)

Appeal Procedures

To Circuit Court, on law only, if proceedings are recorded; for trial de novo in Circuit Court if proceedings in Magistrate Court not recorded (§§ 16-12A-26, 16-12A-27)

Tennessee

Court(s)

Municipal Court or Court of General Sessions

Informative Court Website(s)

None

State Law Website(s)

http://www.lexislawpublishing.com/sdCGI-BIN/ (Click on "tncode") (Searchable by expandable contents or words)

Vehicle Laws

Tennessee Code, Title 55 (Motor & Other Vehicles)

Speed Laws

Above, Ch. 8 (Operation of Vehicles/Rules of the Road) §§ 55-8-152 to 55-8-157 (ABSOLUTE)

Speed Detection

Pacing, aircraft, radar, laser

Trial by Declaration

No

Jury Trial

Yes, on de novo appeal to Circuit or Criminal Court

Appeal Procedures

Appeal for de novo trial to Circuit Court or Criminal Court (§ 27-3-131); thereafter, on law only, to Court of Criminal Appeals

Texas

Court(s)

Municipal Court or Justice of the Peace Court

Informative Court Website(s)

Texas has several trial and appellate court sites, with no useful information on traffic court. Houston Municipal Court's traffic site gives info on paying fines only

State Law Website(s)

- http://www.capitol.state.tx.us/statutes/statutes2.html
  (Searchable by words only)
- http://caselaw.findlaw.com/cgi-bin/getcode.pl
  (Click on "Texas, Statutes")
  (Searchable by expandable contents or words)

Vehicle Laws

Vernon's Texas Code, Transportation Code, Title 7 (Vehicles & Traffic)

Speed Laws

Above, Subtitle C (Rules of the Road) 545.351-545.362 (PRESUMED)

Speed Detection

Pacing, radar, laser

Trial by Declaration

No

Jury Trial

Yes

Appeal Procedures

On law only, from Municipal Courts "of record" to County Court; for trial de novo in County Court, from Municipal Court "not of record" and from Justice of the Peace Court; thereafter, on law only, to Court of Appeals. (Govt. Code §§ 30.00013, 30.00393, 30.00823, Code of Crim. Proc. Art. 44.17)

Utah

Court(s)

Circuit Court, Justice Court

Informative Court Website(s)

None

State Law Website(s)

http://www.le.state.ut.us/
(Searchable by expandable contents and words, and has option to download files in WordPerfect 6.1 format)

Vehicle Laws

Utah Code, Title 41 (Motor Vehicles)

Speed Laws

Above, Ch. 6, §§ 41-6-46 to 41-6-48.5 (ABSOLUTE in school zones, otherwise PRESUMED)

Speed Detection

Pacing, aircraft, VASCAR, radar, laser

Trial by Declaration

No

Jury Trial

Yes

Appeal Procedures

Appeal for trial de novo from Justice Court to Circuit Court (§ 78-5-120); from Circuit Court, appeal is on law only, to Court of Appeals

Vermont

Court(s)

Judicial Bureau

Informative Court Website(s)

Vermont Traffic Bureau/Judicial Bureau: http://www.cit.state.vt/us:80/courts/vt6/trfcmp.htm

State Law Website(s)

- http://www.leg.state.vt.us/statutes/statutes.htm
  (Searchable by expandable contents or words, downloadable in WordPerfect 6.1 format)
- ftp://ftp.cit.state.vt.us/pub/leg/html,
  (Downloadable Zip files by title numbers)

Vehicle Laws

Vermont Stats., Title 23 (Motor Vehicles)

Speed Laws

Above, Ch. 13 (Operation of Vehicles §§ 1003, 1007, 1081 (ABSOLUTE))

Speed Detection

Pacing, radar, laser

Trial by Declaration

No

Jury Trial

No, at first trial. Yes on trial de novo (at driver's option)

Appeal Procedures

A Jury Trial is allowed on de novo appeal at driver's option, or the court can solely consider questions of law (4 VSA § 1107).

Other

Under administrative procedure, standard is "clear and convincing" evidence, "hearing officers" hear cases, officer must appear, no prosecutor is present. See 4 VSA §§ 1101-1108, 23 VSA §§ 2302-2305.

Virginia

Court(s)

General District Court

Informative Court Website(s)

No General District Court sites give significant traffic-court information. Fairfax Gen. Dist. Ct. gives info on paying fines only

State Law Website(s)

http://leg1.state.va.us/000/src.htm

Vehicle Laws

Code of Virginia, Title 46.2 (Motor Vehicles [Etc.])

Speed Laws

Above, Ch. 8 (Regulation of Traffic) §§ 46.2-862, 46.2-870 to 46.2-876 (ABSOLUTE)

Speed Detection

Pacing, VASCAR, radar

Trial by Declaration

No

Jury Trial

No, at first trial. Yes, on de novo appeal to Circuit Court

Appeal Procedures

Appeal for trial de novo to Circuit Court (§§ 16.1-132, 16.1-136); thereafter, on law only to Court of Appeals

Other

Radar detectors are illegal. § 46.2-1079.

Washington

Court(s)

District Court, Municipal Court

Informative Court Website(s)

- Seattle Municipal Court:
  http://www.pan.ci.seattle.wa.us/seattle/
  courts/tickets.htm
  (Excellent site)
- Master site to Dist. Courts:
  http://198.187.0.226/courts/crtinfo/district/
  home.htm
  (But most Dist. Ct. sites give very limited traffic court info)

State Law Website(s)

- http://www.leg.wa.gov/wsladm/rcw.htm
  (Searchable by expandable contents)
- http://search.leg.wa.gov/basic/textsearch/
  default.asp
  (Searchable by word only)

Vehicle Laws

Revised Code of Washington, Title 46 (Motor Vehicles)

Speed Laws

Above, Ch. 61 §§ 46.61.400 to 46.61.475 (ABSOLUTE)

Speed Detection

Pacing, aircraft, VASCAR, radar, laser

Trial by Declaration

No

Jury Trial

No. RCW 46.63.090

Appeal Procedures

On law only, to Superior Court, which has discretion to refuse to consider the appeal (§ 46.63.090)

Other

1. Traffic violation "decriminalized," burden of proof by "preponderance of evidence," can request hearing by mail, no prosecutor, police officer need appear. RCW 46.63.010-46.63.151.

2. Moving VASCAR illegal. Stationary VASCAR allowed only if distance "accurately measured off." Distances for VASCAR and aircraft speed timing must be at least a quarter mile. RCW 46.61.470.

West Virginia

Court(s)

Municipal Court or Magistrate Court

Informative Court Website(s)

None

State Law Website(s)

- http://www.legis.state.wv.us/sitsrch.html, (Searchable by word only)
- telnet://129.71.161.122
  Crude telnet site, use username=public, password=public. Searchable by section number only

Vehicle Laws

West Virginia Code, Chs. 17 aircraft, 17B, 17C (Motor Vehicles)

Speed Laws

Above, Ch. 17C (Traffic Regulation & Laws of the Road), Art. 6 (Speed Restrictions) §§ 17C-6-1 to 17C-6-5 (ABSOLUTE)

Speed Detection

Pacing, aircraft, VASCAR, radar, laser

Trial by Declaration

No

Jury Trial

Yes, must be demanded in Municipal or Magistrate Court, or lost in de novo appeal. §§ 8-34-1, 50-5-1

Appeal Procedures

If jury trial in lower court, appeal on law only to Circuit Court. If no jury trial in lower court, de novo appeal to Circuit Court without jury; thereafter, on law only, to Supreme Court of Appeals (§§ 8-34-1, 50-5-1)

Wisconsin

Court(s)

Municipal Court or Circuit Court

Informative Court Website(s)

Milwaukee Municipal Court site has no traffic court information

State Law Website(s)

http://www.legis.state.wi.us/ (Searchable by index and word)

Vehicle Laws

Wisconsin Stats., Chs. 340-351

Speed Laws

Above, §§ 346.57 to 346.60 (ABSOLUTE)

Speed Detection

Pacing, aircraft, VASCAR, radar, laser

Trial by Declaration

No

Jury Trial

Yes. Written demand and fee required. See *State ex rel Mattingly v. Municipal Court*, 109 Wis. 2d 53, 325 N.W.2d 75 (1982) and § 345.43(1)(a)

Appeal Procedures

Appeal from Municipal Court to Circuit Court; on law only, from Circuit Court to Court of Appeals

Wyoming

Court(s)

County Court or Justice of the Peace Court

Informative Court Website(s)

None

State Law Website(s)

http://legisweb.state.wy.us/titles/statutes.htm (Searchable by expandable contents and word)

Vehicle Laws

Wyoming Stats., Title 31 (Motor Vehicles)

Speed Laws

Above, §§ 31-5-301 to 31-5-306 (ABSOLUTE)

Speed Detection

Pacing, radar

Trial by Declaration

Some courts allow this

Jury Trial

Yes

Appeal Procedures

On law only, to District Court

Index

■

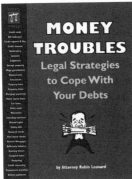

Take 2 Minutes
& Give Us Your 2 cents

Your comments make a big difference in the development and revision of Nolo books and software. Please take a few minutes and register your Nolo product—and your comments—with us. Not only will your input make a difference, you'll receive special offers available only to registered owners of Nolo products on our newest books and software. Register now by:

PHONE
1-800-992-6656

FAX
1-800-645-0895

EMAIL
cs@nolo.com

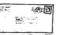

or **MAIL** us
this registration card

REMEMBER:
Little publishers have big ears. We really listen to you.

fold here

REGISTRATION CARD

NAME _____ DATE _____

ADDRESS _____

_____

CITY _____ STATE _____ ZIP _____

PHONE _____ E-MAIL _____

WHERE DID YOU HEAR ABOUT THIS PRODUCT? _____

WHERE DID YOU PURCHASE THIS PRODUCT? _____

DID YOU CONSULT A LAWYER? (PLEASE CIRCLE ONE) YES NO NOT APPLICABLE

DID YOU FIND THIS BOOK HELPFUL? (VERY) 5 4 3 2 1 (NOT AT ALL)

COMMENTS _____

_____

_____

WAS IT EASY TO USE? (VERY EASY) 5 4 3 2 1 (VERY DIFFICULT)

DO YOU OWN A COMPUTER? IF SO, WHICH FORMAT? (PLEASE CIRCLE ONE) WINDOWS DOS MAC

❑ If you do not wish to receive mailings from these companies, please check this box.

❑ You can quote me in future Nolo.com promotional materials. Daytime phone number _____

| BEYT 1.0 |

"Nolo helps lay people perform legal tasks without the aid—or fees—of lawyers."
—USA TODAY

Nolo books are ..."written in plain language, free of legal mumbo jumbo, and spiced with witty personal observations."
—ASSOCIATED PRESS

"...Nolo publications...guide people simply through the how, when, where and why of law."
—WASHINGTON POST

"Increasingly, people who are not lawyers are performing tasks usually regarded as legal work... And consumers, using books like Nolo's, do routine legal work themselves."
—NEW YORK TIMES

"...All of [Nolo's] books are easy-to-understand, are updated regularly, provide pull-out forms...and are often quite moving in their sense of compassion for the struggles of the lay reader."
—SAN FRANCISCO CHRONICLE

fold here

- -

nolo.com
950 Parker Street
Berkeley, CA 94710-9867

Attn: BEYT 1.0